MAYDAY OFF THE WILD COAST

MAYDAY OFF THE WILD COAST

THE EPIC STORY OF THE OCEANOS RESCUE

ANDREW PIKE

SHERIDAN HOUSE

Guilford, Connecticut

SHERIDAN HOUSE

An imprint of The Rowman & Littlefield Publishing Group, Inc.
4501 Forbes Blvd., Ste. 200
Lanham, MD 20706
www.rowman.com

Distributed by NATIONAL BOOK NETWORK

British Library Cataloguing in Publication Information available

Library of Congress Cataloging-in-Publication Data available

ISBN 978-1-4930-5566-1 (hardcover: alk. paper)
ISBN 978-1-4930-5567-8 (e-book)

♾™ The paper used in this publication meets the minimum requirements
of American National Standard for Information Sciences—Permanence
of Paper for Printed Library Materials, ANSI/NISO Z39.48-1992.

For Kazalette, Jeśka and Stefan, whose patience, understanding, love and support for me have been extraordinary and for which I am immeasurably grateful.

A story of sheer courage and heroism in the face of impossible odds. It is a beautiful read, with good lessons for our times. It offers an incredible leadership lesson, too. I recommend it for all those who deal with the perils of the sea and those who take an interest in how extraordinary the South African human spirit can be.'

—Sobantu Tilayi, *acting Chief Executive Officer, South African Maritime Safety Authority*

'The *Oceanos* rescue epitomizes the spirit and passion that ordinary people can bring to saving lives at sea, something the National Sea Rescue Institute of South Africa (NSRI) identifies with in the context of its entirely volunteer rescue crew. This story of civilians who stepped up and provided the necessary leadership to keep passengers calm and then coordinate the successful rescue of hundreds of lives makes for a riveting read. The detailed accounts of the passengers provide a colourful and intriguing insight into the fateful sinking of the *Oceanos*. It is a great read that will give you goose bumps! Read it with respect for the selfless actions of all those who go to save the lives of people they may not know and who may never know them!'

—Dr Cleeve Robertson MB.ChB FEMSSA, *Chief Executive Officer, NSRI*

CONTENTS

AUTHOR'S NOTE

Telling the story of the *Oceanos* – one of the biggest civilian maritime rescue operations in history – has not been without its challenges. As with every great story told some time after its occurrence, some of the detail gets lost as memories fade and witnesses disappear.

Every person mentioned in the book is (or was) real and the facts surrounding that person are, as best as I could ascertain, true. Some names and a few minor details have been changed to protect privacy and reputations; pseudonyms are marked with an asterisk at first mention in the text.

Where I encountered similar stories from different sources, but some of the facts conflicted, especially with regard to the timeline, I have used some licence and logic to ensure that the story remains plausible.

The spoken narrative in the book is in part as told to me verbatim by survivors and witnesses whom I interviewed and partly made up by me to be consistent with the facts as told.

For sea measurements, I have used nautical miles (called simply 'miles') for distances and knots for nautical and wind speeds. One mile equates to 1.85 kilometres and one knot equates to one nautical mile per hour.

Finally, some of the technical facts to which I was privy must remain confidential, as they are protected by legal privilege. That said, some descriptions of technical aspects of the sinking have been shared with me, by or obtained from, third-party sources to whom the legal privilege rule does not apply, and I am satisfied that these are either within the public domain or may plausibly be deduced from the surrounding facts.

I share some additional detail in the section 'Postscript' at the end of the book, where readers can delve a little deeper into the facts of the tale.

Andrew Pike
Durban

FOREWORD

This is a story that simply had to be told. Before it even reaches the shelves of the wide readership that the book warrants, it is Africana of a high order and an important record of a signal event in South Africa's colourful maritime history.

As a member of the investigative team after the spectacular sinking of the passenger liner *Oceanos* off the South African coast in 1991, maritime attorney and author Andy Pike was immersed in the catastrophe. He brings to the story the ring of insider authenticity. His factual background is profound and forms a lasting record of perhaps the most spectacularly successful and miraculous maritime rescue anywhere in the world.

Without sparing essential detail, instructive shipping insight and maritime-law background, Andy tells this spellbinding story from a very human perspective. That close to 600 souls were plucked from a wild sea in appalling storm conditions was bound to give rise to extremes of courage and cowardice. By telling it like it was, Andy confirms the utterly extraordinary dereliction of duty by the ship's master and most of his officers.

Perhaps more importantly, he shares with us the truly amazing accounts of how ordinary, non-maritime folk – tour operators, entertainers and passengers – filled that disgraceful vacuum of command and leadership on board the vessel as she sank in the space of less than 24 hours. He records for posterity the selfless bravery of those who rose to the occasion on board and ashore, and the enormous role of the South African Defence Force – especially its helicopter pilots and divers. It was the concerted effort of all these heroes, many largely unsung, that prevented loss of life. They deserved better and lasting recognition: not all got the medals they merited.

Sadly, it seems that the ship's captain also failed to get his just desserts.

The book ends with shared wisdom on how humanity can and does rise to defeat adversity – even when confronted out of the blue by a black swan. The sinking of the *Oceanos* off the Wild Coast of South Africa was the epitome of the unexpected. Yet, through Herculean and concerted effort, the human spirit prevailed.

John Hare
Professor Emeritus of Shipping Law
Cape Town

INTRODUCTION

The Wild Coast is a beautiful but treacherous 300-kilometre-long piece of coastline on the eastern side of South Africa. It stretches from the Umtamvuma River near Port Edward, a small town south of Durban, to Morgan Bay, a beach resort north of East London.

The coastline is that of the territory formerly known as the Transkei, now part of the South African province of the Eastern Cape. It is an area of great beauty and a number of holiday resorts and small settlements, including Coffee Bay and The Haven near the mouth of the Mbashe River, have been established along its length over the years.

The Wild Coast boasts a number of natural wonders and beautiful natural phenomena: Waterfall Bluff, a high waterfall that pours directly into the Indian Ocean and which is one of three such waterfalls in Africa and one of only about 30 in the world; the famous Hole in the Wall, a huge detached cliff with a giant opening carved through its centre by the waves; the freestanding pinnacle of Cathedral Rock, and the kilometre-long rock shelf at Luphuthana against which waves explode high into the air in a beautiful and naturally choreographed sequence at certain tide levels.

The warm Agulhas, the most powerful ocean surface current in the world, flows southwards from Mozambique along the eastern coastline of South Africa. A couple of miles offshore, a Venturi effect due to the curved shape of the country's northeastern coastline accelerates the current along the entire length of this coastline to a speed of 5 or 6 knots (10–11 kilometres per hour and, significant in maritime terms, can increase a ship's speed by up to 40%). The current narrows in the vicinity of Coffee Bay, causing it to reach its peak velocity in that area. Ships travelling southwards will, if conditions permit, sail in the current because of the additional speed and consequent fuel saving.

Prevailing waves travel in a northeasterly direction, arising from storms deep in the Southern Ocean. The wind typically blows from the northeast, but can turn southwesterly as a result of the Roaring Forties, the strong westerly winds that arise between the latitudes of 40 and 50 degrees south.

The combination of the fast-flowing Agulhas current from the north and the waves originating in the Southern Ocean, when coupled with frequent storms and strong winds in the area, often conspires to create enormous rogue or freak waves. These waves are thought to be aggravated by the sudden fall of the continental shelf, a relatively shallow area of the seabed that surrounds every continent, where the depth of the water changes suddenly and significantly.

Sailors on ships traversing the area frequently describe experiencing enormous waves, some in excess of 20 metres. Researchers say that waves in the Agulhas current can reach 30 metres (about the height of a 10-storey building) and move at a speed of up to 50 knots (around 90 kilometres per hour). When a wave that size swamps a ship, thousands of tonnes of water will land on the ship, placing huge downward stresses on the vessel and causing it to sag in the middle. When a ship crests a huge wave, the centre of its hull or keel will hog upwards as the bow and stern sag, while the ship's buoyancy in the water causes the midsection to be supported by the wave. (Hogging is the stress on a ship's hull or keel that causes the centre, or the keel, to bend upwards.)

Ships are, for the most part, robust: they are designed and built to withstand nasty weather and heavy seas. But every ship will have its limits, and these are frequently tested in the seas of the Wild Coast. Around 3 000 ships have been wrecked along South Africa's massive coastline since record-keeping began and the Wild Coast has unquestionably claimed a disproportionate share of these, estimated to be at least half that number.

Some of the vessels that have foundered along this coastline are most famous for the mystery surrounding their misfortune. One of these was the *Waratah*, a 500-foot (150-metre) passenger steamer. In July 1909, en route between Durban and Cape Town, it disappeared somewhere along the Wild Coast with 211 passengers and crew aboard. Despite periodic searches for the vessel over the decades, no trace of the ship – not even flotsam – has ever been found.

In 1782, the *Grosvenor*, said to have been carrying a treasure of diamonds, rubies, gold and silver, foundered on the rocks off Lambazi Bay near the mouth of the Umzimvubu River during her final voyage from India back to England. Although many of the crew and passengers of the *Grosvenor* survived the wreck and made it off the ship, 27 perished in the waves and on the rocks. The 123 survivors set out on foot for Cape Town, a distant 1 500 kilometres away; only 18 of them made it, the rest dying along the way of starvation, illness or at the hands of hostile indigenous tribes.

Numerous other ships have been wrecked in the area over the years including, in more recent times, the *Jacaranda* (which ran aground in strong winds in 1971), the *Nagos* (which sank in heavy weather in 1993), the *Aster* (which went aground near Umngazi in 1995), the BBC *China* (which went aground at Lambazi Bay in 2004), the dry bulker *Kiperousa* (in 2005) and the bulk carrier *Kiani Satu* (in 2013).

It was along this stretch of water, perhaps best described as South Africa's equivalent of the Bermuda Triangle, that the *Oceanos* was to sail in August 1991. It would be her final voyage. It was also in these hostile waters that, with the odds overwhelmingly stacked in favour of a catastrophic loss of life when the *Oceanos* foundered, one of the greatest and most successful maritime rescues in history was staged.

CHAPTER 1

A DEAL TOO GOOD TO MISS

'Have you seen this?'

Turning to her colleague, Tanya Stoddart, travel agent Debra le Riche held up a telefax from TFC Tours which had been circulated in-house at Rennies Travel in Port Elizabeth. The heading read 'Opportunity to Cruise' and contained a special offer for travel agents to take a trip on the *Oceanos* from East London to Durban at a hugely discounted rate. It was mid-July 1991 and the Greek cruise liner had started plying her trade in southern African waters the previous month.

'Are you keen?'

Tanya took the memo and carefully read through it. 'Wow! Let me talk to my hubby, but I'm in.'

That evening Debra mentioned it to her family around the dinner table. Her two children, 8-year-old Raymond and 5-year-old Megan, were raring to go. Her husband, René, responded in more measured tones. 'How much is this going to cost?'

'R200 per person,' replied Debra. 'This offer is just too good to miss. It will be the experience of a lifetime for all of us.'

And with that, the decision was made.

A number of Debra's colleagues had seen the same memo, and eventually the Le Riche family and four other couples decided to hire a Kombi to drive the three-odd hours to East London and join the ship there. The plan was that they would sail overnight to Durban and then fly back home to Port Elizabeth.

Johan Venter* was bored – with his job as the managing director of a successful luxury-car dealership in Port Elizabeth, with his wife, with his life.

'Janet!' he called out to his PA of three years.

Janet Harrison*, a platinum-blonde forty-something divorcee and career secretary, came tottering in on her cork-wedge heels.

'Yes, Johannie?' She came over to his desk and her scent wafted over him.

'Janet, Piet* tells me that there's a special deal for a trip on a ship called *Oceanos* from East London to Durban in two weeks' time.'

'Yes?' She waited for him to continue.

'What do you think about coming on a cruise and spending a couple of days in Durban?'

'You want *me* to come?' Janet was not entirely sure of what was being offered. 'You've got a wife. What are you going to tell her? And why do you think I'd want to come with you anyway?'

'Ag, Janet. We've known each other for long enough. It's time we stopped playing games. We both know what we want and here's a perfect opportunity. *Jy weet ek is lus vir jou* [You know I want you],' he growled, lapsing into Afrikaans, his mother tongue, to express his true intentions.

'You can't just spring this on me,' Janet said, without much conviction. 'I need to think about it …' Her mind was in turmoil. Sure, she was half in love with her boss, seduced by his power and success, but she was also torn by the inappropriateness of a looming affair with another woman's husband.

Johan Venter rarely took 'no' for an answer. 'Well, don't think too long,' he said, gruffly. 'I might withdraw the offer. When you've thought about it, go and book for you, me, Piet and Mary-Anne*. You can book a couple of nights in Durban for after we get there.' Piet Mynhardt was the floor manager at the dealership and a good friend of Johan; Mary-Anne Cummins worked in the accounts department, and she and Piet had been having an affair for a while.

---

* Pseudonym

An advertisement for cruises on the *Oceanos* that appeared in *Fairlady*.

'You still haven't said how you're going to deal with this at home,' Janet said, weakening. Johan was not an unappealing man: a little overweight but tanned and with the chiselled jaw and strong features of the Afrikaner stock from which he came, he was generally not a bad package for a single mom with a routine life. And he had money, which was never a bad thing.

'I'll tell Marlize* that I'm going to a conference in the Eastern Transvaal. She's never interested in what I do and she'll believe that.'

'Is Piet alright with this? Has he sorted it out with his wife?' Janet asked.

'Ja. He's going to the same conference.' Johan laughed at his joke. 'You can book as Mr and Mrs Venter and Mr and Mrs Mynhardt.'

In Durban, South African Airways (SAA) employee Michael O'Mahoney was on a five-minute break when a colleague casually tossed a brochure from travel company TFC Tours across the desk.

'We're thinking of going on a cruise this year,' he said. 'There are some pretty good deals here. You should consider it too.'

When Michael started thumbing through the brochure, his eye was caught by an overnight cruise from East London to Durban. His wife, Yvette, had been all-consumed for the past three months with the role of mother to a newborn baby girl, Meghann. He was sure she would appreciate the break, or at least the change of scenery.

'That sounds so good,' Yvette said when he asked whether she would like to go. Neither of them had cruised before. 'Why don't we ask the Shaws if they want to join us?' she added.

Michael called their friends, Neal and Robyn Shaw, and the deal was struck. The Shaws decided to bring their daughter Kirsten with them, but to leave their infant child with Robyn's mother. Michael and Yvette brought along their 4-year-old son, Liam, a great friend of Kirsten Shaw, and their infant Meghann.

As an SAA employee, Michael could both cruise with TFC at discounted rates and fly cheaply to East London, so the trip represented a good value-for-money weekend break for the family.

A few days later, Michael was watching television one evening. 'What are you watching?' asked Yvette as she walked into the sitting room.

'A documentary about the *Titanic*,' replied Michael, without looking up.

'Well, you're tempting fate watching that before we go on our trip,' declared Yvette.

'I'm not superstitious,' said Michael. 'It's just a TV programme – nothing will go wrong.'

The *Oceanos* was named after the Greek god of the seas. She was a 153-metre ship with a 7-metre draught (the vertical distance between the waterline and the hull, and the minimum depth of water a vessel can safely navigate), refurbished to carry 516 passengers and about 200 crew.

Originally built in France as a general cargo vessel and launched in July 1952 as the *Jean Laborde*, she was used on the Marseilles–Madagascar–Mauritius cargo service. She underwent several name and ownership changes and in 1976 was registered in Piraeus, Greece under the name *Oceanos*.

The ship was converted in 1983 to carry passengers. Despite her Byzantine décor and other modernisations, given her origins, she was arguably not a model of passenger-ship aesthetics or design.

She had a number of decks, all named after Greek gods and goddesses. These were, from topmost to lowest, Jupiter, Apollo, Venus, Dionysos, Poseidon and Nereus.

The Jupiter deck housed the Old Athens Bar, the Odysseus lounge, the casino, the disco and the swimming pool. On the Apollo deck, immediately below, were the Adonis beauty salon, a sauna, passenger accommodation and the Four Seasons lounge. The Venus deck was largely for passenger accommodation, but included a shop and the purser's office. Dionysos accommodated a dining room, a hospital and more passengers. The Poseidon and Nereus decks accommodated crew.

Beneath the crew decks were the bowels of the ship, including the engine room, the auxiliary (generator) room and other machinery such as the propeller shafts, which ran from the ship's huge engines to and out of the stern, where they turned the giant propellers.

The company that owned the *Oceanos*, Epirotiki Lines SA, had originally carried passengers and cargo along the river Danube in Europe. In the early 1900s, Epirotiki moved its headquarters to the Greek harbour city of Piraeus, where it continued its operations on Akti Miaouli, the main street of this powerful shipping hub and a must-have address for any serious Greek shipowner.

After the Second World War, Epirotiki narrowed its focus to the cruise industry, operating principally in the Aegean Sea and the Mediterranean, and later extending its operations to the Caribbean. It continued to expand its passenger fleet until, by the 1970s, Epirotiki was the largest cruise-ship business in Greece, with in excess of 20 ships in the fleet. The company later diversified its operations into cargo, adding dry bulk carriers and oil tankers to its fleet.

Epirotiki had suffered two major casualties, in 1988 and 1991, with the loss of the cruise ships *Pegasus* and *Jupiter*. The *Jupiter* was struck by an Italian freighter in the Piraeus harbour in 1988 and sank with the loss of two lives out of the 580 passengers and crew on board. The *Pegasus*, which had been the flagship of the fleet, suffered a minor explosion and then a fire while berthed in the Venice harbour, resulting in the evacuation of the ship. Italian firemen, fearing another explosion, which might have damaged the city, ordered the flooding of the vessel, which subsequently sank at her moorings.

In 1988 the *Oceanos* completed a successful cruise season in South Africa. She returned three years later when she was taken on an eight-month charter by South African company TFC Tours, a family-run business founded in the 1950s by John Foggitt, a legend in the travel industry. Foggitt pioneered a number of local travel-industry firsts, including the first flights and tours to a number of destinations previously difficult to access for South Africans, such as Bangkok, Istanbul, the Far East and Seychelles. He also started the South African cruise industry, eventually growing TFC Tours into the largest travel firm in the country.

The company later changed its name to Starlight Cruises, after which it was acquired by MSC Cruises SA of Geneva.

When TFC Tours launched their cruise business, they would typically charter a ship for the six-week cruise season that started in mid-December and ran through to late January. However, the *Oceanos* was different. She was chartered in mid-June 1991 for a cruise season that would run for eight months, until the following January, sailing up and down the South African east and south coasts and to and from the Indian Ocean islands of Réunion, Mauritius, Bazaruto and Comoros.

This was a big commitment for the company – in fact, the longest charter they had ever undertaken. There was huge excitement and enthusiasm for this project, accompanied by a massive sales-and-marketing drive. Thousands of brochures were distributed around the country, and all TFC staff were required to cruise on the ship at least once and learn everything there was to know about cruising generally and the ship in particular.

At that time, Lou Tolken was the TFC manager in Durban. She sent all of her staff on the ship as soon as possible after the vessel came on charter, leaving herself to be the last in the office to cruise. She booked herself and her husband, Ernie, and assistant Louise van den Berg onto the ship for late July.

In 1991, the *Oceanos* was under the command of Captain Yiannis Avranas, a Greek ship's master (captain) with 30 years' experience at sea, 20 as a ship's officer. He had a crew of about 200 sailors serving under him, principally Greeks and Filipinos, with the officers and senior crew for the most part being Greek.

On the vessel's arrival in South Africa at the beginning of the 1991 cruising season, a journalist reporting for the South African edition of *Travel Times* had an opportunity to interview Captain Avranas. In answer to one of her questions about what would happen if the ship were to sink, the captain joked: 'I will be on the first lifeboat off the ship!'

Captain Yiannis Avranas

Musician Christopher 'Moss' Hills and his wife, Tracy, joined the *Oceanos* in Durban for a seven-month tour when she was taken on charter by TFC Tours in June 1991, along with a group of other musicians and entertainers, all employed by TFC Tours. Moss and Tracy performed as the musical duo Crosstalk, with Moss principally on vocals and playing lead and rhythm guitar and Tracy on the bass guitar and doing backup vocals. Before joining the team on the *Oceanos* they had worked on a number of relatively small cruise ships, such as the *Harmony*, the *Rhapsody* and the *Achille Lauro*.

Musician Moss Hills on the deck of the *Oceanos*

Their colleagues on the *Oceanos* included the Green Dolphin Showband Trio from Cape Town, jazz singer Tina Schouw, magician Julian Russell and the dazzling dancer Kevin Ellis. They were accompanied by comedian and singer Terry Lester, as well as Tony Shielder, Tom Hine and Terry Fortune – all household names in the entertainment industry at the time.

Then there was Alvon Collison, who became famous for his award-winning performance as Pharoah in the 3 000-performance run of the 1974 musical *Joseph and the Amazing Technicolor Dreamcoat*.

Another particularly well-known entertainer on board was Marah

Dancer Kevin Ellis (in white shirt) was part of the entertainment team.

Louw, who would later go on to become a soapie star. She started singing with a senior choir at the age of ten and later toured the world with musical shows; she performed for Queen Elizabeth in 1975 and at the Mandela Concert at Wembley Stadium in 1988.

Magician and comedian Robin Boltman,[1] whose lifelong ambition to become a magician was matched only by his hankering to go to sea, supported what began as a hobby by earning money as a banker. He was eventually noticed, while doing one of his moonlight magician gigs at a club in Cape Town, by a senior executive at Safmarine, the national shipping carrier of South Africa in the 1980s. He was asked to join the Safmarine passenger flagship, the *Astor*, on which he did a lengthy spell of duty and later worked on the *Achille Lauro*. In 1991, Robin joined the *Oceanos* at the Seychelles port of Mahé and sailed to Durban with his

---

1   Robin Boltman was the acting cruise director for this *Oceanos* voyage, to allow TFC representative Lorraine Betts, who usually served as cruise director, to plan the next trip (to Madagascar).

good friends, Tom Hine, Terry Lester and Alvon Collison.

In addition to the group of entertainers, TFC Tours had another 15 to 20 staff members to assist in all aspects of the tour and passenger administration and entertainment, including the able and experienced TFC representative Lorraine Betts.

'This ship is unseaworthy. It's the worst ship I've ever sailed on. It rolls around like a whore, the curtains in this cabin are torn, the décor is scruffy, we have this damn coffee-vending machine outside our cabin, the lifeboat fittings are rusty … It's a mess!'

David Gordon was having a sense-of-humour failure, and it was only the first day of a 12-day cruise on board the *Oceanos*. A leading senior advocate at the Durban Bar, with a speciality in maritime law, he was a veteran cruise-ship passenger and knew that the way this vessel was rolling on relatively calm seas was unusual for a passenger ship.

David had booked the Indian Ocean islands cruise package for himself and his wife, Anne, through TFC Tours. They departed from Durban in mid-June and, once aboard, he re-engaged his interest in cruise ships, wandering around the ship and filming everything he could see with his video camera, including lifeboats and safety equipment – and finding very little to his satisfaction.

As valid as David's complaints may have been – he also did not like the food – it was unlikely that the vessel was unseaworthy, as it had been allowed into South African waters on a long-term charter carrying the highest Lloyd's Register classification standard, 100A1. (All ships need to be classified as seaworthy, that is, safe, before they are permitted to sail. Lloyd's Register of London is one of about 50 classification societies in the world and is one of the most credible. These societies have a classification system that attributes numbers and letters to ships depending on their state of seaworthiness.) In addition, TFC Tours would almost certainly also have had the ship surveyed for seaworthiness when she came on hire under the charter, and the South African Department of Transport is unlikely to have allowed a passenger ship to ply South African waters over a long period without official assurance that the vessel was seaworthy.

For David and Anne the voyage proceeded uneventfully, if somewhat uncomfortably, until the ship reached Réunion. As the ship sailed from the harbour, David and a colleague were standing on the port side of the vessel, with David filming the ship's departure. Suddenly, his colleague exclaimed: 'We've just touched the bottom!'

David pointed his camera downwards, towards the water, as the ship exited the harbour at the end of the concrete breakwater. Mud and sand could clearly be seen, churning up close to the vessel's port-side hull.

That evening David and Anne dined at the captain's table, something of a privilege on a passenger ship. The captain, a typically Mediterranean-looking man with good-looking, if somewhat heavy features, thick, black curly and slightly greying hair, high cheekbones and thick eyebrows, dominated the conversation. During the dinner, David asked Captain Avranas: 'Did we hit the bottom when we sailed out of Réunion harbour?'

The captain replied in his thick Greek accent: 'It was nothing. We touch an underwater buoy.'

'Why would there be a buoy underwater? Is it for the Réunion submarine fleet?' David asked facetiously. 'Surely the vessel touched the ocean floor?' He was not letting this one go.

'It's nothing,' said Avranas. 'I know what I'm talking about. It was buoy. You doubt me.'

Avranas's arrogance cut short the conversation, and the dinner continued uneasily.

CHAPTER 2

ALL ABOARD

The official cruise schedule of the *Oceanos* advertised voyages from Durban to Cape Town and back, with a stop in Port Elizabeth on the return leg, departing in the latter part of July. This particular voyage, however, which departed from Durban on 28 July, would call in at East London instead of Port Elizabeth on the return leg, where passengers could enjoy two nights ashore before completing the voyage to Durban. The reason for this diversion was that an East London businessman had chartered the ship for his daughter's wedding for two days.

From Durban, the ship had sailed south to Cape Town, where she discharged a few passengers and collected some new ones. She then set sail again, in huge seas, on 31 July for her voyage around Cape Point and up the south and east coasts. The ship was guided out of the harbour by the pilot, a skilled mariner employed by the port authority and whose job it is to guide ships in and out of the port.

A pilot boards each vessel from a helicopter or a small launch (known as a pilot boat) when the ship is approaching the harbour mouth, then steer the ship, or give steering instructions to a helmsman, as well as generally directs the speed of the ship. The pilot accompanies the ship most, if not all, of the way to the ship's berth.

When the ship departs from its berth, the pilot again accompanies the ship and directs her navigation until she has exited the harbour, usually up to or just beyond the breakwater wall, but sometimes further if there is a long channel out of the port. The pilot then disembarks by launch or helicopter.

The pilot uses his local knowledge of water depths, channels, currents, weather and anything else that might affect the ship's course to direct the master as to which course to steer and how to avoid calamity. Importantly, he is required to direct the ship towards and into the middle of the entrance channel to the port. Almost without exception, every port has a marked channel that is deep enough (through dredging or the action of underwater currents) for ships to navigate safely without touching the bottom. Channels, which can be relatively short but in some ports run for many miles, are marked with red buoys on the ship's port (left) side and green buoys on the ship's starboard (right) side.

Disembarkation of the pilot usually takes only a few minutes, but can be hazardous, especially in heavy seas, as the pilot boat travels at the same speed as and closely parallel to the ship and the pilot has to climb onto or off a ladder hanging down the side of the ship.

When the *Oceanos* sailed from the Cape Town harbour on Wednesday 31 July, the ship was shadowed by the pilot boat, as is usually the custom. (Although pilot boats are still often used, some ports now embark and disembark pilots by helicopter.) However, once outside the harbour, the swell was so huge that it became too dangerous for the pilot to climb down the ladder and hop onto the launch. The pilot boat was surging up and down against the hull of the *Oceanos*, frequently squashing the rubber fenders hanging off the pilot boat against the bigger vessel and almost making contact with its charge; if the pilot braved the ladder, there was a real risk that he could be crushed against the ship.

The *Oceanos* eventually had to turn broadside to the wind to create a lee in which the pilot boat could position herself without fear of smashing the boat and crushing the pilot. Finally, an hour later, the pilot managed to land safely on the deck of the boat.

This was to be the pattern of weather for the next two days as the *Oceanos* made her way northeast towards her next stop in East London, as well as during her sojourn there.

The newlywed couple: Linith Sadh and her groom Christopher Maytham

Linith Sahd was a teacher at a school in East London and a bride-in-waiting. Her father, Winston Sahd, was a wealthy businessman who had made his fortune in the furniture and interior décor trade and wanted a grand wedding for his eldest daughter.

Sahd commissioned Mercia Schultz, travel manager of Rennies Travel in East London, to charter a ship for a wedding ceremony out at sea. As an add-on, Sahd wanted to host a party on board for his business associates and son-in-law elect.

On Sahd's instructions, Mercia arranged that the vessel, the *Oceanos*, would call at East London rather than the originally scheduled Port

Elizabeth. The plan was that, while the vessel was in East London, TFC Tours would arrange for all the passengers to stay in hotels ashore for two nights, while Sahd, his family and friends of the bride and groom took the ship on charter. The TFC entertainers were to stay on board and entertain the bridal couple and guests throughout.

The plan was to have a function on the Thursday evening, combined with a short cruise, and the wedding then on the Friday evening, combined with an overnight cruise. The ship would return to East London on the Saturday morning and fetch all her other passengers, before setting sail again in the afternoon to complete her voyage to Durban.

As East London was not a standard stop for cruise ships visiting South Africa, the local travel agents had had very limited exposure to the cruise industry. Bookings for the vessel after the wedding were relatively low, so Mercia persuaded TFC to offer a special last-minute reduced rate to her travel-industry colleagues for the onward leg to Durban, to give them first-hand experience of cruising as a holiday option.

The *Oceanos* berthed as planned on Thursday 1 August in the East London harbour, the only river port in South Africa and situated just inside the mouth of the Buffalo River. When the ship had docked, all the passengers disembarked and were whisked off to the local Holiday Inn for their first night ashore, which would be followed by a stay at the more luxurious Fish River Sun Hotel and Casino the next night.

That evening the ship set sail for a cruise to nowhere and back, returning to port at around midnight.

On the Friday, the weather began deteriorating rapidly. Nonetheless, wedding guests started to stream onto the ship before lunch and a huge party broke out on the upper deck. At around 2 pm the *Oceanos* set sail with attending tugs spraying the ship with pillars of seawater in celebration of the East London wedding of the century.

No sooner had the vessel exited the harbour than she encountered tempestuous waters and started rolling like a barrel. Two lunch sittings had been planned, but many guests retreated to their cabins with rising nausea. Those who made it to lunch sat and, for the most part, stared vacantly at a fixed spot, trying to ward off the inevitable. After a couple of hours at sea and with most guests incapacitated by seasickness and vomiting, the ship returned to port with the wedding ceremony yet to take place.

As the vessel entered the calmer waters of the port, guests started to emerge from their cabins, like rabbits from a warren over which the nausea wolf was no longer standing watch. The party started up again. The bride was, however, desperately unhappy at the prospect of her marriage vows being said on board a ship stuck in a grubby harbour and was determined that the ceremony should take place at sea. Under pressure from Linith and following a debate between her father and Captain Avranas, they set sail for the second time late that afternoon, once again into a heaving sea.

The wedding ceremony was performed on a stage in the Four Seasons lounge, with guests having gathered to observe the ceremony sitting in sofas around lounge tables.

The minister had some difficulty getting everyone's attention. 'If you could all extinguish your cigarettes and put down your drinks, we can get on with the ceremony!' he finally shouted above the general din. Slowly some semblance of order and solemnity came about.

As the vows were being said, musician Moss Hills watched from the stage how the guests, when called on by the minister to stand, swayed first to the left, then to the right, then back, propelled by the unrelenting swell into a novel wedding dance.

The organist, greener than the two enormous flower bouquets that Moss had placed strategically in front of her, soldiered on during the signing ceremony, but eventually had to rise from her seat and scurry to a corner of the lounge to vomit. Moss quickly found a bucket for her, into which she continued to retch from time to time as she played out the rest of the ceremony.

This was not the fairy-tale wedding Linith had had in mind when she originally planned her dream day. The moment the ceremony was complete and despite the original plan to stay out at sea all night, the vessel headed back into the sheltered waters of the East London harbour.

Entertainer Moss Hills and his wife, Tracy

There, once again, guests emerged from their lairs to resume the party.

Rough seas and a demanding bride were not the only challenges that the captain had to deal with on the evening of the wedding, however. While the ship was out at sea, a mystery woman telephoned the Port Control office at East London with a disturbing message: 'There's a bomb hidden in the wedding cake on the *Oceanos*,' she said.

In some panic, Port Control telephoned the South African Police to report the call.

On the ship's return that evening, waiting police demanded access to the vessel, but were denied it by the captain. After a lengthy stand-off between the captain and police, TFC Tours smoothed things over by advising the police that there was in fact no wedding cake on board; also, they said, the ship had been searched by security personnel and no bomb had been found.

As the guests regained their composure in the relative calm of the harbour, dinner was served and the TFC entertainers performed in shifts from sunset to sunrise. Moss and Tracy played first, followed by

Julian Russell, the Green Dolphin Showband Trio, Terry Lester, Robin Boltman, Marah Louw and the others.

The party raged on all night. There was an open bar, compliments of the father of the bride, which inevitably proved to be a suitable catalyst for the festivities. (The bar bill would never be paid, as all the till slips disappeared with the rest of the ship two days later.)

Following the all-night marathon of the wedding party, the entertainers tried to catch a few hours of sleep. Guests started to stagger off the ship late in the morning. After some rest, Moss walked into town to buy a few supplies. On his return to the ship, he found himself leaning into a gale and horizontal rain. It promised to make for an interesting trip to Durban.

Eduardo Abellar, one of the kitchen hands, went ashore with some Filipino friends from the galley to look around the town and buy a few things. On their way they met a priest who invited them to his small chapel. As Catholics, they respectfully entered the chapel, dipping their fingers into the font and crossing themselves with holy water. They each genuflected approaching the altar.

Unusually, pictures of sailors adorned the walls.

'Who are the people in the pictures, Father?' asked Eduardo.

'They were survivors of shipwrecks who were saved by the grace of God. I sheltered them here,' the priest responded. Pointing to a map of the coastline, he added: 'This coast is famous for its shipwrecks.'

The priest loaded the *Oceanos* crew into his car and drove them back to the ship. The priest's words were still swirling around in Eduardo's head as he made his way back on board.

Two incidents back on the ship did not do anything to ease Eduardo's mind. First, a fellow crew member told him about a bad dream: a ball of fire was flying in the air, floating and chasing him. And then one of the Greek sailors, apparently drunk and disconsolate after being ditched by his girlfriend, leapt overboard in what was either an ill-considered suicide attempt or, more likely, an attention-seeking stunt. A rubber dinghy was quickly deployed to recover the sulky swimmer.

On the big day, Saturday 3 August 1991, the O'Mahoney family was awake bright and early. Neal, Robyn and Kirsten Shaw arrived at their house, from where they all set out for the short ride to Louis Botha Airport, formerly Durban's international airport. On the southbound flight they encountered massive turbulence caused by, they were told by the captain, a storm approaching from Cape Town. Despite strong crosswinds almost causing the flight to be diverted, and a gut-wrenching descent into East London, the plane landed safely, albeit with most of the passengers looking green about the gills.

With the plane stopped at its berth and the steps rolled up, the purser made several attempts to open the aircraft door. But every time she shoved it open, the wind blew it closed again. Eventually Michael jumped out of his seat to assist and, with some effort together, they finally managed to open and secure the door.

The O'Mahoneys made their way carefully down the swaying steps, Yvette clinging to baby Meghann in the gale while Michael tried to manage their hand luggage and hold on to little Liam. Michael leaned into the wind as they crossed the tarmac and Liam clung to his dad's hand, his legs regularly being gusted off the ground.

The two families were greeted by SAA personnel, who told them that the port had been closed to shipping because of the weather; they could wait in the business-class lounge at the airport for further news. An hour or two later the port reopened, but ships could sail only at the discretion of each vessel's captain.

A minibus whisked the two families down to the harbour and the waiting *Oceanos*. In the howling wind and squalling rain, they hurried up the gangplank and into the lounge – only to be told to disembark, check in properly and pick up their boarding passes. Michael and Neal dutifully trooped down to a container on the quayside, which had been converted into a makeshift shipping office, to exchange their tickets for boarding passes.

Yvette, already feeling seasick, opted to stay with baby Meghann in the family's cabin on the Venus deck. Michael and Liam went up onto an outside deck to watch the ship's windy departure from the harbour into the heaving sea.

Lou Tolken, the Durban manager for TFC, had flown to East London on the Thursday to help with the wedding preparations, and then to assist with the embarkation of passengers on the Saturday for the voyage on to Durban.

She greeted passengers returning to the ship from the Fish River Sun who told her what they had seen while driving to the harbour: some corrugated-iron roofs were dislodged from their huts by the massive winds and flew across open veld and into the road, and huge concrete dustbins had been blown over in the appalling weather, they said.

The wind was gusting up to 75 knots (about 130 kilometres per hour – hurricane force) and the sea was in turmoil, with huge, foamy waves and spray streaking southwards through the grubby air. Black clouds disgorged buckets of soaking rain on the embarking passengers, while awnings, bins and other structures around the harbour were blown over and destroyed.

On arrival at the ship, some of the passengers simply booked flights back to Durban, refusing to re-embark given the discomfort and sea-sickness that so obviously lay ahead.

After checking in at the container serving as the makeshift passenger terminal, Johan Venter, Janet Harrison and their colleagues Piet Mynhardt and Mary-Anne Cummins boarded the ship. Janet was excited – it was her first sea cruise.

'We're going to have such fun tonight, Johannie,' she gushed, clutching his elbow. 'I've brought my party clothes – and a brand new silk negligee,' she added, using her best seductive voice.

Weather was the last thing on Janet's mind, but the TFC hostesses were well aware of it. 'The departure might be a bit delayed on account of the weather, Mr Venter,' one of them told Johan. 'The captain will make a decision later. Hopefully the wind will drop a bit in the afternoon.'

'That's okay,' said Johan. 'We'll spend the afternoon in the cabin. We need some rest,' he added, leering lasciviously at Janet.

Early on the morning of 3 August, the Le Riche family and their friends set off for the drive north from Port Elizabeth to East London, travelling along the Eastern Cape coastline, through the so-called independent homeland of Ciskei. They arrived in the late morning and boarded the *Oceanos* around lunchtime.

As they were boarding, Debra noticed a tiny door in the hull of the ship, just above the waterline. 'That's my escape route when the ship capsizes,' she joked to her colleague, Tanya.

Given that a gale-force wind was howling around them, Tanya did not find it particularly funny. 'Don't say that, Debra! You'll bring bad luck on the ship.'

But Debra persisted, excitedly: 'You know, like in the movie, *The Poseidon Adventure*. No one could get out of the capsized ship. If they'd had a little door, everyone could have escaped.'

As they boarded they were warmly welcomed by the Greek crew and served bite-size pizzas and cocktails. Spiro, one of the Greek waiters, was especially taken by little Megan's charm. 'What a beautiful girl and what beautiful hair you have,' he said, fussing over her and making sure she was well looked after.

The adults and children made themselves comfortable in the ship's lounge, with the wind howling outside under the overcast skies. Looking around, Tanya said: 'Is this ship listing?'

Debra replied that, if it was, it was probably due to the bad weather. She remembered that one of her other colleagues at the office, a classic Job's comforter, had told them before they left that they could expect high seas and inclement weather.

Finally, everyone was aboard. Among the passengers was a large contingent of SAA personnel and travel agents, lured by the promotional TFC Tours offer to the travel industry. These included Mercia Schultz from

Rennies Travel in East London, who had arranged the Sahd wedding, her parents, her husband, Leon, and their 10-month-old baby, Krystin.

Lou Tolken joined her husband, Ernie, who had already boarded. Both of them felt very uneasy about the weather.

'That wind looks shocking! We'd better not break down in that ocean,' Lou exclaimed.

'You're right,' her husband said. 'There won't be much help out there.'

CHAPTER 3

SETTING SAIL

The vessel's departure, which had been scheduled for 3 pm on the afternoon of Saturday 3 August, was delayed in the hope that the wind would abate.

Resuming his shift, kitchen hand Eduardo, on an errand to one of the outside decks, looked out at the surrounding dock and pier area. Even inside the harbour, the waves were significant. He wondered how much worse the waves must be on the ocean.

A rumour spread that they would not be sailing owing to the bad weather. Some of the Filipino crew yelled excitedly, thinking they would stay ashore for the night and have some fun.

Two hours later, however, and despite 6- to 10-metre waves forecast at sea and the storm that had raged for the whole day, Captain Avranas decided to sail. He ordered the engines to be started at around 5 pm.

It is always the captain's decision whether to sail or not. Safety of the vessel would be a primary consideration in making that decision, but in this case it is possible that Captain Avranas also had at the back of his mind the concern that the vessel was due to depart from Durban to Madagascar the following day, Sunday 4 August. Had he delayed the departure from East London for much longer, the *Oceanos* would probably have ended up leaving Durban late too, inconveniencing passengers and upsetting the ship's schedule.

When the ship finally sailed, it was very much against the will of the junior crew members, especially those who had made the acquaintance of the priest earlier in the day. The general consensus among them was that Captain Avranas was crazy.

In days gone by there was always something magical about the atmosphere at the quayside when a cruise liner was about to sail. Passengers would start arriving, with friends and family in attendance to wave them goodbye. The highlight was when the ship cast off her moorings and graciously moved off her berth: streamers flowed from the upper weather deck, people waved frenetically and the ship played out a happy farewell song over the loudspeakers and blew her horn.

Although the custom has waned somewhat in modern times because of the increased security measures in ports, when there was a sail-out from Durban harbour many years ago, droves of people would line up with their cars along the breakwater, all hooting and waving goodbye as the great liner started her journey.

There was no such sail-away for the *Oceanos* that day in East London. After the anticlimax of the long wait, coupled with the abominable weather, few passengers had stayed out on the deck. A handful of cars were parked along the port breakwater, hooting and flashing lights at the ship in the gloom, with a few bedraggled onlookers braving the elements to stand and wave with what enthusiasm they had left to those of their departing friends and relatives who were still visible on board.

The chief mate was reluctantly standing watch on the weather-blown bow of the ship, the southwesterly gale blowing into the port entrance making his life a misery; the second officer was cowering behind sparse shelter at his departure station on the poop deck aft of the ship. The master, third officer and a lookout were stationed, dry and warm, on the bridge as the tugs connected bow and stern lines to the vessel and pulled her off the quay wall of the sheltered harbour.

With the ship clear of her berth, the engineers down below in the engine room responded to the 'slow ahead' signal from the bridge. With two tugs in close attendance, the *Oceanos* slowly picked up speed and made her way past the southern quay walls in the mouth of the Buffalo River and headed towards the harbour exit.

The mandatory pilot provided by the port authority stood next to the third officer, who was helmsman at the time, directing him through the channel and towards the end of the long breakwater. As the vessel attempted to direct her bow in a northerly direction, she found herself being buffeted by the huge southerly gusts, hitting her starboard-side accommodation section and directing the bow section towards the concrete dolosse of the breakwater on the southern side of the port entrance. The rudder was inadequate to correct the problem while the engines were turning at low speed.

The pilot, realising that a situation was developing which could see the vessel catastrophically grounded on the breakwater in no time, immediately took action. 'Stern tug!' his instruction came over the VHF radio. 'Urgently push with full power on the port side! The bow isn't coming round in this wind.'

The pilot knew that a shove on the port side would push the stern of the ship to starboard and bring the bow around to port and allow the pumping gale to be more following than beam on. Once the ship had the wind more behind her, it would be easier to steer a straight course, especially when the engines picked up speed.

The master of the after-tug immediately directed his vessel towards the engagement point on the port-side stern quarter of the ship and gave the command to his engineers to shove with full power. Slowly the bow of the *Oceanos* came around to port.

As the vessel approached the beginning of the breakwater, the pilot turned to the master and said: 'Captain, I will need to disembark as we pass the entrance to the port. Will you be alright to take the vessel from there? If not, I have to travel to Durban with you.'

'No, it is fine,' said Captain Avranas, knowing that carrying a pilot to Durban would bring additional costs for his employers and leave East London short-staffed.

As they approached the end of the breakwater several hundred metres on, the pilot ensured that the ship was properly aligned and that his accompanying launch was safely alongside. 'Captain, are you sure you're

happy to take full control from here and you need no further assistance?'
he asked again. He needed to be sure the captain would not complain
later that he had deserted him.

Captain Avranas nodded.

'In that case, I'll leave the vessel to you now. Have a safe voyage. The
sea looks wild ...'

With that, he left the bridge, climbed down the several flights of stairs
to the main deck and exited into a flurry of rain, driven horizontal
by the gale. The pilot went to the side of the ship, now abeam of the
inner breakwater, and clambered over the rail and down the ladder. In
the heaving sea, it was all he could do to avoid being crushed between
the ship and shadowing launch. He leapt ungraciously across the gap,
landing uncomfortably on the deck as the *Oceanos* ventured onwards
into the open and storm-tossed sea.

As the ship crossed the sand bar after exiting from the harbour and
headed northeast, a huge, persistent swell pounded the starboard bow
of the vessel, rolling her uncomfortably over to her port side before
allowing her to bob back to starboard. This – the worst possible rolling
of a ship for passengers and crew – was to be the pattern for the next
several hours.

On board, members of the crew were carrying out their many and varied duties: setting places for dinner, battening down lifeboats, preparing
the casino, settling guests, tending the engines and generally keeping the
passages clear, while others rested, for the most part in their cabins, in
preparation for their next shift.

The entertainers had broken with the tradition of a sail-away party on
the pool deck and moved the proceedings indoors to the Four Seasons
lounge. If a party in the rain and wind did not seem all that much fun,
the festivities in the lounge were not a whole lot better, with the huge
swells turning Moss and Tracy's rock'n'roll into unpleasant pitch'n'roll.

'We'll provide the rock and the ship will provide the roll!' Moss kept
up his banter as they played.

The band, TFC staff and passengers manfully tried to keep the party going with music, streamer-throwing, dancing and heartiness. However, a combination of collapsing conga lines and seasick guests eventually dampened enthusiasm for further partying, and when entertainers Terry Lester and Julian Russell knocked each other over and together landed on magician Robin Boltman, the party was finally called off.

Two hours into the voyage, Captain Avranas stood on the bridge with his chief officer, watching the waves wash over the bow as the ship pitched, yawed and rolled in the foul conditions. Typically, Chief Officer Stavros Nikolaidis* would be the officer in charge of the navigational watch from 4 pm to 8 pm each day, accompanied by an able seaman acting as helmsman. However, departing from a port, traditionally the captain would be on the bridge to ensure that all was well.

Chief Officer Nikolaidis* was busy checking the course he had plotted against his instruments, to determine his first waypoint before the ship turned more northwards. Spray was lashing the bridge windows, high as they were above the main deck, making visibility difficult. The helmsman's eyes flickered between the bridge windows and the radar screen. A debris of waves and spray peppered the radar screen, making it difficult to determine if any vessel lurking in the huge waves posed any threat of a collision.

In this weather, fishing vessels became a particular hazard as they were low in the water, therefore difficult to see among the waves and even harder to detect on radar, which, in heavy weather, tended to pick up wave crests rather than small vessels.

Down in the engine room, the engineers were acting on the instructions received from the bridge to increase the vessel's speed as best they could. The engines thumped louder as the vessel ploughed on at half ahead (half of the engines' maximum speed), surging through the relentless swell. The ship was unable to go any faster as the propellers emerged repeatedly from the water when the ship went through each trough. If they had been going any faster, they would have been unrestrained, turned over too fast and consequently damaged the engines.

Chief Engineer Panayiotis Fines was standing in the auxiliary engine room, also known as the generator room, which was located just forward of midships. He was watching the fourth engineer, who was trying to remove a portion of a long venting pipe. The function of the pipe was to clear the build-up of noxious gases such as methane from the sewage tank.

Passengers had been complaining of a bad smell on the ship and Chief Engineer Fines suspected that there was a sewage blockage in the venting pipe. It was an old system on a ship that had, after all, originally been designed to carry cargo, so when it came under pressure of a ship full of passengers it tended to get blocked from time to time.

In modern ships, sewage systems are relatively sophisticated, with proper separation tanks and treatment plants for grey water (used water from basins and showers) and black water (water flushed down toilets). The processed water can then be recycled for non-potable uses on the ship.

However, the system on the *Oceanos* was more basic. Grey and black water drained from the cabins through a series of pipes that all eventually fed through two inlet pipes into a large tank in the sewage compartment. The inlet pipes each had a valve that could close off the flow of sewage into the sewage tank. When the ship was at sea, the tank would be emptied by pumping the raw sewage through an outlet pipe into the sea.

If the holding tank became too full, sewage would build up and escape into the venting pipe, which could then become blocked. As the system was close to the lowest passenger deck, it was inevitable that passengers would start complaining about unpleasant odours if these could not escape.

The venting pipe that the engineers were trying to remove was about 4 metres long and 10 centimetres in diameter. It ran down the generator-room bulkhead (a metal wall) and then through a hole in the bulkhead into the sewage-tank compartment.

The motorman, whose usual duties included routine checks of the machinery, tanks, bilges and pump rooms, along with the daily operation and maintenance of the machinery, was assisting the fourth engineer.

The wiper, whose functions included cleaning the engine spaces and machinery, stood by and awaited instructions.

The engineers toiled at their job. The flanges holding the piece of venting pipe were partially corroded and stuck and the men did not want to break the pipe during its removal or damage the hole through which it passed. Nonetheless, brute strength was required to resolve the problem.

Panayotis Megaloikonomou, the barman, was the muscle needed for the job. The wiper was sent in search of him.

Upstairs, the chief cook and his assistants were well along the path of preparing the evening meals. Making dinner was proving to be challenging, with the ship bucking around and scalding hot pans and pots threatening to slide off the stoves and do an injury to the cooks.

The first dinner sitting was scheduled for 7 pm each day. A show was usually scheduled for the same time, so that those eating dinner at the second sitting could watch the first show. A second show was then put on at around 9 pm for those who had attended the first dinner sitting.

However, the first show, which was to have involved dancing, had been cancelled earlier following a mini-mutiny by the dancers who feared broken or twisted ankles. The cruise director had also agreed to start the second show later, at around 10 pm.

The chief steward was a worried man. As his team of waiters made up the table settings in the dining room, cutlery was sliding around faster than it could be laid. The waiters had dampened the tablecloths in an effort to stop things from sliding around, but this reverse Heath Robinson solution was a poor match for the forces of nature.

Most of the passengers had retired to their cabins. Those who were susceptible to seasickness knew that their only salvation might be in lying prone on their beds and ensuring that they knew the most direct route to the toilet bowl. Those who were impervious to the green sea monster very quickly worked out that lying down was going to be a whole lot more comfortable and secure than trying to stagger around, bouncing off the narrow corridor walls.

Yvette O'Mahoney was one of those suffering badly from seasickness. However, her more robust husband, Michael, had gone upstairs for a beer with his friend, Neal Shaw. As the 7 pm dinner sitting approached, some passengers started to leave their cabins cautiously and make their unsteady way towards the dining room, although it was obvious that many were going to give dinner a miss. By the time the dinner gong sounded, several passengers were already seated, with others slowly filing into the dining room, among them Michael and Neal.

As passengers were seated, waiters started delivering their meals. A few plates crashed off their trays, leaving food and broken crockery strewn on the heaving floor. Meals that made it to the tables started sliding off the damp tablecloths with whatever else was not actually nailed or screwed down; some of the tables themselves were starting to capsize and crash to the ground. The *Oceanos* tables, unlike those on some of the more modern and luxurious ships, did not have rims to prevent items from sliding off, so it became something of a game to see who could keep their tables fully equipped. It was a hopeless challenge, and for the most part passengers just laughed, realising that they were in for a long night.

Michael returned to his family's cabin at around 8.15 pm to find Yvette on all fours in front of the toilet, retching relentlessly and violently, her diaphragm aching from the force of each heave. Liam was still awake, wide-eyed at his mother's suffering.

Michael gave what assistance he could to Yvette: passing tissues, persuading her to drink some water and rehydrate, having her lie down between bouts of vomiting. Then Meghann started to cry and Michael had to turn his attention to the baby.

After a quick and uncomfortable dinner in the crew dining room with officers and other entertainers, Moss and Tracy went to collect their wages from the purser's office at around 7.30 pm. As they passed the doors to the main dining room and peered in, they realised just how badly the ship was rolling. Through the doors they saw passengers sliding around on their chairs, usually nimble waiters dropping trays, and plates and cutlery sliding off tables. Moss started having second thoughts about whether they could perform at all that night.

Tracy returned to their cabin. She was shocked to discover that the porthole, which previously had a minor leak, was now letting in a steady stream of water. Her bed, beneath the porthole, was soaked, as was part of the floor.

She wedged towels all around the porthole and, although alarmed by the leak, was so tired from the previous two nights of almost nonstop entertainment that she lay on Moss's bed and dozed off.

Just after 9 pm a tremendous lurch of the ship woke her as the cabin contents were flung around, including three heavy steel trunks, which flew about 2 metres through the air and crashed into the opposite wall, spilling their contents all over. The cabin was in a shambles and the noise of the pounding sea on the side of the ship was overwhelming. She felt the first pangs of alarm and quickly started to gather some personal effects together into a small bag.

Earlier, Moss, who was worried about his equipment, had gone to the Four Seasons lounge to secure his microphone, instruments and their stands. He took his speakers down and put them on the floor, then went back up onto the stage to secure the cymbals. As he was doing that, the white grand piano – which was carefully secured on non-slip pads – came sliding across the stage and slammed into the drum kit.

Having settled into their cabins, Debra, René, Raymond and Megan le Riche were among those heading up to the dining room for the second dinner sitting at around 8.30 pm. The crew in the dining room were still scurrying around, trying to straighten things up and serve food without spilling it. Far from finding the situation stressful, the Le Riche family, none of whom had succumbed to seasickness, were still abuzz with excitement and considered the chaos just part of the adventure.

Every time the ship rolled, something else fell somewhere in the dining room, and when a cupboard flew open and a stack of crockery crashed to the floor, the Greek waiters just looked on, making no attempt to clear it up.

'Typical,' joked Debra. 'The Greeks will break plates at any opportunity.' The family roared with laughter.

A waiter turned to her, unamused: 'Madam,' he said, 'it is much worse than you think.'

After dinner, 8-year-old Ray started to yawn. 'Can we go to bed now, Mom?' he asked Debra.

'We're going to watch the show,' she replied, 'but I suppose we can put the two of you to bed first.'

She asked one of the crew members if it would be safe to leave the children in their cabin.

'Yes, ma'am,' the young Filipino attendant said, confidently. 'They will be fine. Very good ship.'

By now the ship had been sailing for over four hours, yet there had been no safety drills for passengers. Had the Le Riche, O'Mahoney or Shaw families – or indeed anyone else who had boarded the vessel for the first time in East London – wanted to know where their life jackets were stowed, they would not have had the faintest idea.

CHAPTER 4

MAYDAY!

At around 8.30 pm, Robin Boltman was in the Four Seasons lounge chatting to one of the TFC hostesses and the barman, Panayotis. The latter was a big man, well over 2 metres tall and immensely strong. Whenever there was a job on board requiring physical strength, Panayotis was the go-to guy. He also helped out with odd jobs and minor problems on the ship.

All of a sudden, one of the engineering staff rushed in, yelling at Panayotis in Greek, the whites of his eyes showing.

'You watch bar, Robin!' shouted Panayotis as he ran out.

Robin assumed he was going to break up a crew fight downstairs, but 20 minutes later Panayotis walked back in, smelling terrible and with muck spread up to his elbows.

'Look at me!' said Panayotis holding out his arms. 'I'm covered in shit!'

'What have you been doing?' asked Robin.

'Bloody sewage system is broken. Now me, barman, must remove pipe. The engineers are too stupid.'

'Did you manage?' asked Robin, fully expecting to hear that Panayotis had been the man of the moment.

'Yes,' replied Panayotis. 'I take out blocked pipe which is full of shit. Engineers must clean it.' He left to wash himself.

After Panayotis returned to take charge of his bar, Robin headed to his cabin to prepare for the show scheduled for 10 pm. The ship continued rolling unpleasantly as he dressed in his suit and tie. He gathered his

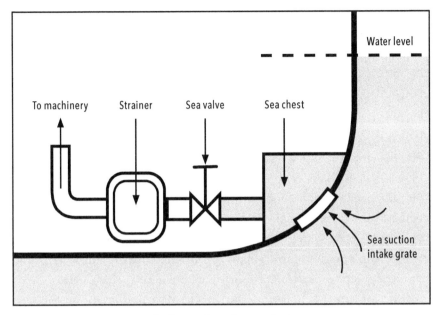

To machinery   Strainer   Sea valve   Sea chest

Water level

Sea suction intake grate

An illustration of a sea chest

props for the show. The next moment, the ship took a huge lurch. Loose personal effects in his cabin fell to the floor and the lights went out.

Down below in the engine room the powerful MAN B&W diesel engines were still turning valiantly, straining in the massive seas. Every time the ship ploughed through a deep trough, the propellers would pop out of the water and surge, causing a roar of discordant noise in the engines.

Close by in the auxiliary engine room, which housed the diesel generators that powered all the lights and electrical equipment on the ship, the engineers were still toiling over the sewage system, trying to dig out the packed poop in the bottom half of the pipe. It was hard work in the hot, enclosed space. Water and muck had spilled onto the floor, so to compound the general misery of the stuffy space, there was also a terrible, gagging stench. Despite years at sea, some of the engineers were starting to feel queasy.

Chief Engineer Panayiotis Fines, a burly man, was standing over them, sweating, exhorting them to hurry up and sort out the problem. He had not eaten since lunchtime and was in a hurry to get back to the crew dining room.

A huge wave suddenly crashed against the port-side hull, sending the engineers reeling. As they struggled to regain their footing after the sharp roll, their ears were assaulted by an ear-splitting roar as the sea chest ripped off the inside hull and water gushed through a half-metre-wide hole into the space where they were working.

The sea chest is a steel box through which piping systems draw water from the ocean for cooling and other purposes through a grating connected to the outside of the ship. The chest is usually welded onto the inside of the hull. Water intake is controlled by a valve and pipe that exit into the ship's plumbing and supply cooling water to the ship's generator, lube-oil coolers, air coolers, fresh-water cooler and other devices.

In the case of the *Oceanos*, the sea chest was mounted on the port side beneath the gratings on the floor that covered the bilges. (Bilges are like drains or gutters where the curved part of the hull meets the vertical sides and where dirty water collects.) It had ripped away from the side of the ship, exposing a huge hole through which volumes of seawater were gushing.

The water knocked the third engineer off his feet and rapidly covered the floor. Pandemonium ensued.

Above the din, the chief engineer was screaming out instructions as he fought his way through the water to the dislodged sea chest and futilely tried to force it back into place, slashing his inner arms in the attempt. The head on the incoming jet of seawater was enormous, aggravated by the depth of the engine room some metres below the ship's waterline. Short of somehow plugging the huge hole from the outside, there was no way of resisting the force of the water. The engineers knew that they could not stop this flood; the floor was already ankle deep in water and the level was rising rapidly.

Chief Engineer Fines was overcome with a sense of déjà vu: he had been on the *Jupiter* when she had sunk in 1988. Apart from the owners, ships' captains and chief engineers probably take it hardest when their ships sink.

The chief engineer and third engineer splashed their way into the main engine room. Fines called up to the bridge and screamed the news in Greek to the chief mate. 'There's water pouring into the auxiliary engine room! The generators will flood and short! We have to stop the generators!'

'Why can't you stop the leak? You're an engineer!' the chief mate barked.

'It's impossible!' yelled Fines. 'The leak is huge! The sea chest pulled off the hull! There's water everywhere. We have to abandon ship!' It was too complicated to explain about the missing pipe.

Fines slammed down the phone and summoned the third engineer. They shut down the generators, ran through the sewage compartment into the engine room and closed the watertight doors behind them, sealing off the auxiliary engine room and sewage spaces from the rest of the ship and fled upstairs to the bridge, pausing in their cabins on the way to collect their life jackets. The ship was now running on a limited store of power, with only bare essentials such as emergency lighting and certain of the ship's instruments capable of working.

By the time they reached the bridge, Captain Avranas was there, talking animatedly to the chief officer. The engineers, who had run up eight flights of stairs, explained breathlessly what had happened below.

'We have to abandon ship!' the chief engineer said again. 'It's going to sink!'

'Did you close the watertight doors?' Avranas asked.

'Yes, of course, Captain.'

'Then why will the ship sink?' Avranas asked impatiently. 'It cannot sink if only one compartment is flooded.'

'The ship will sink,' repeated Fines. 'We didn't have time to replace the venting pipe or close the valves to the sewage system.'

When he explained that they had been working on the sewage system, Captain Avranas understood: no matter how tightly the watertight doors had been sealed, water was still going to escape from the auxiliary engine room into the sewage tank. It would then flow through the sewage pipes that ran through the entire ship, first flooding the forward section of the ship and then spreading aft.

'Get the crew to start handing out life jackets,' he ordered the chief officer, 'but don't cause panic. Just tell everyone this is a precaution because we have some engine trouble. We must abandon ship, but I think we have time and maybe we can wait until help arrives. Do not cause panic and do not tell anyone what has happened.'

With that, he ran to his cabin, a short distance from the bridge, to tell his wife, Davina, what was happening – and to pack a bag, just in case.

Back on the bridge, he asked his chief engineer: 'How long will it take for the water to spread through the ship?'

Fines gave a Mediterranean shrug: 'Ten hours, maybe more.'

'And how fast will it reach each level?'

The chief engineer gave another shrug. 'Maybe two hours for each level.'

They discussed the ship's list to starboard, and whether it would increase the flow of the water through the vessel, and at what rate.

'Do the calculations!' Captain Avranas ordered the chief officer. He needed to know how much time they had before the ship would capsize or sink.

Nikolaidis started doing stability calculations.

An hour had passed since water had started pouring into the ship.

In the ship's corridors, dim emergency lights came on. Robin hurried from his cabin, making his way through the rolling ship towards the lounge, staggering like a drunk. He knew passengers were gathered in the lounge waiting for the show and he did not want them to be sitting confused in the dark, although he was not entirely sure what he would do when he reached them. Nonetheless, he was usually the host of the show, so would be the one expected to make any announcements to passengers.

He arrived to find passengers milling around in the half light. Although one or two entertainers had reached the lounge before him, Moss was not there yet, nor the dancers. Robin was not sure how he was going to start a show with no power and none of his main acts.

Having secured his equipment as best he could, Moss set off for his cabin just after 9 pm to find and chivvy Tracy. On his way he saw a commotion outside the lounge. Crew members wearing life jackets were running around with arms full of life jackets. Moss found this strange, as no emergency drills has been scheduled. In fact, as he thought about it a bit more, they had not done an emergency evacuation drill at all since leaving East London and there were new passengers on board.

As he emerged onto the Venus deck, he saw three security men running towards the aft of the vessel. Sensing trouble, Moss followed them to the crew stairwell on the Dionysos deck.

Crew were scurrying up the stairwell, some soaked, many carrying small kit bags, and most wearing life jackets. Others were ducking into cabins to throw their personal effects together, then rushing back out again. A few officers were shouting at them to calm down, adding to the unfolding scene of chaos. Moss guessed that there must be a serious problem on board.

Moss ran back to his cabin to warn Tracy. She was already shoving a few clothes and personal effects into a bag. 'I'm really worried, Moss,' she said as he entered. 'Something doesn't feel right.'

'Get changed quickly! Jeans and track shoes! We might have to abandon ship,' Moss said with restrained urgency. He explained what he had just witnessed. 'The crew seem to know something we don't.'

Quickly, he also packed a small bag and they started back up towards the lounge. As they climbed the stairs, the power went off. They were left in the pitch dark for a moment or two before the emergency lights popped on, throwing an eerie half-light into the rolling corridors.

As they made their way to the lounge, Tracy asked: 'How are we going to do the show without any power?' A true entertainer, she believed the show still had to go on.

'We could go all acoustic,' said Moss. 'The passengers are expecting a show and we have to do something.' Entering the dimly lit lounge, he could hear the assembled passengers grumbling. Robin was standing on the stage.

'Sit down, everyone!' Moss shouted. 'We're going to start the show shortly. We just need to find out where our power went.'

Moss left the passengers with Robin and found Lorraine Betts outside the lounge. 'Lorraine, what's going on? I saw crew running around in life jackets.'

'I'm not sure,' Lorraine said, shifting into cruise-director mode. 'I'm going to speak to the captain.'

There had been no alarm or other official announcement, yet crew members were running around frenetically and in some panic. Something was seriously wrong and Lorraine needed to find out what. She and Moss followed a couple of the scurrying crew members, all officers.

'Where are you going?' demanded Lorraine of the second officer. At this time of the evening he would usually be nowhere to be seen – his standard shift was from midnight to 4 am, and it was just after 10 pm.

'Captain says we must launch lifeboats. Just precaution, understand?' Despite his thick Greek accent, the second officer could not disguise the fear in his voice.

'Why do you launch lifeboats as a precaution if we're not abandoning ship?' asked Lorraine. 'Are we sinking?'

'No, no! No sinking! We just launch lifeboats in case,' replied the flustered Greek sailor.

Lorraine was not convinced. As a cruise director, she knew as much about ships and cruising as most other full-time crew members. She was also fully alive as to when you launch lifeboats, and when you do not. There had to be a compelling reason for their launching of the boats with huge seas running.

The second officer rushed off after his colleagues, with Lorraine and Moss in hot pursuit. They ran out onto the deck, where their worst suspicions were confirmed. Deck hands were frantically trying to release two lifeboats and several officers were already seated in each.

The wind was howling and Lorraine could hardly make herself heard above the din. 'What the hell's going on?' she shouted. 'No alarm has been sounded. Where are you going?'

She could not hear the reply from the officer she had accosted, now ensconced in the lifeboat.

She ran back into the show lounge, where she spotted Robin. 'Take this, Robin,' she said, handing him one of the on-board megaphones. 'We have no power and it's the only way you're going to communicate with the passengers. We need to keep them calm. I don't know what this power outage is about or why crew are trying to launch lifeboats, but I have a bad feeling about it.'

Robin took the megaphone. 'Attention, passengers! This is your magician speaking. We're working to manifest some light, but to brighten up your evening we're going to have a party. Just give us a few minutes to set up.'

Robin hurried back to his cabin to collect his acoustic guitar. Back at the lounge, in the twilight cast by the emergency lights, he quickly launched into a rendition of Jeremy Taylor's iconic 'Ag Pleez, Daddy'. The passengers joined in the singalong.

Back in his cabin, Michael O'Mahoney was changing baby Meghann's nappy when the lights went out. In the gloom of a small emergency light it had become eerily quiet. The engines' comforting rhythmic background thumping had been replaced with the swishing of huge waves passing across the cabin's portholes in the darkness outside, but otherwise nothing.

A sudden and urgent knock on the door a couple of minutes later made him jump.

'Who is it?' Michael asked through the door.

It was one of the TFC Tours staff. 'Sir, please can you put on your life jackets and go upstairs to the lounge?'

'Is this a drill?' asked Michael, thinking of the still-unchanged baby Meghann and his ill wife.

'No, sir, this is not a drill. Your life jackets are in the bottom of your wardrobe.'

Yvette, overhearing the conversation, struggled to her feet groggily.

Michael pulled the life jackets from the wardrobe, threw one across to Yvette and began pulling his on. Holding up the remaining two jackets, he could see immediately that they were both adult sized. There was none for Liam and of course nothing that would fit baby Meghann.

'What do I do about children's life jackets?' he asked, exasperated.

'There are children's life jackets upstairs,' the TFC staff member replied. 'Now, please hurry to the lounge. Leave any personal belongings behind.'

They made their way as quickly as they could along the dimly lit passage from their cabin, Meghann wrapped in a small sleeping bag and clutched to her mother's chest, Michael leading Liam by the hand. When they arrived in the lounge, they found dozens of passengers already there, everyone wearing life jackets, some people seated, others lounging on the floor. The incongruous strains of a singalong were audible above the general din and chatter of anxious and confused passengers.

Around 9.30 pm, as Debra and René le Riche walked through the casino on the way to the lounge, a roulette table crashed over onto its side, spilling chips. Some passengers started screaming and everyone clutched onto whatever they could as the ship lurched from port to starboard and back.

'I want to go back and check on the children,' Debra said anxiously.

Together they hurried back to the cabin where the children were fast asleep in their beds, although every loose item in the cabin was lying strewn on the floor.

Crew members were darting around outside in the corridors, some moving with purpose, others apparently aimlessly. René called out to them: 'What's happening? Why are you running?'

A babble of replies came back, mostly in foreign languages, all unintelligible. A Filipino crew member said to them: 'Sir, grab your life jackets and get upstairs immediately!'

'Are you serious?' asked René. But the Filipino was gone.

It did not take them long to discover four life jackets in the cupboard: three were for adults and one was for a child. The child's life jacket fitted Ray perfectly, but that left an adult life jacket for 5-year-old Megan. They secured it around her as best they could, hoping it would not be necessary for them to wear the life jackets for long.

Locking the door behind her, Debra set off up the corridor with her family, heading for the Four Seasons lounge. Suddenly, all the lights went off.

'We're going to die in here!' exclaimed Debra in the darkness. Feeling their way along the passage walls, dim emergency lights came on, again showing them the route to the stairwell and up towards the lounge.

Moss returned to the lounge, which was quickly filling up with passengers wearing life jackets. He took the baton from Robin, pulling out his own acoustic guitar and hammering it hard to be heard above the general hubbub. He and Tracy led the singalong, with a dash of Neil Diamond, Albert Hammond and other old favourites. Robin and a few other entertainers joined in for the choruses, the added voices partly making up for the absence of an amplifier.

The passengers half-heartedly got up for 'Sweet Caroline' and 'Piano Man'. When Moss called 'American Pie' to Tracy, she whispered in his ear: 'We'd better change the line that goes: "This'll be the day that I die ..."'

Moss roared with laughter.

Suddenly, the attention of everyone in the lounge was caught by a loud rumbling noise, a bit like a passing race of horses' hooves. Moss looked out of the large windows and was astonished to see the silhouette of a lifeboat being lowered.

He went cold with fear. He was almost certain the lifeboat contained officers. Who could or would have the authority to launch the lifeboats? Given the running around in the corridors he had seen earlier, and his conversation with Lorraine and the second officer, it could only be senior crew in the lifeboat being lowered past the lounge windows. Were the officers abandoning the ship and leaving everyone behind?

Passengers started shouting at him: 'What the hell's going on, Moss?' There had been no official announcement or instructions from the ship.

Trying to hide the anxiety in his voice, Moss told everyone to sit tight while he went to find out what was happening.

While they had been playing, Robin saw dancer Kevin Ellis come into the lounge wearing a life jacket. He jumped off the stage and hurried over to Kevin. 'What do you think you're doing? Take that life jacket off!' Robin shouted at him. He knew that it would only cause the passengers to panic if they saw a member of the entertainment team wearing a life jacket. It is one thing for passengers to be asked to wear life jackets as a precaution, but when staff and crew also start to don them, a more serious message is conveyed about the state of the ship.

'All the crew downstairs are wearing their life jackets, and if they're wearing theirs, I'm wearing mine,' Kevin replied defiantly.

Moments after Moss had gone in search of further information, the staff captain, also wearing a life jacket, came rushing into the lounge and screamed, 'Everybody lie down!'

'Are you insane?' asked Robin. 'This isn't a bank robbery. Get the fuck out of here. You're causing panic and we've only just managed to calm the passengers down.'

Robin advanced on the staff captain and the latter backed out of the lounge. However, he and a few other officers with him, also dressed in life jackets, told some of the TFC staff to go and fetch life jackets for everybody. All available staff rushed downstairs and ransacked cabins, pulling blankets off beds and grabbing life jackets. They brought everything upstairs to the lounge.

Moss also returned to the lounge, not having learned anything new about what was going on. 'I'm going down below to see if we're sinking,' he announced, picking up his video camera.

'No, you're not!' exclaimed Tracy. 'It could be dangerous, Moss. Please don't go.'

'I need to find out what's going on,' he replied. 'If we're sinking, we need to know.'

'I'll go with him,' magician Julian Russell said and, to Tracy's relief, walked quickly after Moss.

Together, the two entertainers went down the stairs, descending from Apollo to Venus and then down to Dionysos. They could hear voices gabbling away from the lower Poseidon and Nereus decks in Greek, Filipino and other languages. Moss and Julian spotted some crew members coming up the stairs carrying backpacks and suitcases.

'What's going on down here?' asked Moss as he descended towards the Poseidon deck. There was no acknowledgement of the question from anyone and no answer. The crew simply rushed around and past them.

The two men carried on walking along the prop-shaft tunnel, on the lowest level of the ship and aft of the engine room. 'Well, this is dry,' Moss pointed out. 'Perhaps we're not sinking, but the shafts aren't turning. Clearly there's no power from the engines.'

They forged on through the ship towards the engine room. There was no sign of crew anywhere.

Eventually they reached a closed watertight door. Moss put his ear to it. 'Julian, listen to this. Can you hear water sloshing? It sounds like there's a lot of water behind this door.'

Julian also put his ear to the door. 'I just don't know, Moss,' he said, raising his voice against the commotion. 'It's hard to tell if we're hearing waves or something else.'

'I don't think it would be too clever to try and open this,' said Moss.

They retreated up to the Four Seasons lounge, not much wiser. With the mood in the lounge growing gloomier, they tried to resurrect the singalong.

At 10.45 pm Captain Avranas reluctantly turned to the chief radio officer. 'Make a Mayday call now!' he said.

Owing to the listing of the vessel, the satellite communications were not working, so the chief radio officer started transmitting the message in Morse code, working on the distress frequency of 500 kHz (also known in slang to radio operators as '5Ton'). Following the international radio telecommunication protocols, he tapped out: 'SOS SOS SOS DE SZPK SZPK SZPK'.

SOS is the Morse-code version of the voice-telephony distress signal 'Mayday'. Contrary to popular belief, it is not an acronym for 'save our souls' or 'save our ship'; it stands for nothing. The DE derives from the French word meaning 'of' and denotes the calling station of the sender. SZPK was the call sign of the *Oceanos*.

It was 10.50 pm when the duty officer at Port Elizabeth Radio heard the auto-alarm bell in the radio room urgently signalling that a distress call had been received. This auto-alarm would have sounded in the radio room of any ship or coastal radio station within about 400 nautical miles of the sender. Simultaneously, the Durban and Cape Town coastal radio stations also picked up the message, albeit distorted.

These three radio stations were vital to shipping along the south and east coast of South Africa. Their function was to communicate with all maritime traffic in the area, principally to coordinate search-and-rescue operations, pass on distress calls, issue weather and navigational warnings, and generally ensure that ships at sea and those interested in them on land stayed properly informed.

A faint message followed the alarm signal: 'SOS DE SZPK. Vessel taking water in engine room. Require urgent assistance. About to launch lifeboats. Position 32.07S 26.06E.'

All three radio stations acknowledged the call. As communications were poor on the 5 Ton frequency, the various stations then moved to the much clearer radio-telephony on the 2182 kHz medium frequency, where they received a voice message.

'Mayday! MV *Oceanos*! Call sign SZPK. We are three miles off Mbashe Point, heading 15 degrees. We are in huge seas – sea state is Beaufort 10 to 12 [hurricane force] with wave height up to 14 metres. Vessel taking water rapidly in the auxiliary engine room and must shut down main engine. Require urgent tug assistance. About to launch lifeboats.'

Port Elizabeth Radio immediately radioed the Maritime Rescue

Coordination Centre at Silvermine near Cape Town.[2] 'We have a report of a passenger ship in distress off Coffee Bay,' the duty officer relayed. 'It is the *Oceanos*.'

'Thank you, PE. We've already had a report from a Norwegian radio station, Rogaland Radio, which also picked up the same signal. What is the position you have?'

A port authority tug based in East London, the *Jan Oelofse*, listening in, interjected. 'MRCC, this is tug *Jan Oelofse*. We have plotted the position. The given longitude is wrong. It is nowhere near Mbashe Point.'

Silvermine then responded directly to the *Oceanos*: 'MV *Oceanos*! We require a sitrep [situation report]. Please clarify your coordinates and advise how many passengers you have on board.'

Captain Avranas rechecked his navigational chart, quickly measuring off the coordinates. After a moment the radio officer responded: '32.07S and 29.07E. Repeat: 32.07S and 29.07E. Nearly 600 passengers and crew.'

'MV *Oceanos*, have you given the order to abandon ship?'

'Not yet,' came the reply. 'We must abandon ship. Ship already listing five degrees to starboard. Slightly down by head. We put both anchors to stop drift to shore and we launch lifeboats.'

The ship responded to Silvermine's further requests for clarification, and when all the necessary information had been relayed, the radio operator said: '*Oceanos*, we will put out a call for help to all traffic in the area and mobilise the Air Force. Good luck. We will remain in contact.'

At 11.35 pm the Silvermine centre formally took over the full rescue coordination. The Durban and Port Elizabeth radio stations were instructed to transmit to all shipping in the area: 'All vessels: MV *Oceanos* position 32.07S and 29.07E sinking. Abandoning ship. 600 passengers on board taking to lifeboats. Please assist.'

Just after midnight a ship called the *Varda* advised them that it would be on the scene within an hour. Shortly thereafter the *Nedlloyd*

2   Among the shipping community, the Maritime Rescue Coordination Centre is usually colloquially referred to as 'MRCC' or 'Silvermine'.

47

Mauritius said it was about three hours away. Other merchant ships and fishing vessels in the area also reported that they were making their way to the casualty site.

Peter Kroon, the principal officer of the Department of Transport (Maritime) in East London, had in the meantime been awoken by Captain Terrence Cook, the East London harbour master, and told about the crisis. Cook told him that Silvermine knew about the casualty and was in contact with the *Oceanos*. Cook wanted guidance on what the port should do.

Although he knew that, realistically, no harbour tug would be able to go to sea safely in the conditions, Kroon ordered that all harbour tugs be on standby. Nonetheless, the crew of the *Jan Oelofse* took it on themselves to set sail from East London in search of the *Oceanos*, despite the huge seas with which they were faced and without orders to proceed. Given that it was a small harbour tug, not designed for deep-sea passage or salvage work, this was a brave decision, verging on the foolhardy.

Captain Avranas left the bridge immediately after completing the communications with Silvermine. As he exited, he bumped into Lorraine Betts, the experienced TFC cruise director.

'What's going on, Captain?' she asked. 'I saw the crew running around with life jackets and lifeboats being prepared.'

Despite her petite stature, Lorraine was a no-nonsense type of woman, and the captain knew it would be difficult to pull the wool over her eyes. Even so, Captain Avranas could not bring himself to tell her the full truth. 'We have some engine trouble. Maybe it is necessary to abandon ship. We give life jackets as precaution.'

Lorraine looked at him suspiciously. 'Why would you abandon ship if you have only engine trouble? Engine trouble is engine trouble. A tug can come and help us. Are we sinking?'

Captain Avranas avoided her eyes. 'No, I don't think, but maybe. There is some water in engine room.'

'If we're sinking, how much time do we have before the ship goes down?' Lorraine asked.

'Five, maybe six hours,' Avranas muttered.

'Then why haven't you ordered everybody to abandon ship?'

'I'm not sure if we sink,' he replied. Before she could argue further, he turned on his heel and quickly walked away.

Lorraine followed him half-heartedly, trying to digest what she had just heard, but then saw Lou Tolken in a passage. Going up to her, she took both of Lou's hands in her own. Looking her in the eye, she said, 'Lou, we're sinking.'

'How long have we got?' Lou asked quietly.

'Five hours. We have work to do.'

CHAPTER 5

ACTION STATIONS ASHORE

Brigadier Theo de Munnink was already in bed and nodding off when his phone rang. Offensive as it always was this late and after hours, he answered anyway.

It was an occupational hazard that came with his senior position in the South African Air Force (SAAF). De Munnink had made a long and successful career for himself in the SAAF and was a veteran of the Border War of the 1970s-1980s. After holding leadership positions in a number of different combat and non-combat postings in South Africa, Scotland and South West Africa (now Namibia), he was appointed Officer Commanding Southern Air Command at Silvermine in 1988.

'Theo, it's Manie.' His brother-in-law, Manie Bezuidenhout, was on duty that night at Cape Town Radio. 'We've just had comms from Durban Radio about a passenger liner, the *Oceanos*, which is sinking four miles off Coffee Bay.'

Theo was wide awake now. He could not believe what he was hearing.

'The ship has lost power, it's taking water and there are 600 passengers on board. The weather is very poor: the wind is gusting at 40 knots and there's a huge swell – in excess of 10 metres,' Manie continued.

If Manie was correct with his information – and there was no reason to doubt him – this was a crisis of monumental proportions. De Munnink immediately called his second in command and Senior Staff Officer Operations, Colonel George 'Tiny' Hallowes, and recounted what had been relayed to him. 'Tiny, I need you to go to Silvermine, contact all support staff and start organising this rescue.'

They discussed for some time the initial steps needed, the people to be contacted and the resources to be deployed.

Twenty-five minutes after De Munnink had first been contacted, Silvermine received a call from the Durban port captain, advising of the maritime disaster that was developing off the Transkei coast.

The Maritime Rescue Coordination Centre at Silvermine is located in the hills behind Muizenberg, some 25 kilometres from Cape Town's city centre, and overlooks Tokai, Constantia and False Bay. Its primary role is to respond to the maritime search-and-rescue requirements of the Department of Transport and interact with government and non-government entities involved with rescue at sea.

The Department of Transport itself has overall responsibility for South African Search and Rescue. While they are able to prescribe policy and provide funds, they do not have sufficient assets, such as aircraft, helicopters and ships, mountain climbers, medical support and so on to do the actual rescue work. The operations coordination is accordingly given to two rescue coordination centres. One, situated at the Air Force headquarters' operations room in Pretoria, covers most of the overland and internal situations, like aircraft crashes inland, floods and fires. The seaward rescues are handled by the centre at Silvermine.

At the time, Southern Air Command – where Brigadier De Munnink was the officer commanding – had a joint operations room with the South African Navy and was tasked as the search master during rescue operations. The Southern Air Command personnel formed the staff of the Silvermine coordination centre when they went into search-and-rescue mode. However, the Air Force bases at Durban and Pretoria did not fall under the jurisdiction of Southern Air Command, so Air Force headquarters was required to deploy these squadrons.

The Silvermine centre was established by the Department of Transport a number of decades ago and has always had a major role in responding to the maritime search-and-rescue needs of the SAAF. In 2002 it was appointed as a regional hub to coordinate maritime search-and-rescue operations for South Africa, Angola, Comoros, Madagascar, Mozambique and Namibia.

The Maritime Rescue Coordination Centre works closely with all of the organisations involved in search and rescue, including the Air Force, the National Sea Rescue Institute (NSRI), the Mountain Club of South Africa, the Medical Response Team at Karl Bremer Hospital in Cape Town, the various port captains around the South African coast, the South African Army, the South African Medical Services, the South African Police Services, the Department of Transport and air-traffic centres. Given that they shared their operations room with the Navy, it was easy to arrange for Navy divers to accompany an Air Force mission such as that undertaken for the *Oceanos*.

This distress call was unique; De Munnink knew that maximum effort and resources would be required. The position at which the *Oceanos* had foundered was on as remote a stretch of the South African coastline as the country has to offer. It was approximately midway between the tiny establishments of The Haven and Coffee Bay on the Transkei coast. These were both remote holiday destinations for tourists not necessarily seeking luxury, but rather the extraordinary natural beauty without the bother of droves of competing holidaymakers.

Access to these resorts was challenging at best, with single-track dirt roads from the Transkei capital Umtata not particularly well maintained and almost undrivable in wet weather. Both The Haven and Coffee Bay had small hotels and an outcrop of residents' houses, for the most part built with dubious title to the land and even less official building approval. At this time of year, August, the weather could be bleak; there were no school holidays and many of the home-owners and hoteliers had closed up and were awaiting summer.

Communication was going to be challenging: mobile telephones were not yet commercially available in South Africa and radio or satellite telephony was generally not used by civilians, so the only realistic form of communication with the outside world at The Haven and Coffee Bay was by way of unreliable land lines, mostly prone to collapse in stormy weather.

After taking the call from the De Munnink, Colonel Hallowes raced to Silvermine. There, he immediately mobilised two Puma helicopters stationed at Air Force Base (AFB) Ysterplaat near Cape Town, although he realised that two helicopters would be hopelessly insufficient for an emergency on this scale. He called the Air Force Command Post in Pretoria for assistance, asking Commandant Dawid van Rensburg for additional air support from Durban and Pretoria. He also asked Commandant Van Rensburg to alert the Navy Command Post in Pretoria.

In Pretoria a shrill ring ripped Dick Lord out of a deep sleep. Gathering his jarred thoughts, he recognised the unwelcome interruption as the telephone next to his bed and reached across to answer.

Of course, it was not the first time Lord had had to respond to an emergency call in the middle of the night. An English-speaking South African, who for political reasons had joined the Royal Navy in the UK, Richard 'Dick' Stanley Lord later became an air-warfare instructor and did a two-year exchange tour with the United States Navy, flying Sky Hawks and Phantoms. He literally wrote the book for the US Navy, penning its air combat manoeuvering manual, and his teachings filtered into the prestigious US Navy Fighter Weapon School, better known as Top Gun.

He returned to South Africa in 1970 and joined the SAAF, fighting in the Border War and flying fighter planes against MiG fighter aircraft piloted by Cubans. He later directed SAAF operations in Namibia.

Having worked his way through the ranks, Lord had been promoted from the rank of commandant to brigadier only two days before the *Oceanos* drama and was simultaneously appointed Officer Commanding the Air Force Command Post, giving him overall responsibility for Air Force operations on a national basis.

On the other end of the phone he heard the voice of Commandant

Dawid van Rensburg, the senior duty officer of the Air Force Command Post in Pretoria.

'I'm sorry to wake you, Brigadier,' said Van Rensburg, 'but this is urgent and I need some guidance.'

'What is it?'

'There's a ship in trouble off the Transkei coast. It's a passenger liner with 600 people on board and I've been informed it's sinking.'

He had Lord's full attention. 'Continue,' he ordered.

'Brigadier, at 22h50 on Saturday evening, the port captains of East London and Durban picked up a distress call from the *Oceanos*. The ship reported that she has 581 persons on board, has a flooded engine room, is continuing to take water and is listing to starboard. The position given was 32.07S and 29.07E, approximately 80 miles north of East London and two miles from the Transkei coast.'

'Call out all rescue helicopters,' Brigadier Lord instructed Van Rensburg. 'This is huge and we need every helicopter available. I'm coming into the office.'

He quickly dressed, then set out on a high-speed 15-minute dash to join Commandant Van Rensburg at their office.

As soon as he arrived, his colleague briefed him on what had occurred and what had been done up to that point. 'The distress call was relayed by the East London and Durban ports to all the maritime rescue agencies, including Silvermine, Sir. The vessel is technically sinking in Transkei waters. The government of the Transkei simply cannot mount a proper sea rescue on this scale. It has no assets, insufficient manpower and no experience. MRCC should take command of the operation, Sir.'

Prior to 1994, the Transkei was ostensibly an independent state, declared such by the apartheid government. In an act designed to deprive black South Africans of almost all their democratic rights – including rights of citizenship and land ownership – the government identified a number of so-called homelands, typically in sparse and unproductive parts of South Africa, and granted them 'independence', as if they were fully autonomous states.

Transkei, which was then governed by Major General Bantu Holomisa, was struggling economically, but determined to hold on to the artificial independence granted to it by South Africa. Without the cooperation of the Transkei government, the entire SAAF operation could be thwarted. Technically, military aircraft could not fly over the sovereign territory of another country without official authorisation from that country. More seriously, if the aircraft were unable to refuel in Transkei, they would be forced to fly all the way back to South Africa and lose precious time. Access to Transkei airspace was going to be a challenge for the SAAF, with the relationship between the two countries at the time fluctuating between cool and openly hostile.

Brigadier Lord called the Command Post of the South African Department of Foreign Affairs, a 24/7 operation in its own right, with a request that they seek the cooperation of the Transkei government. He asked that the Umtata air field be made available to SAAF aircraft for the duration of the emergency and that the Umtata air-traffic personnel cooperate fully with the SAAF; that all fuel at Umtata be reserved for SAAF use and that any fuel stored in drums be transported by road to Coffee Bay for SAAF use; and that a restricted flying area immediately be imposed over a radius of 5 nautical miles around the *Oceanos* and up to a height of 5 000 feet above sea level.

As if by a miracle, in the context of the then strained relations between Pretoria and Umtata, the duty officer of the Department of Foreign Affairs was able to confirm to Brigadier Lord within ten minutes of the request that the South African ambassador in Umtata had spoken directly to Major General Holomisa, explaining the problem and requesting his assistance, and that the latter had immediately understood the gravity of the situation and agreed to cooperate.

SAA had, in the meantime, made available a Boeing 737, crew and paramedics to be mobilised from Durban to collect rescued passengers from Umtata. They had also mobilised their emergency response unit.

In 1991, the only two dedicated Air Force bases at which aircraft were stationed to deal with maritime emergencies were Ysterplaat and Durban. Given the distance between them – over 1 600 kilometres directly along the coast – any rescue mission by the SAAF to a locality between the two was going to take time, despite the speed advantage of an aircraft. AFB Durban was closer to the casualty site, with the AFB Ysterplaat helicopters having to travel over 1 000 kilometres to reach it.

Although there was a paucity of dedicated maritime rescue helicopters, all other Air Force bases around the country permanently had two helicopters and two complete crews on readiness, a situation necessitated by the ongoing political violence in South Africa during the early 1990s.

The Pumas at Ysterplaat and Durban had been mobilised, but Brigadier Lord knew that four helicopters would still be hopelessly inadequate for the task at hand. Although he was still short of information – he had no idea whether or how many lifeboats had been launched, how many people had evacuated the ship, or indeed whether there were people in the water – he was fairly certain that many people, if not all on board, would have to be airlifted off the ship.

Whatever the situation, four helicopters were not going to cope, so Brigadier Lord ordered a further two standby Pumas from 19 Squadron stationed at AFB Swartkop outside Pretoria. These had further to travel to the *Oceanos* than those stationed at Durban.

In the meantime, the commander of 30 Squadron at AFB Ysterplaat had called out additional crews. As they started arriving at the base, they were greeted by frenzied activity, with hangar doors open and Pumas being towed out by tractors onto the floodlit tarmac.

Long-range fuel tanks were being fitted into the cabins and filled with aviation fuel. Co-pilots were busy plotting the route to the Transkei, flight engineers were checking aircraft systems and maintenance crews were preparing the aircraft for the long haul. Arrangements were also being made with AFB Port Elizabeth for refuelling en route.

At 35 Squadron in Cape Town, three Dakota fixed-wing aircraft fitted with Aid Life were mobilised to fly to the scene. Aid Life was a system developed in South Africa for dropping survival supplies from fixed-wing aircraft to people in or on the water.

At AFB Swartkop in Pretoria, although only one Puma helicopter was on standby, the base had managed to mobilise two of them on Brigadier Lord's instructions. They faced the particular challenge of not being equipped for maritime rescue missions: although they each had a hoist, the helicopter crews had no flotation gear or maritime rescue equipment such as a dinghy. Most significantly, they had almost no experience in hoisting or hovering over the sea, an exercise requiring special skills and plenty of practice, especially on a night such as this. Captain Tarri Jooste, one of the Swartkop Puma pilots mustered for the *Oceanos* rescue, had once done some hoisting training at 5 Recce in Durban harbour with the Navy frigates, but that was the sum total of his experience.

Nonetheless, it never crossed their minds that they were about to take part in a rescue of such a nature with no suitable training or equipment. In fact, what they were about to embark on was technically illegal. The urgency of the lives to be rescued at the time weighed up far more heavily than the fact that legally the aircrew were neither current on their maritime rescue training nor equipped to undertake such a rescue.

Captains Tarri Jooste and Jacques Hugo, the pilots of the two Pumas, were both up for the task and took off with their crews at 3 am on Sunday 4 August. Captain Jooste's co-pilot was Anton Botha and Captain Hugo's was Len Pienaar, with flight engineer Francois Schutte. They flew to East London for a full briefing, then went on to assist in the evacuation, each crew flying almost nonstop for nearly 12 hours that day.

To create an on-scene command post from which messages could be relayed to the various bases and flight crews, Brigadier Lord deployed a C-160 Transall crew from 28 Squadron at AFB Waterkloof near Pretoria. The C-160 Transall is a fixed-high-wing long-range twin turboprop aircraft, typically used for military cargo transport. The Transall, also fitted with Aid Life, set off in the early hours of Sunday 4 August and arrived on the scene, some 600 kilometres from its base, at 5.30 am.

As a number of aircraft were to be involved in the operation, a mobile air-operations team was deployed to the scene under the command of Major Louter van Wyk, an operations officer in Southern Air Command and an experienced maritime helicopter pilot. This team's role would be to take control of all air operations in the immediate vicinity of the sinking ship.

Major Van Wyk and his team of operational clerks and radio operators hitched a ride with one of the Pumas from AFB Ysterplaat to Coffee Bay. Also loaded up was all the equipment they were likely to need: radios, maps and map boards, spare batteries, sleeping bags and tents, food, water. One of his missions was to identify a suitable landing site on the shore, erect all communications equipment and control and coordinate whatever air activity there would be in the restricted zone around the *Oceanos*.

A decision was taken to dispatch three Dakota fixed-wing aircraft and two Alouette light helicopters from Durban to assist in the visual search for survivors in the water. Brigadier Lord surmised that the helicopters would be perfect for any shoreline search for survivors.

Finally, one of the issues Lord anticipated was that elderly passengers would have difficulty in getting into a helicopter hoisting strop. His solution was to mobilise six Navy divers stationed at Simon's Town and Durban, made available by the South African Navy and who would be transported to the stricken vessel aboard the helicopters.

Activity in the Command Post started to wane in the early hours of Sunday morning, once all arrangements had been made. Shortly after 3 am, Brigadier Lord called the senior officer on duty at the Navy to ask whether the three strike craft had sailed from Durban, and was advised that, in fact, four had sailed: the SAS *Oswald Pirow*, *Jim Fouché*, *Frans Erasmus* and *Jan Smuts*. The vessels were loaded with hundreds of blankets, extra rations, soup, plastic cups and whatever else could be sourced in the time available to them.

Given that each strike craft carries a crew of 47, the Navy had managed to muster and deploy 188 sailors and provision and sail four ships in the space of a few hours after midnight – an extraordinary response by any standard.

Next, Brigadier Lord called the officer commanding at 15 Squadron at AFB Durban. 'Are your two Puma helicopters airborne?' he asked.

'Yes, Sir. In fact, all four helicopters have been deployed.'

The story was the same at 30 Squadron at AFB Ysterplaat. 'Five helicopters are airborne,' he was told.

The C-160 Transall, having arrived at around 5.30 am, was already circling above the *Oceanos*. A total of 11 Puma helicopters were making their way towards the sinking ship. The remaining Dakotas and Alouettes would depart from Cape Town and Durban as soon as it was light enough to fly.

CHAPTER 6

TO THE LIFEBOATS

The *Oceanos* had taken an uncomfortable and obvious list to starboard and it had become obvious to all that something was seriously amiss. When it became clear that singing was no longer doing anything to calm or comfort the passengers and entertainers, Moss and the others stopped trying to distract the passengers, but talked quietly among themselves on the stage, discussing what to do next.

Passengers were continually coming up to Moss and asking him what was happening with the ship, but he had still not heard anything from the crew. Although Captain Avranas had spoken to Lorraine about abandoning ship, and at least one lifeboat had by then rumbled down the side of the ship into the darkness, Moss thought that it was not really the place of the lead guitarist to give the order to abandon ship. In any event, he had no operational authority on the ship. Nonetheless, he knew that some action had to be taken: he could not stand by and do nothing in the hope that somehow and at some time the captain and crew would start to take responsibility for the growing chaos and confusion on board.

In the meantime, Lorraine had returned to the lounge and given instructions to the TFC staff to start handing out life jackets and move people towards the lifeboats.

Moss decided to return downstairs, once again flouting the strongly protesting Tracy's wishes. This time, after grabbing his video recorder and walking again with Julian, he decided to use the forward staircase.

As they descended towards the bottom level of the ship once more, with Moss leading the way, they first heard and then saw, shimmering in the gloom of the emergency lights, water running down the stairs. The water had already filled the ship to halfway up the stairs, just above the Nereus deck.

'My God, we're sinking!' Moss said to Julian, switching on his camera to record the sloshing, sinister water running down and lapping at the stairs. He provided a commentary for his footage: 'We're right down below now ... There's water everywhere! It looks like it's flowing in reasonably fast. It's sloshing about from side to side.' Recording the time as 12.05 am and date as 4 August, he added calmly: 'So I guess we're going down.'

Suddenly, a Greek-accented voice shouted down the stairwell at them: 'Hey! You come upstairs! Hey! You go upstairs! Go upstairs!'

'Yes. Did you see the water down there?' Moss called back, remaining friendly.

'No! You come up! Up!'

'Jeez! Ja, going up. But there's water everywhere.'

The sailor was in no mood for engaging in conversation: 'Up! Up!' he insisted.

As they started climbing back up the stairwell out of the gloom, Moss turned to Julian and said: 'Did you hear? Robin had a look down there just now as well.'

As they reached the top of the stairs, the Greek sailor realised that Moss had been filming the situation below and became very agitated. 'You drop the camera!' he said.

'Yeah, I took a bit of a camera down,' Moss replied, maintaining his composure.

'Drop! Drop!' The sailor was incensed.

'I keep the camera everywhere,' explained Moss.

'No!' The sailor was adamant.

'Ok, I won't go down there with a camera,' Moss said, dropping it to his side, but continuing to film surreptitiously.

When they got back to the lounge, Moss walked quickly and directly to Tracy.

'We're sinking,' he said quietly, not wanting anyone else to hear and so create panic. He told a few of the other entertainers: 'I've seen the water. We are sinking. We have to do something.'

He summoned over the rest of the TFC staff, who got in a huddle to confer and strategise. A plan was hatched.

Moss instructed entertainer Tom Hine to stop everyone from returning to their cabins. Moss did not want passengers going anywhere near the cabins or seeing the rising water.

After agreeing on a plan with the others, which included launching the lifeboats, Moss himself ran through all of the passenger cabin areas, banging on doors to wake anyone who might still be downstairs and asleep. He had been told earlier by one of the TFC staff that Louise Holmes, the daughter-in-law of two of the passengers, was missing. She had not been seen upstairs and Moss thought that she might be sleeping through the drama.

When Moss knocked on the door of the cabin number he had been given for her, there was no answer. He carried on banging until he heard a sleepy voice.

'Who's there?' Louise asked in a croaky voice and semi-comatose fashion. The sleep-inducing seasickness tablets that she had taken had knocked her out.

'It's me, Moss Hills, the guitarist from the ship!' he replied, urgently. 'Wake up, get your life jacket on and come upstairs!' he instructed her.

'Why must I come? I'm sleeping!' she replied grumpily, an element of suspicion also creeping into her voice.

'You have to trust me,' replied Moss more urgently. 'Come now! Everyone must get out of their cabins!' Moss was still reluctant to tell her that the ship was sinking, but he knew he had to persuade her to come out of her cabin.

Eventually, Louise opened the door and trundled out wearing her life jacket. 'This had better not be a joke,' she grumbled and walked unsteadily along the passage towards the lounge.

Moss had instructed all waiters and band members to go through the ship, knock on cabins and move passengers up to the lounge. He also told them to gather life jackets, despite the fact that there was still no announcement and no alarm had been sounded on the ship.

Life jackets, which had been gathered from the cabins by the TFC and waiter staff, were dumped in the reception area outside the lounge. Passengers had by then started complaining that the toilets were backing up and flooding and that there was a terrible smell of sewage on the ship.

As the toilets on the ship had become useless, Kevin Ellis got creative. One of his dance routines involved a bucket and a mop. His bucket found a new use for the passengers as a backstage toilet. With passengers getting sicker and sicker, the temporary short-drop toilet was quickly brought into use.

The rest of the TFC staff were instructed to walk around, smile a lot and pretend that all was well, or at least that there was no need for panic. When the TFC staff were all present they started handing out life jackets and Robin took charge of teaching the passengers how to don them, giving his instructions with the help of a megaphone. The passengers who had joined the vessel in Durban or Cape Town had already done lifeboat drills and knew what they were doing with the life jackets, but the new passengers from East London for the most part were not too sure if they were wearing them correctly. The group of SAA staff who made up a portion of the East London passengers helpfully showed the passengers who were struggling how to fit their life jackets properly.

Robin went onto the main deck to see what was happening with the lifeboats, having earlier seen one being lowered while the entertainers had been in the lounge. To his horror he discovered that several lifeboats were already being boarded by senior crew members. They were all carrying their baggage.

After running through the ship, Moss went up onto the main deck and saw some Filipino crew.

'Start launching the lifeboats!' he ordered when he saw what was happening. They were reluctant to do so.

'We can't launch the boats, Mr Moss,' said one of the deckhands. 'We wait for order to abandon. We must listen to the officer,' he whined.

'There aren't any officers on board the ship any longer,' said Moss sternly. 'They've taken a lifeboat and gone already. Now prepare these lifeboats for launching!' He remained certain that the lifeboat he had seen through the lounge window was full of officers.

The Filipinos scuttled off, the gravity of what Moss had said galvanising them into frenzied action.

To launch a lifeboat on the *Oceanos* it had to be carried to the embarkation deck, fixed to the launching davits, filled with passengers and then launched. However, given the already 15- to 20-degree list to starboard and rolling of the ship, lifeboats that had been set up for launching on the starboard side were swinging up to 4 metres away from the ship, then back again and crashing into the side of the vessel. For anyone embarking there was every risk of being crushed between lifeboat and ship, or falling into the frothing sea below, or both.

Moss explained the grim dilemma to passengers – they either had to face the risk of maiming or worse by trying to board the lifeboat or stay on the *Oceanos* and go down with her.

'This ship is sinking. We don't know when it will sink and we don't know if it will capsize first. All we know is that we have to get off or we will all go down with it,' he shouted above the general din. This was incentive enough to persuade passengers to board the lifeboats.

Although he had no formal standing on the ship as a crew member, Moss became the de facto officer in charge. 'Help me remove these railings,' he said, mustering all the authority he had, speaking to a couple of the male passengers standing on the deck with him. 'They're going to hinder passengers trying to get onto the lifeboats.'

Once removed, they were thrown overboard.

'Organise yourselves into groups of 20,' he shouted above the wind at the fast-growing group of passengers who had joined him outside.

'Kevin, try and keep them all calm and stop any sense of panic,' he said quietly to Kevin Ellis, the dancer.

'Everyone, load your pockets up with sweets from the lounge,' he ordered the passengers around him, who were now hanging on his every word. 'Kevin, I want you to fetch sweets, share them out and keep sending people outside to join me here.'

Kevin quickly started rounding up those who had remained indoors and out of the weather.

Lifeboat 3

Michael O'Mahoney and his wife Yvette had been sitting around on the floor of the lounge for what seemed like a long time with no information forthcoming. Eventually Geraldine 'JD' Massyn, one of the hostesses from TFC, approached them.

'We need women and children to follow us to the lifeboats, please,' she said. The calmness of her manner belied the urgency of the situation.

'Yvette can't look after a young child and a 3-month-old baby on her own,' objected Michael.

'We'll assign someone to accompany her and assist with your son, sir,' Geraldine replied reassuringly.

Moss had by then already started loading the first lifeboat he had come upon, which happened to be Lifeboat 3. His plan was to include at least one SAA or TFC person in each, someone who was familiar with lifeboat and emergency drills.

The *Oceanos* carried four rigid lifeboats each on its port and starboard sides, with two of the boats covered with a hard shell and the other six open to the elements, but with the option to erect tarpaulins on light-weight frames. Each lifeboat was able to carry 90 people, fully laden.

The covered lifeboats were powered by small yet efficient motors, while the open boats were propelled by what is known as Fleming gear. Invented by the Fleming brothers in Liverpool in 1938, the apparatus had oscillating levers coupled to a bar with cranks and shafts, which, when pushed back and forth by someone in the lifeboat, turned a propeller.

Although a poor substitute for a motor, it gave the lifeboat some form of propulsion, albeit feeble. The Fleming gear was a relatively efficient way of propelling the lifeboat in calmer waters, but in the mayhem of a Wild Coast storm it would be quite ineffectual.

Lifeboat 3 was one of the Fleming-propelled vessels.

Moss would put a leg on the lifeboat as it swung towards the ship to try and hold it as close to the vessel's hull as he could and then quickly load up a couple of passengers before it swung away again. The passengers, many of whom were scared out of their wits, had to time their leaps into the lifeboat to ensure that it was as close to the *Oceanos* as possible when they jumped. As the lifeboat swung away from the vessel, Moss would jump back onto the *Oceanos* while it was still in range. This was to be Moss's modus operandi for each lifeboat with which he assisted. (Had there been any senior crew around to assist in the evacuation, they would almost certainly have used the standard apparatus known as tricing pendants to pull the lifeboats close to the ship and prevent the dangerous swinging caused by the rolling *Oceanos*. Moss and the TFC staff could not have been expected to have known how to use the tricing pendants.)

'Watch your legs as you board!' he shouted to the terrified passengers. 'Jump only when I instruct you to jump and don't fall in the water.'

The exercise became harder and harder as Lifeboat 3 became heavier and heavier. It soon became too hazardous for Moss to stabilise the huge swinging load with his leg. As the weight of the lifeboat increased with more and more passengers embarking, it started crashing heavily into the ship, with pieces splintering and breaking off.

After Michael had accompanied his family to Lifeboat 3 he helped them struggle aboard to relative safety with a throng of about 30 other women and children. The next moment they were joined by 12 crew who pushed passengers aside and jostled among themselves to get aboard.

Challenging as the boarding of the lifeboat was, it turned to mayhem as Greek sailors yelled and lashed out at one another to make room for themselves. Once aboard, the crew would not allow the lifeboat to be filled to capacity, maintaining that it would capsize in the big seas if it was full. It was about 45 passengers short of its carrying capacity. Michael and the attending TFC staff were appalled at their behaviour.

It was not clear whether this Greek initiative arose from safety concerns for overladen lifeboats or comfort concerns for themselves, but given that each lifeboat was designed to carry 90-odd people, it is hard to understand why numbers were restricted by the Greek crew to around half the capacity. It is not as if the designers would have added a caveat that the boats could carry 90 people only on calm waters. By the nature of maritime casualties, lifeboats need to be safe and fully operational in all sea conditions.

'We need to launch this boat now,' Moss told the Filipinos working with him. 'If we don't, it's going to break up and we'll lose everyone!'

By now, the lights of some of the ships that had responded to the call for assistance had started to appear sporadically in the darkness and through the wind-driven spray.

Moss called out to Lynne Greig, one of the TFC hostesses: 'You get into this lifeboat and look after the passengers.'

As they were trying to load the lifeboat, Lynne's colleague, JD Massyn, who was standing on the deck assisting passengers, saw Captain Avranas trying to get on board.

'What do you think you're doing?' JD asked. 'You're the captain. You can't get in a lifeboat!'

'I just checking something,' said Avranas, hastily getting out again. Avranas's wife, Davina, and his 11-year-old daughter, Fay, were already in the lifeboat. Davina had boarded the lifeboat carrying a bird in a cage.

Inside the boat, Lynne's anxiety levels were rising. 'How do we start the engines?' she asked Moss, sounding doubtful.

'I have no idea,' replied Moss, 'I don't even think there are engines. You're going to have to figure it out.' He handed her a walkie-talkie and, with that, the davits were loosened.

East London travel agent Mercia Schultz, her parents and baby were already in the lifeboat. Her husband, Leon, had agreed to remain on the ship as the plan at that time was to get as many women and children off the vessel as possible.

Sometime after 1 am Lifeboat 3 started dropping into the dark abyss below.

Moss heard Lynne shouting up at him: 'Where are we going and what do I do?'

Moss shouted back: 'Head for the lights of the closest ship. You're on your own now. Good luck!'

As the lifeboat swung away from the side of the *Oceanos*, it dropped partially and then got stuck. Panicked crew members struggled to free the boat, dangling in the wind and crashing into the side of the *Oceanos* from time to time. Communications with the crew were almost impossible as very few of them spoke English; more disturbing was their inability to deal with the situation of tangled ropes and cables.

Horrified, Michael watched the launching from the ship's deck. In the meantime, Mercia's husband, Leon, had run down to the lower deck and jumped off the *Oceanos* into the lifeboat to try and free it.

After almost an hour of the boat dangling next to the *Oceanos*, the crew somehow freed it with a pole and it crashed down into the water. Leon remained on board the lifeboat with his family as he was unable to climb back onto the *Oceanos*.

As the steel blocks and tackle were released from the lifeboat, they swung free, clanging onto the side of the ship. One of them struck Maria Smythe, the 87-year-old grandmother of Lorraine Betts, on the head. The blow opened a huge gash, which bled incessantly for the rest of her time on board the lifeboat, despite passengers' attempts to stem the flow.

Lynne discovered very soon after the boat landed in the water that, in fact, it had no engine.

The sailors who had earlier boarded tried to work the Fleming gear to create distance between the lifeboat and the ship, but it was repeatedly sucked up against and crashed into the *Oceanos*, towering above and threatening to crush them with its passive, but still perilous propellers. Eventually the lifeboat drifted helplessly away with the wind.

Oceanos crew members, barman Panayotis and another called Marcos, finally managed to work the rowing mechanism properly and the boat slowly moved further away from the ship. The rest of their colleagues in the meantime passed around bottles of whisky and brandy they had brought on board. These proved to have an admirably soporific effect on many of the Greek crew, who slept away much of the uncomfortable night that followed.

All the while, Michael had been watching the drama of the lifeboat being launched into the crazy, tossing sea. His family was gone. As it slowly drifted off into the darkness, he wondered fearfully if he would ever see them again.

Lynne, communicating with Lorraine Betts by walkie-talkie from the lifeboat, shouted above the wind: 'No one knows what to do! Your granny's head is bleeding! Water is coming into this boat! Please bring us back up to the ship.' But that was not an option.

Lifeboat 3 started making for the lights of a ship that were beckoning hazily through the darkness. However, with the lifeboat falling into troughs and then again cresting waves, the lights kept on disappearing and reappearing. The occupants were, for the most part, unable to see the ship because of the huge waves and spray around them and eventually lost sight of their closest hope of rescue.

'Where is the nearest ship?' Lynne asked anxiously into her walkie-talkie. She was speaking to Robin Boltman on the bridge, who replied:

'Let go a flare and I'll tell you if you're headed in the right direction.' A minute or two of silence followed. Robin asked: 'Well, did you let off the flare?'

'Yes,' replied Lynne, 'but it shot into the fucking water!'

She let off a second flare, which took off above the waves but was whisked away by the wind. Despite the flare, Robin could see nothing of the lifeboat. 'Sorry, Lynne. I don't see where you are or where you're headed. Just head for whatever lights you can see.'

Robin felt helpless, Lynne desperate.

As the lifeboat crested a wave, the howling wind ripped the canopy aside and into the sea. What little shelter there had been was now gone. They were open to the driving wind and lashing sea. Both were brutal. The survivors started to freeze.

With a rowing mechanism that was largely useless in the tearing waves and wind and having lost their only two flares, the lifeboat was now at the mercy of the elements. Lynne started digging around in the boat and found a spare cover in an orange box.

'Help me put this up,' she asked a crew member. He shrugged and pointed to three support struts that had broken off in the gust that had ripped away the original canopy. Only one strut was left and, in the circumstances, useless. The passengers and crew continued to be pounded by the 60-knot wind, driving spray and waves crashing over them.

Passengers were helpless as the little boat was tossed around. For the most part their only activity was to vomit. Some resorted to prayer, repeatedly imploring the Almighty to deliver them from this nightmare.

Car dealership employees Janet and Mary-Anne were huddled in the back of the boat, soaked to the skin and shivering uncontrollably. 'I'm so cold and so scared. I knew I shouldn't have listened to Johan and come on this stupid trip,' said Janet, her voice quivering and not far from tears.

'Maybe God is punishing us,' said Mary-Anne.

'Don't be stupid,' replied Janet. 'Piet and Johan are the ones who need to be punished. They're the ones cheating on their wives.' She was oblivious to her part.

'I hope they'll be alright,' said Mary-Anne. 'I'm so scared for them.'

They had left Piet and Johan on the ship. There were still some lifeboats to be launched by the time Lifeboat 3 took to the sea.

'Maybe they'll get off on the next lifeboat,' she added hopefully.

'I don't care about them right now,' replied Janet, her earlier self-pity turning to anger. 'What's he going to say to his wife? How will I ever look her in the eye again? She'll know – she can't not know – and I'll end up taking the brunt and being fired. Just you wait and see. It'll be my fault. I'll be the whore who seduced him.' Mary-Anne just sat quietly, weeping softly.

For what seemed like an eternity, the lifeboat ploughed through the sea, passengers being drenched by spray and waves. Yvette O'Mahoney, clinging onto baby Meghann, kept placing her hand into the child's sleeping bag to check that she was still alive.

In the trauma of the evacuation, Yvette's milk had dried up and she was unable to feed Meghann. No one could find whatever emergency rations were supposed to be on board. There was no relief for anyone who may have become hungry or thirsty during the long hours in the lifeboat.

In the end, Lifeboat 3 spent six-and-a-half hours on the open sea. Its occupants had to face wild winds, towering swells, seasickness and terror before it finally closed in on the bulk carrier *Great Nancy*. By then it was already light, but although the wind had dropped to around 45 knots (84 kilometres per hour) and the swells had reduced to around 10 metres, conditions remained atrocious.

In the first few moments there was a palpable sense of relief among the shipwrecked passengers. But when it came alongside the vessel, their relief turned to dread as the waves threw it hard against the hull of the *Great Nancy*. Time and again they tried to tie up alongside, but eventually, with the lifeboat receiving a terrible battering, they cut their ties with the vessel and headed back into the swirling sea, aiming for a new set of lights.

An hour later they reached the Polish reefer vessel *Kaszuby II*. The ship had manoeuvred herself around to intercept and make contact with the lifeboat. As the boat slammed repeatedly into the side of the rolling *Kaszuby II*, Lynne yelled at Panayotis and Marcos: 'Get us away from here! This ship will kill us.'

The two rowed for all they were worth, steering the lifeboat away from the towering vessel and moving it just out of range.

As the *Kaszuby II* approached them again, mothers and children started screaming: 'Go away! Go away!' They were terrified that they were going

AIR AND SEA RESCUE ACTIVITY

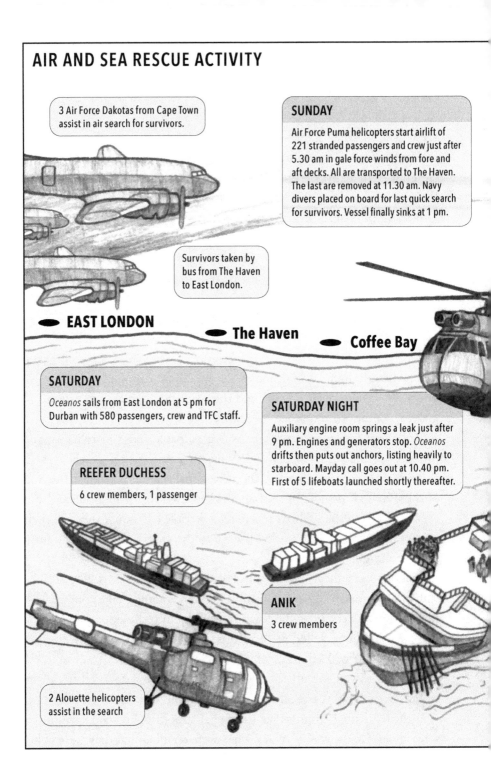

3 Air Force Dakotas from Cape Town assist in air search for survivors.

SUNDAY

Air Force Puma helicopters start airlift of 221 stranded passengers and crew just after 5.30 am in gale force winds from fore and aft decks. All are transported to The Haven. The last are removed at 11.30 am. Navy divers placed on board for last quick search for survivors. Vessel finally sinks at 1 pm.

Survivors taken by bus from The Haven to East London.

EAST LONDON　　　**The Haven**　　　**Coffee Bay**

SATURDAY

Oceanos sails from East London at 5 pm for Durban with 580 passengers, crew and TFC staff.

SATURDAY NIGHT

Auxiliary engine room springs a leak just after 9 pm. Engines and generators stop. *Oceanos* drifts then puts out anchors, listing heavily to starboard. Mayday call goes out at 10.40 pm. First of 5 lifeboats launched shortly thereafter.

REEFER DUCHESS

6 crew members, 1 passenger

ANIK

3 crew members

2 Alouette helicopters assist in the search

DAWN, SUNDAY MORNING

28 Squadron Transall C160 from Waterkloof arrives 5:30am and co-ordinates arrival of airforce helicopters.

Total of 11 Puma helicopters leave in the early hours of Sunday morning from Ysterplaat, Durban and Swartkop.

DURBAN

4 Navy strike craft sent from Durban

NEDLLOYD MAURITIUS

51 survivors

GREAT NANCY

176 survivors

KASZUBY II

106 people, mostly passengers

to be crushed and drowned. Somehow, remaining in a lifeboat, which stank of seasickness and human filth and was in danger of sinking, seemed preferable to the fate of being dealt a crushing blow from the vessel.

At 8.30 am two crew members from the *Kaszuby II* were hoisted down to the lifeboat as it again drifted up to the vessel. They tied the lifeboat fast so that passengers could climb into nets that had been lowered. The nets, carrying several passengers at a time and who flopped like huge fish, were then hoisted up using the vessel's crane. Among the rescued passengers were three toddlers, whose terrified, sobbing mothers could only look on and pray as their children were loaded into the nets and hoisted onto the huge vessel.

Mercia Schultz's 10-month-old daughter was so small that she would have fallen through the mesh. The crew, realising the dilemma, lowered a bucket inside the net. Mercia's baby was loaded into the bucket and one of the other children from the lifeboat then also went up in the net, holding onto the bucket to ensure that it did not tip.

The rope ladder that the *Kaszuby II* crew had lowered was soon smashed between the lifeboat and hull of the ship. The net used to haul passengers up the side of the ship was eventually ripped and torn from the repeated contact with the lifeboat. Waves were lifting the lifeboat above the level of the *Kaszuby II* deck, with lifeboat passengers able to look down on the vessel. Once aloft, the lifeboat would then surf down a wave, dragged repeatedly against the ship's side each time.

The *Kaszuby II* eventually managed to lower a harness as an alternative to the nets, which was fastened around one elderly woman. As she was lifted, so the lifeboat rose with her. Passengers screamed for fear that she would be crushed between boat and ship.

With the makeshift hoisting devices of the *Kaszuby II*, it was inevitable that there would be injuries. One woman's leg was crushed between the heaving lifeboat and hull of the bulker. She was unconscious by the time she was hauled on board.

The lifeboat finally disintegrated soon after the last passenger had been evacuated and its pieces floated away. The rescued passengers lay wet, freezing and exhausted on the deck of the *Kaszuby II*, with the Polish crew encouraging them to go inside and warm up.

In keeping with traditional Polish hospitality, the crew members were extraordinary in their kindness. The seamen understood suffering and they also knew how they would want to be treated if they had just been rescued from an ordeal at sea. They gave up their cabins, shared rations, made hot drinks and even looked after babies by finding cotton wool to make diapers. Nothing was too much trouble within the confines of their resources.

When there were no more survivors to be rescued, the *Kaszuby II* later set sail for Durban.

CHAPTER 7

15 SQUADRON MOBILISES

Captain Slade Thomas, one of the SAAF helicopter pilots based at AFB Durban, was at a big rugby match at Kings Park earlier that day. He was not on duty that weekend, so he headed for the hospitality area after the match to join friends for a barbecue and embark on the customary match post mortem.

After an evening of chewing the fat with his friends and some philosophical, if not heated, debate, Thomas headed home, tumbling into bed just after 11 pm and falling asleep virtually as his head hit the pillow. Almost immediately, so it seemed, he was jarred out of his sleep by the telephone.

It was the duty sergeant in the operations room at AFB Durban, where 15 Squadron was housed. In slow motion, he reached over to pick up the receiver.

'Sir, there's a ship sinking off the Wild Coast. We're going to need you here asap.'

'But Chas is on stand-by this weekend. Use his crew!' Thomas objected, referring to Captain Charles 'Chas' Goatley.

'Yes, Sir, Captain Goatley's crew is on stand-by, but we understand there are 400 people trapped on this ship. My instructions are to muster all available resources in the squadron.'

'I'll be there in 45 minutes,' said Slade resignedly. He was wide awake again. 'This is going to be a loooong day,' he thought to himself as he ran a bath and pulled out his uniform.

This photo from *The Natal Mercury* shows most of the pilots who were involved in the *Oceanos* rescue. In the front row are Capt Slade Thomas (second from right) and Capt Chas Goatley (far right). Captain Hennie Meintjies is in the back row on the left.

Captain Slade Thomas had qualified as a helicopter pilot from the SAAF in 1985, achieving first position overall following his enlistment in 1983. By 1991 he had served as Puma Fleet Flight Commander at 15 Squadron, AFB Durban for three years, managing 11 Puma helicopters, 22 pilots and 11 flight engineers. His role was to ensure the operational readiness of all aircraft and personnel, the serviceability of the aircraft and the well-being of all crew.

Little did he know when he joined the SAAF how important a role he would have in preparing the staff of 15 Squadron for the biggest maritime rescue in history. In his wildest dreams he could never have imagined the scale of peace-time operation to which he would be called to respond.

In the early 1990s, the SAAF decided to phase out the Super Frelon helicopters and replace them with Pumas. Thomas questioned the wisdom of this, especially given that the Super Frelon fleet was relatively new and fully serviceable, whereas bases like 15 Squadron in Durban had to work with hand-me-down Pumas that were barely serviceable when they arrived in Durban. The Puma was a four-blade medium-utility helicopter with space to carry up to 20 passengers.

During the transition period, 15 Squadron had, on average, only one or two operational Puma helicopters each day, a hopelessly inadequate number for the potential tasks at hand. Given that the squadron had crew and support staff for at least four helicopters, many airmen were sitting around for long periods with nothing to do.

The base was abuzz when Thomas arrived.

Despite having had only one serviceable aircraft and one rescue hoist during the previous week, in a confluence of mysterious forces of synchronicity, the squadron's engineers had managed to get four Pumas serviceable the previous day and had four rescue hoists available. They were at as full a strength as they had ever been.

Captain Charles Goatley was the stand-by officer for the weekend. An outstanding helicopter pilot in his own right and senior to Captain Thomas, Goatley was perhaps best known for the support he had given to Colonel 'Mad Mike' Hoare as a mercenary in a bungled coup in the Seychelles in November 1981. Following their hijacking of an Air India plane from the Seychelles, carrying 44 mercenaries and forcing it to fly to Durban, the group surrendered to police and were arrested upon arrival in Durban. All but one of the men, including Colonel Hoare and Goatley, were tried and all sentenced to imprisonment. When Goatley was released five years later, he rejoined the SAAF with the rank of captain.

On this particular evening, being the official stand-by pilot for the weekend, he had taken charge of the rescue preparations at the base. By the time Thomas arrived, Goatley had already worked out the flight times and the amount of fuel needed for the operation and had given instructions for the preparation of the Pumas. Each aircraft was to be fitted with two ferry tanks, each filled with 400 kilograms of fuel, which would provide an additional 40 minutes of flying time each. The usual range of a Puma was two hours and 15 minutes, so the ferry tanks extended this significantly. In addition, four or five extra drums of fuel were loaded into each aircraft.

The flight engineers[3] loaded up everything they thought might be needed in addition to sufficient fuel. All four helicopters were equipped with flotation gear. Apart from the standard lifting hoists and strops, the engineers also loaded up Mae West life jackets, flares, medical kits and two rubber dinghies. They were also concerned that passengers might be in the water, especially if the ship sunk before they could evacuate everyone, so cargo hooks and nets for fishing people out of the water were also loaded.

Shunters Arms, a popular watering hole and restaurant in downtown Durban was, as usual on a Saturday night, buzzing with activity on 3 August 1991. A small group of national servicemen and friends stationed at the South African Navy base on Salisbury Island, situated on the southern side of the Durban harbour, were on an unauthorised night out. The group included Able Seaman Paul Whiley, who was employed as a Navy diver.

Whiley had wanted to be a diver since he was a child, living close to the sea and employed from the age of 14 as a commercial fisherman and boat skipper at Thompsons Bay near Ballito on the Natal north coast. He had been recruited to the Navy for his mandatory national service and, while there, had been selected as one of a handpicked group of volunteers for a diving post in Durban.

---

3   Flight Sergeant Philip Scott was standing in as Goatley's flight engineer.

At around midnight, a naval cadet on duty at Salisbury Island, who knew where Paul and his friends were to be found, overheard a message that there was a ship in trouble and that Navy divers were being called out. He scurried off his duty post, leapt into a rubber duck and raced across the Durban harbour.

After beaching the small boat on the northern side of the harbour, he ran the kilometre or so to Shunters Arms. Bursting in breathlessly, he told Paul and the others that there was trouble afoot and they needed to get back to the base urgently before anyone missed them.

Everyone rushed out of Shunters, ran down to where the rubber duck had been beached and raced back to the base, where they leapt into bed and pretended to be asleep before the inevitable call-out.

With a loud knock on Paul's door, the camp's commanding officer, Lieutenant Commander Hoffman, called out: 'Wake up, Whiley! We have an emergency!'

Paul got out of bed, pulled on some shorts and opened the door, trying to look both sober and sleepy. 'What's happening?' he asked.

'There's a ship sinking off the Cutting [an area just outside the port of Durban] and three or four people are missing. The Air Force needs divers to help with the search and rescue,' he added grimly. '15 Squadron are coming to fetch us and take us to the Cutting.'

With this piece of misinformation, whether deliberate or otherwise, Paul had no clue about what lay ahead. A call-out like this was exciting and challenging in and of itself, one of the reasons he had signed up for the job.

Now fully alert, Paul threw some clothes and equipment into a grab bag, pulled on a Speedo and wet suit and quickly made his way to the duty room to await orders, arriving at much the same time as three of his colleagues, including Gary Scoular.

A short while later a Puma helicopter from 15 Squadron landed and whisked the group off to the base at Louis Botha Airport, some 20 kilometres away. When they arrived, lights were on in the hangers and Air Force personnel were scurrying around, checking fuel, stacking equipment onto the helicopters and making them ready for a long journey.

The divers were bundled into the helicopters as soon as they arrived.

Captain Goatley gave a full briefing to everyone and then the helicopters took off, departing in loose gaggle formation at about 3.30 am, with Goatley and Thomas leaving first.

Thomas's co-pilot was Major Phillip Fenwick and his flight engineer was Warrant Officer William Riley.

The Puma that carried Paul Whiley was under the command of Captain Goatley, with Captain Johannes (Hennie) Meintjies as his co-pilot. The chopper was stacked with so much spare fuel that Paul and his colleagues had to lie on top of the drums. Owing to the additional weight, the helicopter had to taxi down the runway before it could take off, rather than doing the more usual vertical take-off.

Paul was worried about what he saw.

'How are we going to land with all this weight?' he asked Phil Scott, the flight engineer.

'Oh, we should be fine. We'll burn off a lot on the way down the coast.'

Paul was unconvinced and asked: 'But aren't we only going to the Cutting?'

'Oh no,' Phil replied, 'there's a passenger vessel sinking down the Wild Coast with 600 people on board. That's where we're going.' The enormity of what lay ahead suddenly hit.

The formation of Pumas lifted off in pairs and headed out on the 200-mile voyage to the *Oceanos*, battling with poor visibility and against strong southerly gale-force headwinds and low clouds, which heralded the approaching cold front. Their departure had been timed to ensure that they arrived just before first light.

Although the night was pitch black, with no visible moon, Thomas and the other pilots were guided by the glow of a white highway – the frothing surf pounding the shore below – for the duration of the journey.

The air crews had all trained to some extent with the Navy for sea rescues, although much of their training had been in Alouettes and Super Frelons, very different aircraft from the Pumas, even if the skill set was the same. They knew they were in for a testing time.

The ship's agent plays a vital role in the operation of any ship, especially in the interface between sea and land. When the ship is at sea, she is usually quite autonomous, relying on her crew, instruments, charts and weather reports to navigate from port A to port B. Occasionally, her captain will need to take instructions from her owners or charterers, but for the most part the ship is a relatively free spirit at sea, following her particular route to the next port of loading or discharge.

Once the ship arrives at a port, she has to start interfacing with all sorts of people. Tugs and a pilot have to be arranged to bring her in to her allocated berth upon authorisation to enter the harbour. The ship may need to refuel, so bunkers (fuel) must be arranged for delivery, either while she is at anchor or when she comes alongside the berth. The ship's chandlers provide food and other necessaries and someone needs to order and pay for all of this.

The port authority would want to be paid for the use of its tugs and pilot and will also claim port dues. If the ship is loading or discharging cargo or passengers, dues will be payable based on the volume of cargo or number of passengers.

The crew may need to change, in which case someone needs to arrange to transport departing crew to a hotel or airport, arrange their homeward tickets, collect the replacement crew and deliver them to the ship. Occasionally members of the crew require medical attention, so someone needs to appoint a doctor and arrange for transport there and back.

When dealing with a cargo-carrying ship, someone has to identify and appoint stevedores for the loading or discharge operations, arrange for the cargo to be transported from the discharge terminal and pay for all the services received from the ship.

Passenger ships are somewhat easier in that passengers arrive at a passenger terminal and are processed by staff there. Nonetheless, someone has to make all the arrangements to ensure that the ship calls into and departs from the port safely and efficiently.

The ship's agent is key, the spider in the middle of the web of communications and arrangements required to ensure the uninterrupted, efficient and continued operations of a ship. The agent has a huge responsibility in the sense that he is essentially the owners' representative in whichever port a ship finds herself. A ship's owners will appoint agents in every port at which she is going to call, to be their eyes and ears and to liaise closely with the ship's master when the vessel is in port.

When a problem arises on a ship, such as damage to cargo or, in the odd circumstance where it happens to be sinking, the agent is usually the first to be informed. The agent is also the person closest to the action and must solve or manage the problem as best he can for the ship's owners.

In August 1991, Phillip Simpson, a man who had been in the shipping industry in both South Africa and abroad for decades, was managing director of Polaris Shipping. Polaris was a major South African ships agency, operating in several ports in South Africa and servicing a few of the major international container line operations. They also handled break-bulk and dry-bulk cargoes, with clients including some of the world's major traders and carriers. Most of their customers were ship owners, ship charterers and traders.

Polaris had been appointed by TFC Tours to look after the *Oceanos* for the duration of her operations in southern African waters. As the charterer of the ship, TFC would have been responsible for refuelling the vessel and providing water and supplies. These functions would have been contracted to TFC's agent. The agent was also responsible for attending to all port requirements and general liaison between the ship, the port and customs authorities and TFC. As the owners, Epirotiki, also required certain so-called husbandry services for the ship, such as assistance in dealing with crew matters, Polaris was also appointed by Epirotiki as owners' agent.

Capt Mike Brown, a master mariner who had finally come ashore, was the executive director in control of operations at Polaris.

Duncan Starke was the executive branch manager for Polaris. All the managers in Polaris branches around South Africa reported to him. Starke had been in the industry for over 25 years and was focused on the business of the *Oceanos*.

In the week before she sank, Starke travelled with the vessel to East London to ensure that all was in order and to help prepare for the Sahd wedding. On the Saturday morning, he flew back to Durban as the port captain, Mike Cooper, had invited him to the big rugby match at Kings Park that afternoon.

On the same day, the other two Polaris directors were also at the rugby, entertaining clients in their box at Kings Park. The annual North–South derby was one of the biggest matches on the Currie Cup calendar, and that year Western Province (from the Cape) clashed with what were then the Banana Boys (now the Sharks) from Natal.

After the match, Duncan went home to put his feet up. At around 11.30 pm the phone rang.

'Duncan, it's Mike.' It was Mike Cooper, with whom he had watched the rugby earlier. The port captain was sounding very formal.

'I've just heard that the *Oceanos* is sinking,' Cooper continued.

'What?! You must be joking! You'd better not be fucking around,' exclaimed Duncan.

'No,' said the port captain. 'Durban Radio has picked up a Mayday signal and we have confirmed that the ship is sinking.'

Duncan immediately found the number to call Epirotiki, not really expecting anyone to answer the phone.

'Epirotiki Lines. How can I help you?' a pleasant Greek woman's voice greeted Duncan. It was the telex operator on duty at the Epirotiki office.

'I'm sorry to have to report that the *Oceanos* is sinking,' said Duncan solemnly. For a ship owner, news that his ship is sinking is never good. However, when it is the third ship sinking in as many years, the news is catastrophic. Duncan was expecting incredulity at the very least.

Instead, the woman replied matter-of-factly: 'Thank you for advising us. I will pass the message on.'

Minutes later the telephone rang again. It was a senior employee of Epirotiki. As he answered, Duncan was greeted with what can best be described as an explosive Mediterranean rant.

'What you mean *Oceanos* is sinking? Impossible! Why you are telling us? Why my captain is not telling me?' Questions rained down on Duncan.

When he was finally able to speak, Duncan replied: 'This is information I have received from the port captain of Durban. I have not had any other chance to verify the information, but I have no reason to believe it is untrue. I'm sorry to give you this news, but this is all I know for the meantime.'

After a short silence, the caller replied, 'Okay. Thank you.' He hung up.

Duncan told his wife the news and started getting ready to go to the office. 'I have an idea I'm going to be away from home for a while,' he said.

As he was getting changed, the telephone rang again. It was the same Epirotiki employee to whom he had spoken a short while before.

'Hello, Mr Starke. I'm sorry I sound so angry. You are right. The ship is sinking. You please take all steps to protect interests of passengers and owners.'

Duncan explained that he was on the way to the office to meet with his colleagues and they would start planning how to deal with the crisis. He called Mike Brown and then set off for the office in downtown Durban.

Phillip, in the meantime, had just reached his home in the leafy suburb of Kloof. It was close to midnight and he was headed straight for bed when the phone rang. It was Mike Brown.

'Phillip, I've just heard from Duncan that the *Oceanos* is sinking.'

Not in the mood for a prank call, Phillip said, 'I'm tired. You'd better just deal with it.'

Then, thinking that there might be a grain of truth in the incredible news he had just heard, he asked as an afterthought: 'What are you going to do?'

'I'm going to the office,' replied Mike.

Any fog that may have been clouding Phillip's brain immediately lifted as he realised that Mike was dead serious and they had a crisis on their hands.

'I'll see you there,' he replied.

At the office, the three directors started strategising. Mike, who had experience of a previous ship's sinking and was also able to draw on his knowledge as an ex-ship's captain, led the strategy talk.

They pulled their desks together to form a type of boardroom table and then divided up their responsibilities. Mike was to deal with the port and all of the maritime aspects of the disaster. Duncan was to manage all matters concerning the passengers, including identifying who was on board (or missing), what was happening and notifying their relatives as far as necessary. Phillip took responsibility for media liaison.

As calls started pouring in from sources such as the Maritime Rescue Coordination Centre, Port Control, Epirotiki, TFC Tours and the media, the threesome received more reports about what was happening, including the evacuation of passengers and the role of the surrounding cargo ships. They started making plans for the arrival of these rescue ships in the ports of Durban, Port Elizabeth and East London. Suddenly, from being the agent for the *Oceanos*, they were agents for half a dozen others as well.

By 2 am, they had received reports that the *Oceanos* had taken a huge list to starboard.

Phillip reported this to Mike and said: 'What's going to happen?'

'The ship is going to sink,' replied Mike, calmly, factually and with certainty.

Phillip's eyes welled up with tears as the reality of the looming disaster finally hit. With almost 600 people on board it was hard to imagine how they could all be saved.

Duncan, in the meantime, was faced with a dilemma. As agents, they were supposed to know who was on the ship and be able to keep track of the passengers. It is a standard shipping practice that, when passengers embark or disembark at a port and before the ship sails, a new manifest is drawn up to identify all passengers on board. (The ship's manifest is a list of cargo or, in this case, passengers on board. The manifest also identifies the ports for which the cargo or passengers are bound.)

The ship's port of call prior to East London had been Cape Town. Polaris had a manifest of passengers who had departed from Cape Town. However, they had no idea how many passengers were on board when the ship departed from East London. All they knew was that both free and hugely discounted passage from East London to Durban had been offered to a group of travel agents, SAA staff and others in the travel industry. Included in this group were travel agents who had drawn up the ship's final manifest for the departure from East London. For some reason, the passenger manifest was taken on board the *Oceanos* when she left East London, with no office copy, so there was no formal record. The manifest eventually met the same fate as the *Oceanos*.

Although Polaris had some idea of who was likely to have boarded at East London because they knew what bookings had been made, they were unable to determine whether any passengers had embarked in Durban or Cape Town but left the ship at East London because of the bad weather. They were given to understand that this was the case, but Duncan had no way of verifying numbers.

Duncan's first call was to Allen Foggitt, the managing director of TFC Tours and son of the founder, John. Foggitt was aghast at the news, but said that he would make all necessary arrangements to deal with passengers.

CHAPTER 8

ALL AT SEA

Travel agent Debra le Riche and her husband René had been in the lounge with their children for some time when Spiro, the waiter who had shown so much attention to their daughter Megan upon boarding, grabbed Megan and pulled Debra with him.

'Come with me!' he ordered. Followed closely by René and Raymond, he hastily led them onto the deck.

'Everything going to be okay,' he said. Handing Megan back to Debra, he said: 'Hold her!'

Standing out in the gusting wind, Debra called to René: 'What are we going to do?' People were running around, some of them vomiting onto the deck. Pandemonium abounded.

'I don't know,' said René, lost for initiative in a drama he did not understand and still could not believe was real.

Spiro tugged at Debra's sleeve. 'Come with me! Come with me!' he urged them.

Lifeboat 2

With Lifeboat 3 launched, magician Julian Russell had started to load another. An exit door from the lounge had jammed and was slowing passengers' exit towards the lifeboat. Moss broke it down, removing it from its hinges to open up the bottleneck.

As Debra followed Spiro, with Megan in her arms and 8-year-old Raymond in front, they saw what awaited them. Lifeboat 2 was dangling

Lifeboat 2 swinging away from the ship shortly before
it was dropped into the ocean.

at a distance from the ship, swaying to the ship with each roll and then
swinging away again by a couple of metres. Someone had placed the
door Moss had removed earlier over the gap between the ship and the
lifeboat. To get into the lifeboat, passengers had to cross this makeshift
gangplank across the chasm to the sea far below.

René took Megan from her mother to let Debra clamber into the
lifeboat and then handed her across the terrifying gap as it closed to its
narrowest. Raymond had already skipped across the temporary bridge
with all the agility one might expect of a young boy.

As the passengers boarded, Chief Officer Nikolaidis and another
officer, who were both already in the lifeboat, took command. They
were accompanied by several colleagues, including the ship's overweight

casino dealer, Avgerinos Tsaikas, who also handled the cash in the casino. He clutched a small bag as he boarded.

Chief Officer Nikolaidis told them to all sit down. Through the door of the lifeboat, Debra could see René standing on the deck of the *Oceanos*, looking on helplessly but not boarding. Next to him stood another passenger, John Adamson, husband of Gail and father of three children, including the 17-day-old John Jr, the *Oceanos*' youngest passenger. Gail and her children had already boarded the lifeboat.

Debra turned to the chief officer: 'Can my husband come on board?' she asked.

'No!' he said sternly. 'Women and children only!' The conversation was over.

As the lifeboat started filling with people, a woman boarded with her husband.

'Why is he allowed on board?' Debra asked.

'Because she is very afraid,' he replied curtly. Debra, still unafraid, wondered whether it was not in fact the husband who was very afraid.

The protective husband, clearly embarrassed by being the only man on board the boat other than the chief officer and some crew, discreetly took a seat at the back and sat quietly, looking for all the world like a stowaway who did not want to be noticed.

The chief officer and his colleague set about trying to free the lifeboat from its davits so that it could be lowered into the water. After some effort they successfully freed a davit and the whole lifeboat dropped at one end, but with the other still suspended by the bow. Passengers screamed as they fell against each other. Nikolaidis grabbed a spanner in the boat and smashed it against the stuck davit, trying to free the jammed device. As it came free, the chain lashed through the air and ripped into his hand, almost severing his thumb. Blood gushed from his hand. He partially stemmed the blood from the wound with a handkerchief.

With one hand dripping blood and incapacitated, the chief officer started the motor of the lifeboat and managed to steer with the other hand. Slowly the lifeboat picked up speed through the heaving waves and moved away from the foundering *Oceanos*.

Opposite Debra sat Gail Adamson with her three children, baby John Jr, the 2-year-old Kari and Samantha, who was eight. John was wrapped in a blanket and clutched in the arms of a terrified-looking Gail.

The lifeboat was so full that an 8-year-old boy had to take a seat on Debra's lap. As the boat plunged into the darkness of each trough and then soared up the face of each incessant new wave, Debra's anxiety increased. She knew that Megan's life jacket was too big and would slip off if the lifeboat capsized and her daughter was flung into the water. She also knew that, as a mother, if such a moment arose, she would jettison the child on her lap to save her own. She prayed that she would be spared this 'Sophie's choice' decision.

A mother with three children on the lifeboat, Sandy Logan, was clinging onto her vomit-covered 10-month-old daughter, Lisa. Her sons, 10-year-old Gareth and 9-year-old Jonathan, were squeezed in somewhere away from her. Both had been retching throughout the trip on the lifeboat and were hanging onto whatever they could as the boat was tossed violently about.

A large wave washed through the boat and Jonathan lost his grip. He was swept overboard into the darkness.

'Mommy! Mommy!' he screamed. 'Help me!'

Sandy was helpless. She was trapped where she was, unable to stand up or move and holding onto the baby, Lisa. She could not see Jonathan and screamed at the women in the stern to help.

As the boy drifted down the side of the boat and towards the stern, an elderly Chinese woman reached over and grabbed the child's life jacket, hauling him back on board. Sandy was close to hysterical, thanking the woman and crying in fear, shock and gratitude, all at the same time.

They had launched at around 2 am – shortly after Lifeboat 3 – and it was pitch dark all around. The night made the lifeboat's descent into each trough feel like a plummet into the depths of a black hole, with every particle of light extracted. The darkness was relieved only by the faint glow of scudding clouds, which became visible at the crest of each wave.

With incredible skill, and against all Debra's expectations, Chief Officer Nikolaidis and his colleague somehow managed to weave the boat through the mountainous waves without it capsizing. 'Where are we going?' Debra asked the chief officer, who was sitting next to her, near the engine.

As they crested another wave, he replied: 'You see those lights over there?' He pointed towards a ship in the distance. 'There, we go there. Maybe they pick us up.'

With that the lifeboat plunged back into a trough, triggering another spate of vomiting all around Debra. After some four-and-a-half perilous and tortuous hours, they approached the ship. As the lifeboat ploughed past the bow of the bulker, Debra could faintly make out the name *Great Nancy* through the spray.

The chief officer stopped the lifeboat on the port side of the *Great Nancy* and Chinese crew on the deck threw down ropes with which to tether the lifeboat and stop it from drifting off. Hanging on grimly, the second officer on the lifeboat made numerous vain attempts to tie up the boat, with ropes slipping through his chafed hands with the surge of every wave.

Suddenly, a massive wave smashed the boat against the hull of the ship. Seams opened and the lifeboat was pushed down the side and towards the slowly spinning propellers of the *Great Nancy*, which were partly exposed as the vessel rose and fell over the passing waves.

Passengers screamed and fell over each other trying to get away from the turning blades, which nicked, sliced and splintered the lifeboat time and again. Somehow the second officer managed to haul back on the line, dragging the lifeboat away from the danger.

Finally, after what seemed an interminable time, the lifeboat was secure, but still crashing against the side of the *Great Nancy* as each wave passed beneath it. They had already accumulated a lot of water, but Debra noticed how the water level rose as they continued to be battered against the *Great Nancy*.

Once the boat was secure, the crew lowered a large bucket on a rope. They gestured that children should get in so that they could be pulled up the side and onto the ship. With the crashing of the lifeboat against the ship, volunteers were short in supply.

Eventually Samantha, Gail Adamson's eldest daughter, courageously said: 'I'll go.' The 8-year-old climbed into the bucket and was quickly hauled to safety up the side of the ship and onto the deck. When the bucket returned, Raymond said to Debra: 'Mum, I'm out of here. I'm going.'

'Off you go, my boy. That's very brave!' Debra said. Raymond, who had managed everything the fierce storm had thrown at him up to that moment, walked to the side of the bucket, ceremonially vomited into the lifeboat for the first time since the drama had begun and climbed in. Debra closed her eyes as he was being hauled up: she simply could not watch. She opened her eyes only once another woman called out: 'He's on board and he's safe!'

Debra turned to Megan. 'Your turn now, Megs,' she said encouragingly.

In a scared little voice, Megan declared: 'I'm not going in that bucket, Mum. I want to come with you.'

'I can't carry you, Megs. You have to go in the bucket,' replied Debra.

'Please, Mum,' she begged, 'put me on your back and then you can climb up the ship.'

As this discourse was going on, Gail sent her second child in the bucket and then, in an act of extraordinary trust, placed John Jr into the bucket, stuffed some jackets on top of him and said a prayer as he was lifted away from the lifeboat.

Every lift in itself had to be of impeccable timing. The bucket could be lifted only as the lifeboat crested a wave. Had it been lifted while the lifeboat was in a trough, both the child and the bucket could easily have been crushed between the lifeboat and ship as the boat surged to the top of the next wave. The Chinese crew appreciated the danger and managed the operation to perfection.

Finally, Debra got stern: 'Megan, you have to go in that bucket or you're going to die.' With her mother's tough love jolting Megan into action, she jumped into the bucket and ascended as the last child off.

The *Great Nancy* crew then lowered a harness on a rope. Gail Adamson, as mother of the most children and youngest child, was first into the harness. The crew tried to indicate that she should lie back and walk up the side of the ship in a type of reverse abseil manoeuvre. Gail was not able to master the technique and crashed into the side of the ship several times as they heaved, crushing her hand and breaking three fingers in one of the impacts. Finally, she was on board, weeping uncontrollably, and reunited with her children.

One by one the adults were hauled up the side of the boat, some mastering the lie-back-and-walk technique while others simply dangled and crashed against the ship's side as they were heaved up to safety.

When the turn came for Tsaikas, the ship's casino dealer, he pulled the harness over his large body and started climbing. The size and weight of the man, however, were too much and halfway up the ship's side, the rope parted and he plunged back into the water, drifting off into the darkness.

The remaining passengers on the lifeboat were horrified. Some screamed helplessly. The stowaway husband finally showed some life, leaping into action and shouting for a life buoy to be thrown out. Crew from the *Great Nancy* threw down buoys on ropes to Tsaikas, but he was unable to reach any of them and the sea was too rough for anyone to launch a rescue effort without imperilling himself. The casino dealer drifted around the back of the bulker and out of sight.

Putting the Tsaikas drama out of their minds and showing admirable discipline and restraint in the most dire of circumstances, passengers queued in an orderly fashion and were pulled up in the harness one by one. Eventually half a dozen people were left on the lifeboat: the two officers, a couple of mothers, the stowaway husband and Debra.

When her turn came to climb into the harness, Debra scrambled up the side of the ship. Once aboard, she immediately went in search of her children. Hunting through crew cabins that had been made available to survivors, she eventually came upon Gail and her children. Megan was there, very happy to see her mom. Raymond, almost without a care in the world, had fallen asleep in a bunk bed. The fact that his mother was still stuck in a lifeboat at sea had seemingly not been a matter of concern.

With her damaged hand, Gail was struggling to hold John Jr, so Debra took him. She and another mother tore up a sheet in the cabin to make some diapers for him.

Soon after Debra took him, John Jr started crying insistently, the way only a baby can when he is in need of sustenance from his mother.

'Why don't you feed him?' asked Debra.

'I have no milk,' replied Gail. 'I think it's the shock or something, but I can't feed him.' She looked shattered and had a defeated flatness in her voice.

Debra went in search of food for the child. She managed to borrow a feeding bottle from the mother of another young child and then went to the galley where she mixed up some milk powder the cook had given her. Ten minutes later she returned triumphantly and pushed the rubber teat into the mouth of the protesting child. Despite his initial resistance to the unfamiliar object, John Jr sucked enthusiastically at the bottle and soon fell asleep.

Doing their best to deal with the hoard of refugees who had invaded their ship, the crew gave Debra and the children chicken-flavour instant noodles to eat.

Raymond, in the meantime, had woken shortly after his mother's arrival and, with the irrepressible curiosity of the average 8-year-old boy, went exploring the ship. He came back reporting that he had watched movies with the crew, eaten chicken and fish and exchanged money with them. There is something too wonderful about children and their ability to live in the moment, whatever that moment might be.

Two other lifeboats reached the *Great Nancy* later. As each arrived alongside, Debra stood on the deck, anxiously scanning the occupants in the hope of finding her husband.

The first was Lifeboat 1, filled mostly with *Oceanos* crew, the greater part of whom were officers. They were also heaved aboard by harness. One of them just stood and cried like a baby once he had landed on the deck. It took Debra to comfort him before he calmed down. The irony was not lost on her.

Most of the women from Lifeboat 2 were enraged. The Greek crew in Lifeboat 1 were all men, yet the women's husbands had been left behind on the *Oceanos*. As women heaped abuse on them, some had the grace to hang their heads in shame.

Lifeboat 4 finally pulled up alongside the *Great Nancy*. Debra was overjoyed to be reunited with René, who, as it happened, arrived with John Adamson Sr. With the arrival of Lifeboat 4, and after receiving clearance to leave the area, the *Great Nancy* resumed her voyage towards Durban.

In Port Elizabeth, Debra's father, Eddie Purvis, had been watching the drama unfold on national television. There was no way of knowing what had happened to his family. Eddie eventually phoned Debra's brother, Alistair, who was in Australia then.

'Alistair, are you getting anything on your TV about a ship sinking off South Africa?' he asked.

'Yes, Dad. We're getting all of it here. Why do you ask?'

'Because your sister is on the ship,' he said.

Lifeboat 5

Chantelle Oosthuizen grew up in East London and had recently qualified as a journalist from Rhodes University in Grahamstown. She landed her first job as a cub reporter on the *Daily Dispatch* in East London, which is where she was employed in August 1991.

Her best friend, Tracey Pautz, was a travel agent in East London. Tracey was offered a special, almost-free overnight-to-Durban voyage on the *Oceanos* and invited Chantelle to join her. For the two relatively impecunious friends, this was to be the holiday of a lifetime, even if it was only an overnight cruise.

Chantelle and Tracey joined the ship after lunch on the Saturday, made themselves comfortable in their cabins and then waited to sail into the storm blowing outside. As with everyone else on board, they had experienced the drama of flying crockery and dropped meals at dinner, the lights going out later and the general mayhem of the unannounced vessel evacuation.

As they sat on the floor in the lounge, Chantelle and Tracey watched as TFC staff summoned elderly people and mothers with children to the lifeboats. Being young and single, they had been told that they would have to be patient and would be among the last people to board the lifeboats.

At around 2 am, a TFC staff member came to a group of passengers, which included Chantelle and Tracey, and said, 'We need fifty people'. The two friends needed no second bidding.

Chantelle got up stiffly from the floor and, struggling to walk with the starboard list of the ship, made her way through the foyer and outside onto the deck. As she emerged onto the deck the reality of the cold and brutal weather outside hit her.

Crew members had tied ropes to railings for passengers to hold onto, but several people still fell as they staggered along the rolling and pitching deck. Clinging onto first one rope and then the next, Chantelle and Tracey clambered their way to a port-side lifeboat, which, despite the list to starboard, was swinging alarmingly away and back as the ship rolled.

With Lorraine Betts, Moss Hills and Julian Russell all helping, passengers had to time their jumps to avoid plummeting into the sea, which kept appearing in the 2-metre gap between their lifeboat and the ship. As they jumped, some of the passengers fell awkwardly into the lifeboat, hurting themselves. Chantelle was one of them, bruising herself extensively. All finally made it into the lifeboat without any more serious incident.

Eventually a mixed assortment of about 60 passengers and crew had boarded Lifeboat 5. Before the lifeboat could be filled to capacity, the crew members who were already on board physically prevented more passengers from boarding, standing at the side of the lifeboat and aggressively repelling boarders.

TFC staff shouted to the crew: 'Please take some more! You're not full yet!'

'No more!' the crew shouted back. 'We will sink.'

When it was clear that no more passengers would be allowed on board, Lorraine threw some blankets into the boat and gave the command to lower the vessel. A frantic snatching at the blankets followed, with the crew commandeering one each, leaving the few remaining ones to be distributed among some of the passengers.

There was no obvious leadership or expertise among the crew ensconced in the lifeboat. They were confused about how to lower the lifeboat and screamed at one another all at once in their panic to launch the boat. With their clumsy attempts, first the bow and then the stern would drop and then the bow again. When the rusty davits stuck, a small hammer was used to try and knock them free. The lifeboat banged its way down the side of the ship. Eventually, as the boat slammed into the hard sea below, the davit hooks broke loose and swung around dangerously above the heads of the passengers, who frantically dived for cover. This was an ignominious start to their escape.

The spectacle of the launching of Lifeboat 5 was terrifying to behold and Moss decided that it would be far too dangerous to repeat the exercise with the two remaining boats on the port side. They were subsequently launched empty but with difficulty, scraping and crashing down the side of the *Oceanos* hull. Moss thought that having empty lifeboats in the water might at least offer some place of refuge if passengers ended up in the water.

Once on the sea, Lifeboat 5 started sliding and banging its way along the rising and falling waterline of the *Oceanos*, making its way towards the dangerous area of the stern. Passengers and crew had found some rudimentary oars and were trying to fend themselves off the hull of the rolling vessel. The oars snapped like matchsticks on impact.

The yawing of the *Oceanos* caused a suction force that pulled the lifeboat towards the huge propellers as it bumped along and around the stern. Passengers screamed and prayed out loud for deliverance as the ship heaved in the sea and the propellers crashed down beside the lifeboat, almost wrecking it in the process.

Eventually the boat drifted free of the immediate danger, into the unknown dark sea and sky. Only the dim light of a half-moon behind fierce clouds allowed them some idea of where they were going and a half-warning of the towering waves around them. The Fleming gear was not connected to the propeller of the lifeboat, the rudder was jammed and trying to row the boat with broken oars was an exercise in futility, so they drifted aimlessly and helplessly. Waves splashed over the side and threatened to swamp and sink the boat.

Chantelle was convinced the boat would capsize and moved herself to a position from where she thought she could escape and not be trapped if the little boat flipped over. She also clutched purposefully onto her identity document. If she was going to drown, she at least wanted to be identified when she was found. Ironically, it was the water from the splashing waves, slowly filling the lifeboat, which acted as ballast and steadied the lifeboat in some measure.

Passengers and crew were repeatedly and continually lashed by the freezing wind, spray and waves as they huddled together from the cold, trying as best they could to share body warmth. Water crashing over the sides of the lifeboat was, in a bizarre way, warming those in its path as it hit, but the tearing wind immediately chilled the wet occupants to the bone. When the husband of an elderly woman told Chantelle that his wife was dying from the cold, Chantelle surrendered the blanket she had managed to grab when they first boarded the lifeboat.

Someone had brought a couple of bottles of bourbon and whisky and handed them around to those who were able to keep it down. Sadly, although it may have been of some medicinal value to the others in the boat, the grain spirits never made it past two of the Greek crew, who each hung onto a bottle and eventually drained it. In the end, the primary and fleeting source of warmth for most people in the boat was the frequent and far-flung vomit of fellow passengers. Chantelle, in particular, was so cold that when someone vomited on her shoulder all she could feel was gratitude for the momentary warmth.

Chantelle could see the lights of two commercial ships on the horizon, but the occupants of the lifeboat were unable to signal their whereabouts. Of the three flares they had, two had not worked when they were fired; the third had spurted to life, but died in the water a few metres away.

At 5 am, a low-flying military aircraft roared overhead. Frantically, one passenger started flashing a handheld torch he had brought from the ship. The aircraft circled and flashed lights back. They knew they had been spotted and hope of a quick rescue arose.

The *Reefer Duchess* was a small Dutch-managed refrigerated cargo ship and was the first to reach the stricken lifeboat. It approached the lifeboat at 6.30 am and tried to assist. As the two vessels made repeated contact, the lifeboat was battered against the ship and started breaking up. Wood was falling off in chunks and the metal bars of the awning were bent and ripped off.

On the lifeboat's first contact with the ship, two male passengers leapt across and grabbed the ropes that had been lowered. They scrambled upwards, leaving their families on the lifeboat. As the lifeboat crashed back into the ship, it pinched and severed the ropes where the men's legs had been. Their families were unable to follow, yet a couple of crew members managed to grab the trailing ends of the ropes and scurried onto the ship.

The panic in the lifeboat was palpable as more and more pieces broke off each time it made contact with the *Reefer Duchess*. Passengers were struggling to communicate with Japanese crew members on the vessel, screaming at them to go away and leave the lifeboat alone. The crew of the cargo vessel either could not hear against the wind or could not understand, and kept throwing ladders down, which repeatedly broke.

In an experience similar to that of the survivors who boarded the *Great Nancy*, the lifeboat was sucked along the side of the huge ship towards her spinning propellers, which kept appearing out of the water in the turbulent sea. The captain of the *Reefer Duchess* managed to stop the engines just in time. Realising that nothing more could realistically be done to help, he finally decided to release the lifeboat and sail away.

An hour later, after about four hours at sea, they were approached by the Norwegian fishing trawler, *Anik*. The crew of the trawler, hanging off the side on nets, tried to make the lifeboat fast, but it again started breaking up. Three *Oceanos* crew members recklessly dived at the nets hanging over the side of the *Anik* and made their escape. No one else was willing to try, and again the lifeboat was cut loose when the crew realised that they were unable to help.

An hour or so later, the Polish reefer vessel *Kaszuby II*, under the command of Captain Josef Pelszyk, managed to come alongside and secure the lifeboat. Again it started smashing up against the side of the ship in the crashing seas.

The remaining Greek *Oceanos* crew in the boat yelled at women to climb up the ropes that had been lowered, but they were simply not strong enough. Eventually the *Kaszuby II* crew lowered nets and, as they did, two crewmen from the *Oceanos* leapt into one, abandoning the remaining passengers and crew to their fates.

Passengers were reluctant to follow, but the Polish captain exhorted them to come.

'It is your only chance!' he shouted down. 'You must come now!'

Up until that moment, Chantelle had been too concerned about Tracey, whose strength and spirit had ebbed in the cold, to try and get off the lifeboat. However, when she heard the captain encouraging them, her mindset changed. She jumped into a net with a couple of other passengers and was hauled to safety.

The Polish crew, realising that nets were the only way to rescue the lifeboat passengers, continued to lower nets and pull passengers up onto the deck, including Tracey. As the last passengers were hauled up, the battered lifeboat drifted away in the current, eventually to beach near East London. It was 9 am on Sunday morning.

The Polish crew could not have been kinder. They took everyone's clothing to wash and dry, providing whatever they could as a temporary replacement. When she finally left the ship, Chantelle was still wearing a set of crew trainers, several sizes too big for her. Survivors were given

Reporter and *Oceanos* passenger Chantelle Oosthuizen's
front-page story in the *Daily Dispatch*.

cabins in which to rest, whatever food was available and every support possible.

Chantelle was too hyped up to rest, so she attached herself to the TFC woman who had been dispatched with the lifeboat and had taken charge of the survivors on board the *Kaszuby II*. Later that day she followed her up to the bridge where the captain was allowing the TFC staff member to communicate with the outside world. Chantelle, ever the responsible new employee, wanted to get a message to her office to say she would be late for work the following day. She called Tracey's mother to tell her they were safe and then her boss, who immediately said they wanted a story from her.

Chantelle wrote out her story, something like a diary entry, and finally faxed it through to the *Daily Dispatch*. As a cub reporter she had her first scoop. In the news vacuum that was the wild waves of the Indian Ocean followed by the crowded bridge of the *Kaszuby II*, little did she know just how big the scoop really was.

Michael O'Mahoney and his friend Neal Shaw waited on the deck, now helpless to protect their families who were somewhere adrift in a lifeboat. Slowly the ship increased her perilous list to starboard, through 25 and then 30 degrees.

In the distance they could see the lights of a small settlement or building on the shore. This was the Haven Hotel near Coffee Bay. Despite being only some 2 miles away, they might as well have been 1 000 miles away given the futility of trying to reach them through the furious waves and howling winds.

Despite the ongoing operation to load and launch lifeboats, and resigned to the fact that as men on the vessel they were unlikely to find space for themselves on one of the lifeboats and would have to remain on board, they decided to return to their cabins to fetch warm jackets and retrieve a few valuables – passports, papers, perhaps Michael's valuable camera equipment and whatever else they could easily carry. As they headed for their cabins on the Venus deck below, they encountered a Greek sailor at the top of the stairs, brandishing an axe.

'We want to go downstairs and fetch our passports,' explained Michael reasonably. The sailor ignored him.

'May we go down, please?' he continued, trying to slide past the Greek, who was firmly planted across the top of the stairs.

As Michael made his move, the sailor menacingly lifted the axe. It was not clear to them why the sailor was so determined to keep people from their cabins, but his intent was unmistakeable and his demeanour not that of someone trying to be helpful.

Michael heard an unusual sound and peered over the bannister: water was swirling at the base of the stairs. It was time to retreat. As they walked away they met another friend of Michael and told him what had happened.

'There's another route to the cabins,' said the friend and proceeded to give them directions.

Carefully they made their way along the sharply sloping deck and found their way to the cabins, now shin-deep in water. Gingerly, they waded through and retrieved a few valuables from the cupboards. Michael donned a leather flying jacket and then went in search of Neal in his cabin nearby. Neal had also managed to collect a few personal effects, including his wife's handbag. They returned to the deck through the lounge, grabbing some sustenance on their way out: a few bottles of Southern Comfort and Jack Daniels from the now deserted bar.

On their return to the deck, the bottles were shared out among grateful passengers, each quaffing a shot of golden stomach warmer before passing on the bottle to the next in line.

'Here you go,' said Michael, offering a bottle of Jack Daniels to a windswept, wet and freezing woman standing next to him. She held it to her lips, sucking on the bottle gratefully. 'If we make it out of here,' continued Michael, laughing at her coughing as the liquid hit the back of her throat, 'we'll be friends for life over this bottle.'

It was 3 am and time was dragging interminably. The ship was heeling

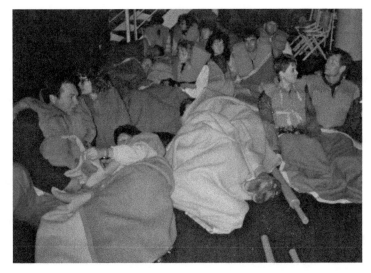

Passengers huddle together under blankets while awaiting their rescue.

hectically, with passengers hanging on grimly. A huge wave smashed into the ship, dislodging Neal's grip. He slid down the deck, grabbing whatever he could and frantically tried to save himself from plummeting into the now empty swimming pool. He stopped himself on a railing and painstakingly climbed back to his position.

Michael needed the bathroom. He got up, made his way along the deck to the lounge area and down to the toilets. They were foul. Raw, stinking sewage was sloshing along the floor to the motion of the ship.

Gagging over the smell of a toilet already blocked and awash with sewage, Michael saw an elderly man who was trying to get out of the toilets and back up to the deck. The ship was heeled right over and it was obvious that the old man was not going to make it. The floor was covered with a smooth short-pile carpet, making it as unclimbable as a ski slope.

Michael managed to crawl up to the railings on the ship's side and picked up some bed sheets, which were fortuitously lying on the floor. As it happened, the TFC staff had earlier brought up blankets from the cabins to give to the passengers boarding the lifeboats and had dropped the sheets on the floor. He spliced a few sheets together, tied one end to a railing and then abseiled back down to his elderly fellow passenger below.

'You're going to have to wrap your arms around my neck. I can piggyback you out of here,' explained Michael.

The old man wound his feeble arms around Michael's neck, half suffocating him. Michael scrambled up the floor with the frail load on his back, finally depositing the older man outside on the deck.

A while later, a couple of the TFC staff approached Neal and Michael. 'Would you be able to assist in getting passengers into one of the lifeboats?'

It was the last lifeboat left out of the eight on board the ship and many of the passengers who were left were elderly and frail. The TFC staff handed Michael and Neal some flares and led them, with difficulty, to the lifeboat, which was on the high port side of the ship and, other than when the ship lurched, resting against the side of the ship. The men were given a short briefing on how the mechanism for lowering the lifeboat worked.

Michael and Neal clambered in and started assisting passengers into the boat. Lou and Ernie Tolken were among them. As the passengers were queuing to embark, the ship lurched and a glass table came crashing down, shards flying around them. Miraculously, no one was injured.

The boat was swinging crazily both forward and aft in the gale and from side to side with the rolling motion of the ship in the heaving sea, away from the *Oceanos* and then crashing back into it. It was not the most stable platform for loading the aged.

As soon as the lifeboat was full, they began lowering it. Suddenly it stuck. The lowering mechanism had either rusted solid or jammed and would not budge. In any event, with the lifeboat resting against the port side of the *Oceanos* for most of the time, it was almost impossible to move it.

'Pass me something to release this!' Michael yelled against the howling wind.

The TFC staff passed Michael a fire axe and he managed to smash his side loose, causing the lifeboat to drop a few feet and leaving it lopsided. Terrified passengers passed the axe along to Neal at the other end so that he could do the same.

With Neal trying to smash his side loose, the boat was bucking like a whitewater raft adrift on the Zambezi, with occupants desperately hanging on for survival. Michael looked around and found a long spiked gaff lying on the floor of the lifeboat. Pushing the spiked end against the side of the ship he partially steadied the boat until a huge wave crashed them against the *Oceanos'* superstructure. The lifeboat compressed against the hull, swung out and then back. When the pole again made contact with the ship's side, it bowed and shattered. Sensation left his hands with the shock wave and his fingernails turned black almost immediately.

Neal eventually managed to smash the winch mechanism loose and his end dropped sharply, more or less level with Michael's. The boat was then just hanging, swinging around in the wind. The crew on deck battled with the electric motors used to lower the lifeboat into the water. Eventually they gave up.

'We have to get everyone out,' said Michael to Neal. 'We're stuck and someone's going to get hurt.' After almost an hour suspended perilously over the side of the ship a decision was made to evacuate everyone from the lifeboat and get them back on deck.

This operation proved more challenging than it had been to load the passengers into the boat. It had dropped a few metres when the davits were freed, so the embarkation deck was then above the level of everyone's heads.

The lifeboat was swinging away from and back towards the *Oceanos* with her rolling. As the boat swung back and into the side of the ship, Michael and Neal scrambled up onto the relative safety of the deck above them. They heaved their exhausted and terrified fellow passengers back to safety, one by one. When it was over they were both drained. Michael still had no feeling in his hands and all they could do was sit down, defeated, in their old spot on the deck.

Eventually they dozed off.

Moss had been trying to keep count of the number of passengers in lifeboats. When all the lifeboats were gone, by his reckoning, there were still about 240 people left on board. The entertainers then decided to find Captain Avranas. Moss believed he would be on the bridge doing whatever captains do when their ships are sinking. He, Tracy, Lorraine, Robin and Julian made their way to the bridge, up the stairs and through the officers' accommodation.

Moss could not believe what he saw when they walked onto the bridge: it was completely deserted, with no one apparently in control of the ship. Log books, binoculars and other loose items were skidding around on the floor. The screens of the instruments were all working, but no one was there. For the first time, Moss believed that they may have been abandoned by the crew.

They thought the best would be to make a Mayday call, as they were never informed that the captain had already done so. However, they had no idea how to do that.

'What channel do we use?' asked Moss.

Robin noticed the radio was connected to a car battery and knew that there was no other source of power for the radio. 'I'm not changing any channel. I don't want to mess with anything here,' replied Robin.

Believing that the VHF radio must have been used earlier, and would therefore be tuned to a channel to which people were listening, they changed nothing. Moss grabbed the hand piece and started calling: 'Mayday! Mayday! Can anyone hear us?'

There was silence for some minutes. Eventually, a foreign voice replied, some sort of Eastern language in their estimation. They guessed that the voice was replying from some ship in the distance, but they could not communicate with each other.

Moss kept on calling: 'Mayday! Mayday! This is the *Oceanos*! Can anyone hear us?'

Eventually, a calm German-sounding voice came back to them through the radio. 'This is Captain Dettmar of the *Nedlloyd Mauritius*. We are already coming to your assistance?' The *Nedlloyd Mauritius* was a container ship owned and operated by the Nedlloyd Group, one of the largest shipowners and operators in the world. Captain Manfred Dettmar sounded, at least to Moss, like someone you would want to have in your corner. Dettmar had received Silvermine's call for assistance earlier in the evening when his ship had been some distance from the *Oceanos*.

'We're sinking!' said Moss. 'We need urgent assistance.'

'How long will you remain afloat?' asked the unflappable Captain Dettmar. 'Please also state your position.'

Moss replied: 'I don't know how long we'll remain afloat. I estimate that the ship is angled over to starboard by 20 degrees or more. We're somewhere between East London and Durban.'

'Thank you,' said Captain Dettmar, 'but what are your exact coordinates?'

'I have no idea,' said Moss. 'All I know is that we are between East London and Durban.'

'Why don't you know the coordinates? What is your rank, please?' asked Captain Dettmar. 'I need to speak to an officer.'

'I don't have a rank,' said Moss. 'I'm a guitar player. There is no one on the bridge.'

A long silence followed. 'I see,' said Captain Dettmar. 'Please try to find your captain. I need to speak to him.' Moss undertook to do so and scurried off in search of Captain Avranas.

Moss knew that JD Massyn had earlier seen Captain Avranas trying to get into a lifeboat.

'Where's the captain, JD?' he asked as soon as he saw her.

'I don't have a clue, Moss. He's disappeared,' she replied. 'I last saw him when I told him to get out of the lifeboat, but I haven't seen him since.'

Moss believed that the captain must still be on board. Moss had, for the last couple of hours, been checking water levels periodically. The last time he had checked the restaurant, which was just below the main deck, it had been flooded and flowers and chairs had been floating around aimlessly. He knew, therefore, that the captain had to be above the level of the dining room, which meant that almost certainly he was somewhere on the main weather deck.

Moss went to the pool deck and found the captain sitting quietly with the radio officer in the shadows, smoking. 'Captain, I need you to come to the bridge and give our position to another ship,' said Moss.

'Not necessary,' he said sullenly.

'The captain of another ship wants to know how we will deal with and fill a lifeboat if he sends it to us,' continued Moss.

'Not necessary for me to speak with him,' repeated Avranas. Although the captain did not seem to be panicking, he had a wild-eyed staring look about him. Moss thought that the captain was all but catatonic.

He gave up and returned to the bridge. It was clear that, even if Captain Avranas had not physically abandoned the ship, he had certainly abandoned his position on the ship and the passengers in his charge. That was the last time that Moss saw the captain on board.

Back on the bridge, Moss reported to Captain Dettmar that he was unable to give any further nautical information as Captain Avranas was unwilling to cooperate with him. Dettmar was incredulous.

'He must come to the bridge at once and control the rescue,' said Dettmar.

'I'm sorry,' said Moss, 'but he refuses to come. You have to deal with us. We will try our best.'

Moss then reported that, in the distance he could see a ship, which probably could not see the *Oceanos* as the latter was showing no lights. He suggested that, if Captain Dettmar could make contact with the ship that Moss could see, it might be able to search for and locate the *Oceanos* in the gloom. Captain Dettmar said that he would try to get information on the other ships in the area via the local port captains.

The group then left the bridge to support the remaining passengers on board.

CHAPTER 9

THE HAVEN

In 1991 P&I Associates was, and even today remains, the largest South African commercial correspondent for ships' Protection and Indemnity Clubs – also known as P&I Clubs – around the world. It has representative offices in every major port in South Africa. P&I Associates represents ships' owners, charterers, agents and mutual liability underwriters from around the world, with a client base that includes all the major international group P&I Clubs and their members.

A P&I Club is a mutual insurance company for ships. The owners of the ships are the members of the Club and they make annual contributions (known as 'calls'), which are used to pay the administrative and running expenses of the P&I Club. These expenses include claims made by members.

The Clubs are usually run by professional managers whose job it is to look after and provide the Club services to their members. These services include third-party liability insurance to cover potential claims for damage caused by the members' ships or compensation in respect of personal injury to passengers, cargo liabilities and loss of personal effects and property, and also for legal costs and support.

Just after midnight, on Sunday 4 August, Captain Chris Green, the managing director of P&I Associates in Durban, received a call from Phil Nichols of the UK P&I Club.

'Sorry to wake you, Chris. We've got a member's ship sinking off the South African coast with 800 [*sic*] people on board. Can you sort it out?'

The UK P&I Club is one of the largest mutual Clubs in the world, with hundreds of millions of ships tonnage registered with it and servicing members in some 350 ports around the world. As with all Clubs, the UK Club employs in-house claims handlers to deal with, for example, crises such as the *Oceanos*. The UK Club had had to deal with the *Herald of Free Enterprise* ferry disaster four years earlier near Zeebrugge in Belgium, so had some current experience of handling shipping disasters involving passengers.

But for Chris Green there was no precedent in recent times of a large passenger ship sinking off the South African coast and there were certainly no protocols or plans in place for such an event. The scenario was so unlikely that it had never crossed his mind how he might set about trying to rescue 800 passengers from a sinking passenger ship.

Captain Avranas did not have time to contact (and is unlikely to have even thought to have contacted) a commercial correspondent. So, despite being only a few hundred kilometres from Captain Avranas at the time the ship started sinking, for Green to have been alerted to the problem the news first had to travel via Port Elizabeth and Durban Radio, the Maritime Rescue Coordination Centre at Silvermine, the ship's agents, the Piraeus offices of Epirotiki, the UK Club managers in London, and finally back to Green, snug in his bed in Durban. In this manner, P&I Associates was eventually appointed by Phil Nichols to assist Epirotiki and the Club in South Africa.

Chris and Phil discussed the details of the casualty as were then available, although what they knew between them at that time could best be described as scanty. Chris then started calling around, first of all speaking to the team at Silvermine, who he knew would be managing and coordinating the crisis. He also spoke to Durban's port captain, Mike Cooper, to find out what he knew. Once he had some more information, he reported back to Phil Nichols and then went to his office in downtown Durban, where he stayed for the next ten days.

From his office, Chris started calling around to see what help he could muster. The first and most obvious people to speak to were Pentow

Marine, the largest salvage and offshore support company in the country, who were contracted to the South African government at the time to handle salvage operations along the country's coastline.

They told Chris that their two large salvage tugs, *Wolraad Woltemade* and *John Ross*, were busy dealing with a 356 000-tonne deadweight oil tanker called the *Mimosa*, whose steering gear had fallen off in the heavy seas. They also told him that derricks had come adrift in one of the ports, some ships had lost containers overboard in the bad weather and essentially there were many casualties all along the South African east and south coasts that required attention.

No proper salvage tugs were available to help with the *Oceanos* and no port tugs were able to leave any harbour in such bad weather. 'I'm sorry, Chris, but you're on your own,' said a sympathetic voice at Pentow Marine.

At the time Captain Nick Sloane was a tug master employed by Pentow Marine (in recent years Sloane became famous for salvaging the wreck of the ocean liner *Costa Concordia*, which grounded and sank off the Italian coast in 2012). On the night that the *Oceanos* got into trouble, he was at sea in one of the only other tugs on the South African coastline that might have been able to assist.

Sloane served at the time as master on board the *Pentow Skua*, the offshore anchor-handler support vessel for the South African FA platform. The FA platform is an offshore oil production platform on a gas field almost 40 miles from Mossel Bay. At the time there were five tugs working around her and she was connected to her accommodation support rig, which had been modified to accommodate over 400 people for the platform construction.

Sloane recalls the weekend of 3 August 1991 being a maritime nightmare.

At sunset on the Thursday, they realised a storm was approaching, but no one expected the scale at which it arrived. By midnight they recorded 80 to 90 knots of wind and swells of around 20 metres near the rig. By 2 am on the Friday, the full force of the storm had reached them and swells were averaging just over 24 metres. He recalls that the swells were so enormous that at times they lost sight of the rig's decks, with just the flare-boom seen above the swells. The captain of the FA platform required assistance with evacuating the 400 people off the rig because he feared that it would capsize in the weather, but Sloane and his team were unable to assist in the prevailing weather conditions. The best they could offer was to stand by and pick people out of the water with their rescue craft in the event of a capsize.

Later that morning, with winds still around 60 knots, they received the *Mimosa*'s 'PAN-PAN' (the international standard urgency signal), from further north of Algoa Bay. She was a fully-laden supertanker and had suffered major structural damage in the storm. The two salvage tugs, *John Ross* and *Wolraad Woltemade*, were mobilised to run to her aid and avoid a looming environmental disaster. The storm was moving north, up against the powerful Agulhas current. They received the Mayday from the *Oceanos* on Saturday night.

After having no luck with Pentow Marine, Chris Green called Silvermine again. Brigadier Theo de Munnink, who was managing and coordinating the rescue from there, was helpful and generous with whatever information was to hand. The public relations officer at the centre subsequently included P&I Associates in the communication loop.

Chris learnt that Silvermine had asked the SAAF to respond and that a helicopter evacuation would commence at first light.

After reporting back to Phil Nichols, he started implementing whatever measures he could. This included instructions from Nichols that he should make preparations for the arrival of passengers in each port. He called Duncan Starke, one of the executives at Polaris Shipping, in the early hours to give him instructions. Ships agents were logistics people and he knew that they would already be making plans.

'Duncan, the P&I Club has instructed us that the most important things to provide to passengers after a casualty are access to a telephone and doctor, transport to a hospital and claim forms for lost personal effects, which should be completed as soon as possible after the passengers come ashore. Please can you organise that in Durban, Port Elizabeth and East London?'

'I'll add that to my to-do list, Chris,' Duncan responded. 'It's getting longer by the hour.'

Duncan had already made a number of arrangements overnight, but some had to wait until the morning.

His first job that morning was to call Telkom, the recently established parastatal telecommunications company, to ask them to start installing additional telephones in the passenger terminal in Durban. He then called Doctor Robertson, the local Durban doctor who specialised in dealing with seafarers.

'Doctor Robertson, we have a looming emergency on our hands. The *Oceanos* has sunk and we will need a doctor on hand when survivors start landing. They're en route already.'

'How many people are we talking about?' the doctor asked.

'I don't know,' replied Duncan, 'but there were nearly 600 people on board the ship, so it will be a good number.'

Silence. 'You want me to treat several hundred people?'

'No,' replied Duncan, more confidently than he felt, 'I'm quite sure only a handful will need medical assistance.' And then as an afterthought: 'But perhaps you had better line up one or two colleagues in case the numbers are overwhelming. The first ship is expected in the early hours tomorrow, at around 5 am.'

Duncan then busied himself arranging for transport to hospitals, placing the nearby St Augustine's and Entabeni hospitals on stand-by to receive passengers, typing up and printing hundreds of claim forms and generally checking and rechecking that everything was in place and ready for the expected flood of survivors.

In the meantime, Mike Brown, Duncan's colleague at Polaris, had ascertained that a number of cargo ships were rescuing passengers who had been put to sea in lifeboats and that some would be ferried to Durban, others to Port Elizabeth and possibly East London. Mike was charged with attending on each of the ships that called to clarify details about their part in the rescue and assisting them with their port arrangements.

He was also liaising with Mike Cooper because port captains are usually relatively inflexible about allowing ships to 'leapfrog' others and berth out of turn. This is because of the cost implications for ships that have to queue to get into a port, so berthing is typically a first-come, first-served scenario in most ports. However, in this case Cooper made an exception and was simply extraordinary in the way he was able to juggle berthing schedules for other ships, so that the rescue ships could come alongside almost as soon as they arrived outside the port.

Boet and Lynette Jacobs were still in bed in their bungalow, having a lie-in on this Sunday morning. They knew that their kitchen staff would be in by 6.30 am to get breakfast going for the sprinkling of guests staying at the Haven Hotel during this low season.

The sound of diesel engines roused them from their half-awake state. Boet looked out of the window to see a 1969 Land Rover, with a 5.5-metre inflatable dinghy in tow, bounce to a stop in front of the hotel in a small flurry of dust. It was followed by three other 4x4 vehicles of various descriptions.

At least 15 men, wearing NSRI uniforms, spilled out of the vehicles and walked to the front door of the hotel. He saw them try the door, and then knock hard when it did not open. Glancing over at the bedside clock he noticed that it was just before 6 am.

As Boet hurriedly pulled some warm clothing over his pyjamas, he could see the men starting to look around for a way into the hotel. As trustworthy as the local community was, petty theft was a persistent problem in the area and the hotel reception area was always locked after midnight or once the last guests had left the bar area, whichever happened last.

Boet walked out of his bungalow, which was some 50 metres from the main hotel and called out to the NSRI men in a thick Afrikaans accent: 'Can I help you?'

One of the men walked quickly over to him. 'Yes, please. Are you the manager here?' he asked.

Boet nodded, a little confused by this unexpected visit.

'I am Geoff MacGregor, the coxswain of the mobile rescue unit of the NSRI East London Station,' the man said. 'We have driven through from East London.'

Boet knew that the drive from East London would have taken anything up to six hours, even when the roads were dry, so the men must have been driving since midnight to reach him.

The NSRI is a South African charity whose mission is to save the lives of persons at sea and any other South African waters. The organisation operates on donations from the public and is run by approximately 1 000 highly skilled, unpaid volunteers who are on stand-by day and night throughout the year. They have rescue bases around the coast and on the larger inland dams used for recreation and water sports. The organisation operates a fleet of rescue boats, rescue vehicles, quad bikes and launching tractors. They also generally have access to a range of helicopters and enjoy a good working relationship with other emergency services.

'The road was terrible,' MacGregor added. 'We were also hit by some sort of tornado on the dirt road. There were roofs of huts and all sorts of other stuff flying around.'

Boet nodded, unsurprised. He knew that the 70 kilometres of dirt road from Umtata, the capital of the Transkei, was in a poor condition: rutted, eroded, muddy and lined in places with the rural huts and shanties of the locals, to say nothing of the cattle, goats and other livestock that wandered around untethered and unenclosed.

'What brings you here?' asked Boet.

'There is a passenger ship called the *Oceanos* sinking near here,' MacGregor said. 'There are still several hundred people on board. We need your help, please.'

Glancing quickly out to sea, Boet could see walls of spray blowing around in the wind and thought he could make out a ship in the distance through the spray. It looked lopsided.

Boet, who was used to having to deal with unusual situations out in the bush, felt an uneasy stirring. He and Lynette had spent the past couple of years as managers at Mkambati Nature Reserve, about 300 kilometres to the north of where they now found themselves, before taking over the managerial position at the Haven Hotel and they were well versed in dealing with crises and working with limited resources. Whatever was required of them now, however, sounded as if it was going to be a big stretch.

'OK, what do you need from us?' asked Boet cautiously.

'First of all,' replied MacGregor, 'we need to make space available for military helicopters to land on your golf course.' The hotel had a small and somewhat unkempt nine-hole golf course. Typical of its genre on this coastline, the course sprawled and meandered its way through the bush, invaded from time to time by local cattle and goats.

'We are also going to need a few bungalows for ourselves, the Air Force and other rescue personnel. We need to set up command posts from where we can direct the rescue.'

'Ja,' said Boet, 'we can help with that.'

'And,' continued MacGregor, 'we are going to need you to provide food and drinks for survivors, whatever blankets you have, possibly places for them to stay, but in any event some shelter. The helicopters will be arriving shortly and will then start ferrying survivors ashore. The survivors will be brought here.'

There was a moment of stunned silence as Boet took this all in. He knew that, at a push, the hotel had room for only 120 people, sharing. As it was, he and Lynette had taken over as managers only two months earlier and were still trying to equip and stock the place properly.

The hotel was old, in need of an overhaul and had a limited amount of crockery and cutlery, so Boet knew that giving shelter to and feeding hundreds of people was going to be a chaotic endeavour, at best.

'Let me call my wife,' said Boet, stalling for time. He turned back to his bungalow, his mind racing. 'Let's see how we can help you.' He stomped off to consult with Lynette.

'HOW many people did you say?' Lynette was horrified when Boet gave her the news. 'You know we've only got 53 cups and saucers!' Together they made their way back to speak to the NSRI people.

'Let's go into the hotel,' said Lynette. The wind was still howling outside making it difficult to hear each other, and it was cold.

They made their way to the hotel, unlocked the main door and went into the lounge. There, Geoff MacGregor told them everything he knew. Together they strategised for the logistics of the operation. They knew that helicopters were on the way. They also knew that there were lifeboats adrift at sea. The difficulty was in not knowing how many people to expect. Potentially several hundred people could converge on the hotel.

Quickly an empty bungalow was allocated to the NSRI and they set up what was named Mobile Rescue 7, a radio command post that could communicate with everyone involved in the rescue. (Station 7 was the allotted number for the East London station of the NSRI. Hence, a mobile station from there was Mobile Rescue 7.) The rescue station had sea and air communication systems and was therefore able to communicate with the SAAF rescue aircraft, Silvermine, as well as the *Oceanos* and any other commercial or naval rescue ships in the area.

Two other bungalows were set aside for the SAAF command centre and whoever else might need one. Thankfully it was low season and only a handful of guests were staying at the hotel. Lynette went into the kitchen and started chivvying her staff.

'We need to make soup for 400 people,' she explained in isiXhosa. Lynette had lived in rural areas for most of her life and spoke fluently in the vernacular.

The looks of utter incomprehension from her staff told their own story. Quickly Lynette tried to explain to the staff what was happening and where all these people would be coming from. The explanation, if anything, confused the staff even more. Helicopters and sinking ships were so far removed from the realm of reality in which the average Transkeian Xhosa person operated, that Lynette could have been describing an invasion from another galaxy, for all the sense she was making.

'*Oceanos*! OCEANOS! Come in, *Oceanos*!'

Tony Bell, another member of the NSRI's Mobile Rescue 7 unit, which had by now established itself in one of the bungalows, kept calling the *Oceanos* to try and make initial contact with the ship. It was around 6.30 am and the first helicopters had arrived and were readying themselves about 10 minutes to the north of The Haven on the rough coastline. In the meantime, it had been agreed that once the helicopters started ferrying survivors off the ship, they would be offloaded onto the golf course, near the main entrance to the hotel.

Eventually a woman's faint voice answered Bell's call.

'This is the *Oceanos*. Who are you?' It seemed a fair question.

'This is Mobile Rescue 7. We are stationed ashore at The Haven. Can you give us a sitrep?' Tony needed a situation report on the vessel's position and current state.

'What is that?' the voice answered.

Tony was taken aback. Any seafarer on the bridge of a ship should know what a sitrep was. 'Who am I speaking to?' he asked, wondering how the rest of the conversation was going to proceed.

'This is Lorraine Betts,' the voice replied. 'I am the cruise director of the ship.'

'Where is the captain?' asked Tony. 'I need to speak to someone in charge of the ship.'

'I suppose we're in charge of the ship,' said Lorraine. 'There are no crew on the bridge.'

Tony was incredulous. 'Why not?' he asked. 'Where are they?'

'Most have left in lifeboats,' said Lorraine. 'I think the captain is somewhere on the deck. The TFC staff are basically in charge of the ship now.'

Tony was stunned. This was turning into a rescue with a difference.

CHAPTER 10

AWAITING THE CAVALRY

With the lifeboats gone and still well over 200 people on board, the mood on the *Oceanos* was for the most part sombre. All the passengers remaining on board now knew that some sort of miracle was required to save them from drowning when the ship finally sank.

Alvon Collison and Robin Boltman circulated among gathered groups of passengers, spending much of the night telling jokes, taking the mickey and generally trying to cheer people up.

Robin eventually decided to open a side door so that people could go out onto the deck and smoke. He used one of the small emergency hammers to break open the door. Passengers started clambering over collapsed blackjack tables to get out. By then, no one appeared to be seasick any longer: everyone was so preoccupied with the sense of impending doom and, with the icy blast of the gale blowing in from the Southern Ocean, seasickness was the least of their worries.

Robin returned to the lounge to fetch soft drinks for the passengers and a few beers for himself and other staff members. The piano in the Four Seasons lounge had by then taken a final curtain call and crashed off the stage.

Robin went over to Tom Hine, still standing guard at the top of the steps, passed him a beer and started a discussion about their situation.

'I think we need to get the passengers out of here, Tom,' said Robin. 'If this ship goes belly up, we'll all have a much better chance of survival if we are on the deck than if we're inside.' Tom agreed and together they started shuffling reluctant passengers out through the open side door to face the elements.

As Tom emerged onto the deck with Robin, the massive angle at which the ship was by then heeling over to starboard became more apparent as the distant horizon became visible.

'Tom, stop moving. You're going to fall off this deck walking around at that angle,' instructed Robin.

Tom, holding an unopened six pack of beers, replied: 'Are you mad? I've spent most of my life at this angle!' It was almost 3 am and the entertainers were still seeing the humour in the situation.

Lorraine came up to Robin to report that the staff had found a life raft and some rubber ducks on the bow of the ship, which could be used as a last resort. She and Robin agreed that they should be tethered properly to the ship because they might be blown off in the gale and should be launched only when it was light enough to see what everyone was doing. Robin wanted someone to watch over them in case they were launched without the agreement of the TFC staff. The only volunteer, a TFC staff member, jumped into one of the rubber ducks and promptly fell asleep.

Once it was light, Robin returned to the bridge, only to find it still deserted. As he walked in he heard a voice saying, '*Oceanos* come in … *Oceanos* come in …'. He answered the radio. It was a ship in the vicinity.

Robin was using emergency channel 16, which theoretically should be kept on and free for all emergencies. Usually channels should be changed once emergency contact had been established as multiple conversations can be confusing on one channel. Robin's conversation was captured on Moss's video footage at the time. It went something like this:

'*Oceanos*, please move to another channel.'

'What frequency? Can you help? Over,' Robin asked.

'OK, now we have two lifeboats close to us,' said a foreign sounding voice, apparently the captain of a ship nearby who had joined the conversation. 'Now we are proceeding to pick up if there are people inside.'

'Okay. No the question was: National Sea Rescue. Need the spare channel. We're on channel one-six. Channel 16 at the moment. Can you give a free channel? Over.'

'Yes, sure, of course. Which channel you want?' The ship responded immediately despite Robin asking for help from the NSRI.

'Which one have you got?' Robin pulled the receiver from his ear, laughing at his ignorance of radio protocols.

'Quick, zero six,' came the reply.

'German vessel. This is National Sea Rescue. Going down to channel six. Channel six.'

'Yes. Channel six,' responded the foreign ship.

'Okay. NSRI, you copy that?' asked Robin.

Then, with a naughty glint in his eye and grin on his face, he turned directly towards the camera and said: '*Dit is "Goeiemôre, Suid-Afrika". Die late-ste nuus is ons is almal in die kak*.'[4]

The radio conversation continued a little later with the *Nedlloyd Mauritius*, which had launched its own lifeboat to pick up people in the water.

'*Oceanos*, we have picked up the passengers from one lifeboat and rescued about 20 from the water,' advised Captain Dettmar. 'Are there any more lifeboats to be launched?'

'No,' replied Robin. 'We have no more lifeboats and a lot of people still on board. Some passengers want to jump into the water in case the ship sinks. We are telling them to wait, but please keep a lookout for any swimmers. Everyone is wearing a life jacket.'

There was nothing more to discuss with Captain Dettmar, so Robin returned to the main deck to check on the passengers.

Passengers were rapidly becoming hypothermic in the icy wind. Ronan, the shopkeeper, went to his locked shop and smashed the window. His keys were in his cabin down below and smashing the window was the

---

4   Translation: 'This is "Good morning, South Africa" [the morning magazine programme on the Afrikaans TV channel at the time]. The latest news is we are all in the shit.'

only option to access the goods in the shop. He started handing out windbreakers, shirts and anything that would help keep passengers warm.

'May I have the blue one?' asked one passenger.

'Do you have this in a medium?' asked another.

'I like the one with the hood,' said a third passenger.

'You must be joking,' thought an incredulous Robin. 'Here we are staring down death's throat and passengers are worried about how they'll look.'

Throughout the night the Maritime Rescue Coordination Centre continued to relay all reports, coordinate shipping movements and monitor developments. By 4.45 am the *Nedlloyd Mauritius* reported that the *Oceanos* was listing between 20 and 30 degrees to starboard with 221 passengers still on board.

Robin and Lorraine periodically returned to the bridge to give to and receive updates from Silvermine and the surrounding ships, who were all communicating with one another.

Just after 6.30 am Robin and Lorraine heard a new voice calling the *Oceanos* on the radio and asking for a report on their current situation. The voice identified itself as 'Mobile Rescue 7', the mobile rescue unit of the NSRI, which had been deployed to The Haven. Lorraine responded to the call. After identifying herself and finding out who Mobile Rescue 7 was, she passed the microphone to Robin to continue the conversation.

'*Oceanos*, give us your position please,' demanded Mobile Rescue 7. The charts had slid off the navigator's table and there was no power on any of the instruments, so even if Robin had wanted and been able to read a chart he could not have.

'Mobile Rescue 7, I have no idea what our position is, but I can see two lighthouses from the bridge. Tell them to switch one off and I can give you a bearing from the compass here on the bridge.' Robin, despite having no acquired navigation skills, had been on ships long enough to use common sense to work out what was going on.

'I must also mention that there are several ships around us, Mobile

Rescue 7. We are the white one with the blue funnel. We're easily recognisable because we are nearly upside down!'

The airwaves bristled with Robin's sense of irony.

'Alright, how many passengers are still on board?' asked the voice. Robin walked out onto the bridge wing, surveyed the passengers and estimated about 270. He reported this back to Mobile Rescue 7.

'Help is on the way, *Oceanos*,' reported Mobile Rescue 7. 'We have 11 Puma helicopters and 2 Alouettes approaching. The first helicopters will arrive from Durban on compass bearing 200 degrees. Others will follow from Pretoria and Cape Town.'

Robin and Lorraine rushed down to the pool deck to share the good news with the passengers. As they arrived, Robin saw all the passengers clustered on the starboard side, watching hundreds of dolphins frolic in the half-light of the early morning. There were no dolphins anywhere else to be seen, only those playing in front of the passengers, perhaps giving some assurance that at least they would be around to assist if all else failed. By now the passengers were sitting in long lines sloping down the deck to the starboard side, each one with their legs wrapped around the next passenger to stop them from sliding into the sea.

Michael O'Mahoney had awoken as dawn was breaking. When one of the passengers pointed to the school of dolphins swimming close to the ship another commented: 'If they're around they'll keep sharks away if we need to jump in.' Passengers were clutching at whatever straws presented themselves.

As the sky brightened around them in the east, Michael heard the unmistakeable sound of an aircraft. He had heard enough aircraft during his lifetime to know that this was a military plane and felt sure that the Air Force was on the way.

Despite the impossible list of the *Oceanos* and the real risk of capsizing or sinking, just the sound of a nearby military aircraft was reassuring. Although he could not at that time know exactly how or when he would be rescued, it seemed as if help was at hand.

Merchant and fishing vessels came to the *Oceanos'* rescue. *Nedlloyd Mauritius* in the foreground.

The four Pumas from 15 Squadron, Durban were the first to arrive at Coffee Bay. The first two landed in the dark just after 5.30 am and the second pair some 15 minutes later. They had chosen to land above one of the numerous cliffs that plunged into the sea on that coastline, exactly abeam of the ship.

A command post was established on the beach. The officer in charge of the command post decided that not all of the divers could be landed on the ship. The mission was too dangerous and there might not be space for all of them.

After some discussion, it was decided to land Paul Whiley on the vessel and leave the other divers on the beach. As they were sitting waiting for the decision, Paul and the others overheard on the radio that the wave-rider buoy at the Mossgas FA oil production platform, which was no more than 100 miles from where they had landed, had measured waves averaging close to 30 metres through the night.

This was going to be no ordinary mission.

From the top of the cliff where the helicopters had landed, everyone could see the *Oceanos* a few miles directly out to sea, listing at a crazy angle. It was clear that disaster was looming.

Everything surplus on the helicopters – drums of fuel, medical kits, cargo hooks, nets and so on – were off-loaded to make space in the cabins for as many passengers as possible. The choppers were then configured for rescue with lifting hoists in place and the assigned aircrew.

As soon as they were ready, the first two helicopters, Rescue 406 and 414, took off and headed straight for the *Oceanos*. Captain Chas Goatley commanded Rescue 406, Captain Slade Thomas Rescue 414. Paul Whiley was with Goatley.

As the helicopters arrived, the dolphins that had been frolicking around the ship earlier disappeared as suddenly as they had originally appeared, as if knowing that help was now at hand for the stricken passengers and dolphin assistance would no longer be required.

In the meantime, the Transall C-160 aircraft dispatched during the night on Brigadier Lord's instruction approached the scene and started providing Silvermine with weather information to be shared with all aircraft involved in the operation. Information was relayed about wind force, the sea state, visibility and the low cloud cover.

On arrival at the scene of the stricken vessel, the aircraft was placed into a low-level orbit around the *Oceanos*. The flight commander also notified Silvermine of the various merchant and fishing vessels in the vicinity, which at the time, were the *Kaszuby II*, *Great Nancy*, *Reefer Duchess*, *Anik* and *Nedlloyd Mauritius*. He also reported that the *Oceanos* had already lowered all possible lifeboats.

The Transall crew could see that one of the biggest challenges of the merchant ships' rescue efforts was to spot the lifeboats in the huge and gloomy seas. The ships used search lights, hunting first left and then right and then forward and back in methodical patterns. They were searching for the bobbing lifeboats, but for much of the time the lifeboats were obscured by swells, spray and the half-darkness.

The *Oceanos* listing dangerously to starboard.

From their aerial vantage point, the Transall crew were able to pinpoint the lifeboats. Its crew started dropping smoke and flare markers to assist the merchant ships in spotting the lifeboats, but battled to get the flares into the right areas because of the massive wind. They therefore had to start the flares well south of the lifeboats to have them drift in and drop close to their targets. The challenge to the ships, of course, was that a large cargo vessel cannot simply manoeuvre like a car, so getting close to the unmotorised lifeboats was something of a hit-or-miss exercise.

Communications between the various aircraft and the disaster scene were not possible as the aircraft were unable to communicate directly with the *Oceanos* or each other. The Transall resolved this problem, becoming an on-scene airborne command post, which was able to relay information from aircraft to aircraft to enable the rescue and coordinate the efforts of the various aircraft and parties involved.

The Transall flew search patterns around the *Oceanos*, with crew members positioned at an open doorway searching for survivors. The aircraft followed this pattern for several hours, circling at a low level and turning left and right to inspect every floating object in the sea. Faced with huge

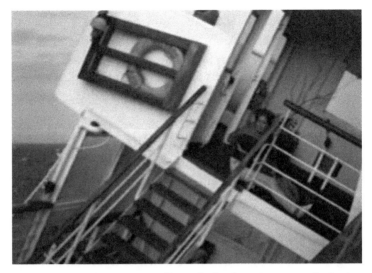

Sunday morning found Tracy Hills on the bridge wing. Note the horizon in the background and the angle at which the ship listed.

air turbulence and a severe wind chill factor, the Transall crew manfully continued the search, despite intense airsickness and icy conditions.

In the meantime Robin, who had come off the bridge to tell passengers about the imminent arrival of the aerial assistance, looked northwards in the half-light that was breaking open the day. 'Look!' he yelled, pointing animatedly.

Everyone followed his pointed arm and saw a formation of helicopters flying low over the water towards the ship. A wild cheer went up from the crowd of passengers, the gloom of their situation instantly replaced by hope and euphoria. Robin raced back to the bridge to speak to Mobile Rescue 7.

'Mobile Rescue 7, this is *Oceanos*. We have a helideck in the front of the ship and we can airlift passengers from two places, the forward helideck and the pool deck aft. Most of the passengers are already assembled on the pool deck.'

'Copy that, *Oceanos*,' came a calm reply from Mobile Rescue 7. 'We'll inform the helicopters.'

As they approached by air, Goatley and Thomas were filled with awe by the sight that greeted them: a ship that had dropped two anchors and was facing into the teeth of the southwest gale, listing 30 degrees to starboard down by the bow, propellers at the stern heaving 10 metres or more into the air as the ship yawed left and right in the mountainous seas, with a wall of water passing periodically over the bows and spraying onto the helideck. Deck chairs were piled up on the starboard railings of the ship, which were low down and closest to the water, while a hoard of passengers were hanging gamely onto the railings higher up on the port side.

'That ship's stern must be moving 40 feet left and right and up and down,' commented Captain Goatley grimly through his headset to his flight engineer. 'We're going to have a hell of a job landing anyone on there.' In fact, one of the other pilots recorded a measurement of 60 feet (almost 20 metres) of vertical movement by reference to his altimeter.

The stricken ship was one thing, but even more disturbing was the multitude of life-jacketed passengers hanging grimly onto the upper rail of a perilous deck. Landing a helicopter on the ship would be nothing short of suicidal.

Passengers waved frantically when they saw the helicopters, with the nervous but both grim and gleeful enthusiasm of a man discovered alive in an avalanche. Some of the terror had been replaced with hope. After the initial burst of excited waving, passengers calmed down, confident that they would be helped, but still unsure of how they would be getting off the ship.

The crew of Rescue 406 were shocked and overwhelmed at the enormity of the task awaiting them. There was nowhere to land and hundreds of people were counting on them. One small mercy was that the lack of panic on the part of the passengers allowed the helicopter crew to concentrate on the job at hand.

What also became apparent as the aircraft drew alongside was just how bad the weather conditions really were. The combination of wind speed, turbulence and sea swell was perilous, more severe and more dangerous

Help finally arrives for the remaining passengers in the form of Puma helicopters carrying Navy divers like Paul Whiley (in the harness).

than anyone on any of the aircraft had previously experienced.

The crew collectively felt a shiver run through them, but it had little to do with the cold outside.

Captain Goatley painstakingly positioned the Puma over the stern of the *Oceanos*, battling to hold the helicopter steady in the southerly 60-knot gale, while Flight Sergeant Scott began lowering diver Paul Whiley onto the deck of the ship, wallowing and bobbing like an oversized and ponderous cork in the huge swells.

Paul had previously participated in exercises which required him to be landed in a harness by helicopter on a Navy strike craft in bad weather. He knew that the Air Force helicopter pilots could usually land a diver with incredible precision on a space the size of a small mat on the deck of a ship, but this was a different kettle of fish altogether. Apart from the yawing and surging stern of the ship, the wildly swaying mast of the *Oceanos* was almost making contact with the rotor blades of the helicopter, with Captain Goatley simultaneously trying to hold position, avoid being struck by the rolling ship and not kill the diver dangling from the harness.

As the Puma hovered above the stern, the passengers could see a small figure being lowered in a harness. It was Paul Whiley. He was being blown like a pendulum beneath the helicopter, but it could not come any lower because of the clawing waves and spray that would choke its turbo-charged engine. Paul swung wildly: first away from the buffeting wind, then back into the wind, then away from the wind again.

At the same time, Captain Thomas, who was hovering close by, watched the stern of the ship rising and falling ominously with the still propellers thrusting into the air and then crashing back into the sea.

Goatley's helicopter was trying to manoeuvre to land Whiley gently, so Flight Sergeant Phil Scott did not dare lower him too quickly onto the deck for fear of his smashing into something.

Scott sat inside the door of the helicopter, looking down as he slowly lowered Whiley towards the deck of the vessel. The mast of the vessel and antennae were swaying ominously towards the helicopter rotors with every pitch and roll of the ship towards the starboard. In the howling wind, it was all that Goatley could do to hold the aircraft steady, let alone keep moving out of the way of the aerial dangers posed by the ship.

Scott was speaking to Goatley constantly: 'Go left, a bit up, down a couple of metres, go right again ten metres ...'

Time and again they tried, with Scott coaching the unsighted Goatley into position. 'Watch that aerial, Chas! Quickly, move right, now down about five metres ...'

As the ship and weather contrived to prevent the landing of the diver, and indeed threatened the very existence of the helicopter and its occupants, Scott said to Goatley urgently: 'You'd better be careful otherwise we are going to kill somebody.'

Goatley, frustrated and furious in equal measure responded: 'If you can do better, then come up front and you fly!'

'Understood,' responded Scott meekly, continuing with his directions to Goatley.

With tempers rising inside the aircraft and Paul realising that he had to disengage from his harness instantly as he landed, he lifted his arm to free the securing 'D' clasp on the harness. Scott, in the helicopter, taking this as a signal to lower Paul, but with the timing wrong as the ship was rapidly rising beneath Paul, released slack onto the harness cable, crashing Paul into the deck.

Slade Thomas, hovering alongside, watched horrified as Whiley hit a railing, flick-flacked over it and fell down two decks.

The audible thump could be heard by the watching passengers, even with the wind howling around them. Whiley tumbled down the second sloping deck until he slowed his fall and regained his footing with the help of the harness, which he quickly released before it pulled him off the ship again. He slowly climbed up the sloping deck back to the railings into which he had been slammed.

His face was bleeding from a gaping gash, but nothing seemed to be broken. He made his way towards the waiting passengers and cheerfully called out: 'Right, who's going up to the helicopter?' There were no immediate volunteers.

As he came closer to the passengers he was filled with dismay. He suddenly discovered that the throng he had seen from the air was a fraction of the number to be rescued. Under shelter of the lounge and casino, Paul saw a multitude of other life-jacketed people.

'I finally know how I'm going to die,' he thought to himself. 'On this ship, trying to save all these people. And a lot of them will die with me.'

Lorraine Betts thrust a megaphone into Paul's hands. 'Right,' she said, 'tell us what has to happen.'

Shoving thoughts of his own mortality out of his head and with blood pouring down his right cheek, the 22-year-old Paul Whiley took control of this huge group of passengers, some of whom were almost four times his age. He shouted into his megaphone: 'We're getting you all out of here. Women and children first. Who's going up in the harness?'

Still no one moved. Having seen what had happened to Paul when he had hit the deck earlier, the passengers were terrified. The sight of a bleeding and battered apparent expert presented little incentive to climb into the harness. He approached about ten passengers and each refused in turn.

He tried to assure passengers that descending was the tricky part, but being pulled upwards was a piece of cake. No one was budging.

Paul quickly realised what the problem was – no one had seen it done. All they had seen was a precarious descent and a klutzy fall by a Navy diver.

'You!' he said, speaking to a woman near the front of the queue who was obviously single and not accompanied by children, 'Come with me. I'll take you up and show you how it's done.'

He took her reluctant hand and led her back along the sloping deck, grabbing the dangling harness as the wind blew it towards him. He placed the harness over both of them, closed the 'D' clasp and Rescue 406 quickly hoisted them up into the chopper.

The aircrew of Rescue 406 realised that chasing a vessel moving in every direction other than forward was very different from trying to land someone on a vessel that was under way. Although the original plan had been for a diver to ascend with every passenger, it was obvious to the helicopter crew that this procedure was going to take way too long. As soon as Paul had boarded the aircraft with the first passenger, Flight Sergeant Scott told him to rather stay on deck and manage the passengers getting into the harnesses.

Paul was dropped back onto the ship's deck with much the same difficulty as the first manoeuvre, although this time incurring less personal wear and tear, and took charge of loading passengers into the harness two by two. It was safer to drop an empty harness and hoist passengers than it was to lower divers and land them safely on the deck, so the exercise started adopting a rhythm of its own once the helicopter crews had worked out how best to interface with each other.

Paul was going to need some help. He spotted a man – he guessed he was in his 40's - sitting calmly slightly away from the throng of passengers, but watching keenly what was going on. The man looked fit and composed and was sitting with a younger man, probably his son. Paul approached him.

'Can you help me,' he asked the man. Piet Niemand answered in a strong Afrikaans accent: 'Yes. What do you want me to do?'

Paul was faced with a mass of passengers milling around and who needed to be organized. He knew he had to start loading them into the helicopters and that it had to be in an orderly fashion, but didn't know who to choose. He didn't want to play God, to be the one who had to choose who went first and who stayed behind. The ship was sinking and he was sure some passengers weren't going to make it.

'Organize them into a queue,' he said. Piet immediately managed to get some order amongst the passengers, taking that on as his role and helping Paul in any other way he could. Paul turned his back on the queue – he couldn't bear to see who was next and who had to wait – and then started working as fast as he could. Having seen Paul and the first passenger hauled up safely into Captain Goatley's awaiting cavalry helicopter, the other passengers found some courage and Paul started loading them two at a time.

He loaded the first two without much drama and watched them all the way as they were winched by Phil Scott into the hovering helicopter.

As he grabbed the wildly swinging hoist and strop on its return to the deck, he turned to load a third passenger. Standing before him was a man in an officer's uniform. It was Captain Avranas.

Paul was at first confused about Avranas's intentions, and then shocked as he realised why he was there. 'You can't get off now, Captain,' said Paul. 'You have to stay until all the passengers are off. We have to get the women and elderly people off the ship first.'

'No! I go look for help and organise rescue,' responded the Captain. Sometime earlier he had told Lorraine Betts that he was going to leave the ship to organise that one of the rescue ships come around and create a lee for the lifeboats that had been launched. The captain's stated plan is hard to understand given that the last of the lifeboats had been launched some hours earlier already.

'Your place is here on the ship, Captain. You have to look after these passengers. You can't just leave them!' Paul was incredulous.

Paul turned to beckon to the next passenger in line. As he placed one of the strops over the head and shoulders of a woman at the front of the queue, Avranas grabbed the other strop, pulled it over his head and signalled to the helicopter to haul him and the other passenger up. Paul was unable to stop him.

Back in the helicopter, Scott was more than surprised to see someone in uniform arrive at the door, but pulled him in. There was no time to speak to each other: the rescue of the other passengers was more important.

In the meantime, pilots Goatley and Thomas had worked out a modus operandi. Goatley's helicopter was hovering on the port side of the vessel, near the stern, with its nose facing into the southwesterly gale. Thomas's helicopter was hovering in the same position, but on the starboard side of the ship.

His flight engineer would then direct Goatley to fly sideways to his right until the aircraft was directly over the pool deck. If the target went missing as the ship yawed in the swell, Scott would have to coach Goatley back into position. A rescue harness would then be lowered, taking account of the bucking movements of the ship. Landing the strop in the correct place felt to Scott like fly-fishing for people. Once he had caught hold of it, Whiley would then load passengers into the strop, one pair at a time.

Timing was everything: as the ship dropped each time, Scott and the other flight engineers would have to hoist. This was the safest moment and the time when any slack on the hoisting line had been taken up.

As the passengers were being hoisted, Scott would coach Goatley away from the ship until the helicopter was safely over the water, so that if any passengers slipped out of the strop they would have a greater chance of survival by falling into the sea than back onto the deck.

When Goatley was clear, Thomas would then manoeuvre to his left, hover over the ship and repeat the exercise in his Puma with his flight engineer directing him in like fashion.

As soon as a helicopter was full, typically with anything up to 20 passengers, sometimes more, it flew back to the shore to discharge its load at the Haven Hotel.

With Paul Whiley in control at the stern of the ship and managing the process there, Goatley then moved his helicopter to the bow of the ship where other passengers were assembled. Flight Sergeant Scott lowered another diver, Leading Seaman Gary Scoular, to just above the level of the mast, which was swaying up to 10 metres in both directions. Each time he lowered the diver further, the mast and cables came swaying towards the diver and Scott would quickly have to hoist the man to safety. The bow was proving unsuitable for hoisting.

However, the helideck was situated higher up and in front of the bridge, so attempts to hoist the passengers were made from there. By way of hand signals, the helicopter directed people who were already on the bow to move to a more accessible position near the helideck.

The helicopters had to establish a comfortable position over which to hover and evacuate passengers off the helideck. The only reasonable compromise was where the flight engineer could keep sight of the bridge and deck below and warn the flight commander of any danger.

A cable that ran above the deck presented a danger to the hoisting operation, so this first had to be removed before hoisting could begin. A decision was made to drop a bolt cutter from the helicopter onto the deck, which could be used by someone on the deck to cut away the cable. Scott tried repeatedly to indicate to the passengers below that he intended dropping something heavy. When he finally made himself understood and the passengers had cleared a space, he dropped the bolt cutter. As it clattered onto the sloping deck, it started sliding down towards the railing. In one of his many heroic acts, Moss Hills nimbly skipped down the sloping deck and grabbed the bolt cutter before it slid into the black sea.

Once a queue had formed near the helideck further forward on the ship and the other two 15 Squadron helicopters, Rescue 407 and 413, had arrived, they started a similar lifting exercise. Navy diver Gary Scoular assisted passengers into their harnesses. However, because of

View from a chopper engaged in the *Oceanos* rescue operation
on Sunday, 4 August.

the configuration of the ship, they were unable to hover parallel to the
Oceanos like the two aircraft operating at the stern, but rather had to
operate perpendicular to the ship. They flew forwards and backwards to
and from the ship, also picking up passengers two at a time.

As helicopters arrived from other squadrons, they started queuing one
behind the other. The front helicopter would pick up two passengers and
then circle around to the back of the queue while the next moved into
position, picked up its two passengers, flew to the back and allowed the
third chopper to move into position. When a helicopter was full, it flew
back to the Haven Hotel and off-loaded its precious human cargo.

The co-pilot or flight engineer of each helicopter would watch the
approaching swells and instruct the pilot to move into position as the
ship rolled to a neutral position. The flight engineer quickly lowered the
strops to the deck, reeling out sufficient slack on the hoist to allow for
the pitching and rolling of the ship, so at times there was more cable on

Moss Hills tied himself to a rope to help Navy diver
Paul Whiley airlift passengers.

the deck than necessary, but when the ship rolled away, the length was about right. The diver would then load two passengers into the strop, the unsighted pilot would be talked into position directly overhead of the loaded passengers and as the helicopter came into position, they would be hoisted quickly off the deck.

There was danger everywhere: the rolling ship's guard rails and overhead awning supports could easily snare a harness and instantly bring a helicopter crashing onto the deck or into the sea. These had to be avoided both during the lowering of the harness and the hoisting of the passengers.

Inevitably, there were several incidents that had not been part of the plan. In one such incident, two women were placed in the strops and hoisted quickly to the helicopter. As they approached the cargo door, terrified out of their wits, first one and then the other grabbed Scott, making him fear for his own safety and that he might be pulled out along with the survivors. Fortunately, he had secured his own safety harness inside the helicopter and, with a combination of strength, agility and sharply worded persuasion, managed to free himself and pull the women safely on board.

In penance, one of these women then helped Scott to pull other survivors onto the helicopter once she had regained her composure, freeing them of their strops and trying to create some order in the tangle of limbs and torsos rapidly accumulating in the back of the cargo area. After 18 passengers were safely aboard, and the helicopter was short of fuel, it returned to shore carrying the numb, sobbing but relieved passengers to The Haven.

By this time, with four helicopters on station, a full-blown shuttle service had commenced, with helicopters fore and aft of the ship, queuing for their turn to lift a load of imperilled but patient passengers.

At one stage of the evacuation, two elderly women were placed in the strops. As the winch was activated to take up the slack on the cable, they lost their balance and started rolling down the deck. Scott tried to slow their slippage by using his gloved hand as a brake on the hoist cable. The slide was eventually arrested, with the women stationary and stuck perilously close to the edge of the ship. If the cable suddenly tightened around someone's limb, it would be severed. If the cable was loosened at all, they would fall off the edge of the ship.

Moss Hills, who had tied himself to a rope attached to the upper railing on the ship, slid down the deck and helped one of the women out of the strop, which had wrapped itself around her leg, and dragged her back up to the railing. The second woman, lying flat on her back, terrified, was then winched directly up into the helicopter.

In all the drama, there were also some moments of lightness. As Scott assisted one woman, adorned in an ostentatious pearl necklace, into the helicopter he inadvertently made contact with the necklace, breaking it and causing a cascade of pearls to be poured onto the floor of the helicopter. Fellow survivors scrambled to help recover the pearls.

An oversized male passenger arrived at the doorway to the helicopter with jeans and underpants arranged around his ankles for reasons known only to himself. Trying to save his dignity before he made his grand entrance into the chopper, he started squirming around in the strop to pull his trousers up. Scott, fearing for the man's safety, beat his hand away, dragged him into the helicopter and told him to be grateful that it was only his dignity that had been lost.

Julian Russell (far left) with a group of Navy divers in one of the helicopters.

In one of the other helicopters, the ship's steward boarded dressed in a suit, bowtie, frilly shirt and little more. Not a pretty sight at the best of times, this apparition also sported a huge protruding stomach hanging over his white meridian underpants, which, in turn, were the source of two thin and hairy legs. The sight was a release valve for the pent-up stress of the passengers, whose mirth was somewhat disproportionate to the event.

As the evacuation wore on and the risk of a capsize increased, diver Gary Scoular noticed some passengers had already jumped off the ship and were at risk of being sucked under the ship and crushed. Handing over the harness-loading duties to Moss, Scoular made his way further forward towards the bow where he had earlier spotted three rubber dinghies.

Attempting to launch one off the starboard bow, which was submerged and the easiest launch point, the first blew away in the wind before he could control it. He loosened a second rubber duck and beckoned to a Greek crew member to come over.

Yelling to make himself heard he said, 'When I get in, hold the rope until I get the engine started.'

With the rubber duck bobbing frenetically, Gary jumped in, landing heavily. His helper immediately released the tethering rope, before Gary had a chance to start the engine. The gale quickly pushed the tiny boat along the side of the *Oceanos* towards the stern. Before Scoular could start the engine, he and the boat had been sucked beneath the stern section of the ship.

As the stern started falling back towards the sea, Scoular desperately grabbed and wrapped his legs around a propeller blade and was driven deep beneath the surface by the ship. For what seemed like an eternity, and with his lungs feeling as if they might explode, he finally sensed the stern rising again, with the propeller blade dragging him back up. Releasing the blade as he surfaced, he sucked air back into his bursting lungs and swam away and forward until he could haul himself back aboard on a rail of the ship. The rubber duck had disappeared.

Drained and with a ripped wetsuit, he crawled to a safe spot and sat there for a few minutes, spent. Eventually, putting the incident out of his mind and with some strength returning, he tried to launch the third rubber duck. No longer able to do so without assistance, he called over a Filipino who held the vessel for him while he started the motor.

Julian Russell, the magician, who had seen some of what was happening with Scoular, jumped into the water and climbed into the rubber duck to join Scoular as they started picking up passengers who were already in the water. They ferried them to the orange lifeboat of the *Nedlloyd Mauritius*, which Captain Dettmar's courageous crew had launched in the appalling conditions.

After making the first transfer of passengers, the rubber duck returned to the *Oceanos*. Scoular instructed Lorraine Betts to persuade other passengers to jump overboard and be ferried to the lifeboat of the *Nedlloyd Mauritius*. This was going to be the only way to speed up the evacuation of the ship.

Lorraine started rounding up younger, relatively fit-looking passengers. Although a number were willing to jump into the frothing water, from where they were hauled onto the rubber duck, several simply refused, preferring to take their chances by waiting to be airlifted off the ship.

In the meantime, fuel supply was becoming a problem for the Durban helicopters, with all the extra fuel carried from Durban consumed. The helicopters headed back to Umtata, almost 100 kilometres away, to refuel. Rescue 414 was the first to run low and Captain Thomas had to leave for Umtata after his first drop-off at The Haven. Clearance to land at Umtata had, in the meantime, been relayed through to the helicopters, but he was nonetheless anxious about landing in what was then the proverbial lion's den.

Over the preceding year or so, tensions between Major General Bantu Holomisa and the South African apartheid government had been rising. In 1987, Holomisa, head of the Transkei military, had deposed the then prime minister of the Transkei, Stella Sigcau, in a bloodless coup and installed himself as leader of the country, insisting that military rule would be better for the Transkei, as a civilian government would just be a stooge of the apartheid government.

Holomisa was seen by the South African government to be getting closer and closer to the ANC, appearing on shared platforms with some of the big names in the ANC at that time: Walter Sisulu, Nelson Mandela and Cyril Ramaphosa, amongst others. The South African government also accused Holomisa of offering support and 'bases' to APLA, the armed wing of the Pan Africanist Congress. South Africa had earlier also imposed sanctions on the Transkei, including a temporary military blockade of the South African–Transkei border.

In this context, it had been years since any SAAF aircraft had landed in the Transkei, particularly in Holomisa's stronghold of Umtata. In addition, Thomas was well aware through military intelligence that the Transkei army, such as it was at that time, had established 23-mm anti-aircraft weapons around Umtata, so he had every reason to feel anxious about his mission, even if it was for humanitarian reasons.

As if airlifting from the *Oceanos* did not provide enough drama, even the refuelling operation in rural Transkei brought some challenges. One of the other helicopters, piloted by Captain Peter Haynes and which had evacuated 22 people on their first lift, landed the survivors at The Haven and then set off for Umtata. Low-fuel warning lights came on indicating critical levels of fuel. Haynes brought one engine back to idle and transferred fuel from that system to the other.

'How far is the airfield?' he asked the pilot of another Puma as they were approaching Umtata.

'It's on the other side of Umtata, still about 15 miles away,' came the response.

As if the question and anxiety had drained the tanks more quickly, the idling engine cut out as the fuel gauge reached zero. The remaining gauge indicated a quantity that was going to make the rest of the trip marginal. They could see the town in the distance, but not the airfield. Haynes decided to carry out a single-engine precautionary landing in a field.

On landing, they were unable to contact any other Puma on the radio, so two of the crew walked to the nearest buildings, which turned out to be a mission station. There they were allowed to use the telephone to contact the airfield, but no help was immediately available. The Mother Superior made them a cup of tea and then drove them to the airbase in her car, some 5 kilometres away. Here they arranged for themselves and a drum of fuel to be flown back to the stranded Puma so that they could re-enter the rescue pattern over the ship.

Meanwhile, after a 25-minute flight to the Umtata airfield, Thomas was, unbelievably, met by General Holomisa himself when he landed. As Thomas climbed out of his Puma, the general was driven up to the aircraft and emerged from his presidential black Mercedes. Even had he not arrived in a cavalcade, Thomas would have recognised him instantly.

Holomisa extended his hand and Thomas shook it. 'Captain, congratulations on the excellent job you are doing,' said the general.

'Thank you, Sir,' replied Thomas. 'I'm glad to be able to help.'

CHAPTER 11

LAST ONES STANDING

After refuelling in Bloemfontein and again at East London, Captains Tarri Jooste and Jacques Hugo of 19 Squadron, AFB Swartkop landed their Pumas at The Haven. They had also picked up investigation and diving teams in East London, before heading out to the scene.

Once he had offloaded his charges, Hugo was instructed to return to East London to fetch and carry senior investigators from the Department of Transport, David Fiddler and Robert Zanders, to the site. Jooste, in the meantime, had gone on to assist with the evacuation.

Neither of the helicopter crews was qualified to operate in a maritime environment and it was both dangerous and foolhardy to try and place divers onto the vessel without the proper training. However, they evacuated and carried smaller loads of passengers from the ship – around eight at a time – which they discharged at the Haven Hotel.

Captain Anton Botha, flying as co-pilot with Captain Jooste, described the perils of the operation in his post-flight report, noting for a start that they had no survival equipment aboard the helicopter.

> With the ship heaving 10 to 12 metres with every wave, the superstructure was 30 feet below the chopper one moment and right alongside the next.
>
> ... We had a very long hoist cable out, which was blowing wildly in the wind ... During one of Tarri's [Jooste] lifts I had time to watch Len Pienaar [Rescue 409] lifting over the front deck. To my

horror, I saw their long hoisting cable swing around the ship's mast. Fortunately, it unwound; otherwise the downward motion of the ship would have dragged the helicopter with it ...

On one occasion while I was lifting, it was the turn of an elderly lady to get into the strop. She seemed to refuse to let go of the ship's railings so that the strop could be placed around her shoulders. The flying conditions up above were very difficult and I can remember using a few choice swear words, while the woman was rigid with fear. Eventually, after a long battle, she was hoisted safely into the cabin ...

I also noticed that the height on the radio altimeter varied by as much as 60 feet as the ship pitched beneath us. At one stage, I watched some people run to the side and jump into the sea as the ship yawed over. A Navy diver in a rubber boat then moved in to pull the people from the water and raced away before the ship [could] yield again.

The diver to whom Botha refers in his report was Gary Scoular.

When the Durban helicopters left to refuel in Umtata, panic started spreading on board the ship as passengers saw their last hope of rescue disappearing over the horizon. The pilot of the orbiting Transall, realising what was happening, relayed by radio to the ship the reason for the helicopters' leaving.

Through the agency of Robin Boltman on the bridge, he persuaded passengers to remain calm and stay on board rather than jumping into the water. Apart from the inherent danger to the passengers of being adrift in mountainous seas, trying to pluck them out of the water would have been difficult, dangerous and time consuming for the helicopter crews.

While the helicopters were refuelling, Paul Whiley went below to search through unflooded decks of the ship to see if any passengers were still in their cabins. Moving from door to door, he eventually found a man in his cabin, drinking and clearly drunk.

'Sir, you need to come upstairs,' said Paul. 'The ship could capsize at any time.'

'Really?' said the passenger. 'That shounds quite sherious.'

'Yes, sir. You must come with me,' Paul insisted, maintaining his decorum, despite every cell in him wanting to slap some sense into the man.

Reluctantly, and with some difficulty, the passenger struggled to his unsteady feet, staggering along the corridor and up the stairs as Paul escorted him onto the deck, where he hoped the cold wind might sober him up.

Paul returned to his search. As he passed from room to room, he noticed basins, showers and toilets filled with dirty water and raw sewage in many cabins, overflowing onto the floors and running out into the corridors. He found no one else in the cabins.

After Captain Thomas's refuelling in Umtata, he headed back to the ship. Here he discovered that aircraft from other Air Force bases around the country had already arrived and were queuing to pick up passengers. He took his place in the queue and did a couple more lifts. During one of these, the hoisting cable snagged on a railing while lifting two more passengers.

When the two passengers had been pulled aboard, the flight engineer examined the cable. 'Slade,' he called through on the radio, 'four strands have gone on the hoist.'

Captain Thomas knew that any more than three or four broken strands on a hoisting cable rendered it unusable – it simply posed too much of a risk of breaking, especially in dire circumstances such as these.

'OK,' he replied. 'We'll have to back off.'

That signalled the end of his lifting operations, but he nonetheless continued to hover nearby to watch the process and at least offer moral support to his colleagues. As it was, the ship was going down fast and Thomas had doubts about how much further helicopter evacuation might be possible.

At 8 am on the Sunday morning, 28 Squadron dispatched a C-130 Hercules Troop Carrier from AFB Waterkloof to Umtata. The aircraft carried – along with huge volumes of survival equipment, medical supplies, stretchers and blankets – 48 doctors, nurses and medical personnel. These were volunteer members of the South African Defence Force's medical services division. Thirty-five other volunteers had to be turned away because the aircraft was full.

On arrival at Umtata, the medics divided into two teams, one of which was designated to remain at Umtata and receive injured survivors, while the other was ferried by road to The Haven. The Umtata Hospital was placed on standby to receive casualties and local Umtata residents with 4x4 vehicles came out in droves to brave the foul weather and search for lifeboats, survivors or bodies washing ashore.

Air Force 41 Squadron dispatched a Cessna Caravan from Waterkloof to Durban, East London and Umtata, carrying medical specialists and psychiatrists to provide post-traumatic counselling for survivors. In the meantime, as the C-130 Hercules left from Pretoria, the Pumas from AFB Ysterplaat arrived at The Haven.

Major Louter van Wyk, the leader of the mobile air operations team, who with his team had hitched a ride on one of them, immediately set up radio communication stations to become the new command post. (Up until that time, the Transall had been acting as an airborne mobile command post.) From there they were able to control the operation of all aircraft within the 5-mile restricted zone around the ship, which was now floundering about 2 miles offshore.

Back at the Air Force headquarters, Brigadier Dick Lord was starting to feel a little more relaxed as reports of the increasing successes started rolling in. Pressure started mounting on him, however, from other quarters.

Everyone who was anyone, it seemed, now needed to be kept informed. Heads of the Air Force and Navy needed to be in a position to field questions if the Chief of the Defence Force asked them what was going on. The latter, in turn, needed to be able to respond to the Minister of Transport's queries, and the Minister was of course answerable to the State President. It would have been a career-limiting mistake not to have answers for the latter or, indeed, anywhere along the chain of command.

By now, the media were clamouring. Reporters from all over the world started calling Silvermine soon after midnight, demanding information. Initially this was managed by personnel actively involved in organising the rescue, but was later delegated in part to the Air Force media liaison. The American press, who had not yet gone to bed, were bombarding the poor media man with requests for information every few minutes. However, despite partial relief of this delegation, the primary media responsibility remained with the public relations officer at Silvermine, as they were coordinating the entire rescue operation.

Some reporters hired aircraft to fly them to the scene so they could take aerial photographs. In view of the restricted flying zone around the ship, all requests for aircraft to approach and take photographs were denied by the air traffic controller in East London. Save for one glaring exception, all civilian pilots obeyed the instructions to stay clear.

A pilot by the name of Alex Karatamoglou, flying a small Beechcraft plane and apparently carrying an American TV crew, ignored all instructions, breached rules and protocol and flew over the *Oceanos* at an estimated 500 feet above sea level. To understand the severity and danger posed by this breach of protocol, the operational context has to be explained.

At the time, about 11 helicopters were shuttling back and forth between the ship and the shore, two Alouettes were searching along the shoreline for survivors or bodies that may have washed up, while four Pumas were hovering over the *Oceanos* herself, hoisting and rotating. Simultaneously, the C-160 and Transall were still orbiting the ship, looking for people in the sea and also having a coordinating role. In addition, three Dakota aircraft were also scouring the waves for survivors. As everyone was focused on the vessel, sea and one another's flight paths, no pilot was on the lookout for a rogue civilian flying a small airplane.

As soon as one of the Air Force pilots spotted the Beechcraft, a warning was relayed to everyone in the area, military aircraft scattered in every direction and all activity ceased until the small plane had left the scene. Apart from the danger the Beechcraft posed to everyone else, its appearance cost a significant amount of lost rescue time and endangered passengers. The manoeuvre was simply unforgivable, reckless at every level.

Miraculously, some good came of the unauthorised incursion. One of the Dakotas that had flown away from the *Oceanos* and was some miles from the vessel turned to head back when an observer on board spotted an orange life jacket in the water below, about 6 miles from the wreck. The Dakota circled again and saw that a person was adrift.

Holding its pattern over the spot, the Dakota summoned Captain Jacques Hugo's helicopter, then carrying photo journalists over the wreck site. The survivor was plucked from the sea and winched to safety at around midday. It turned out to be the casino dealer, Avgerinos Tsaikas, who had drifted away into the darkness after his ill-fated attempt to board the *Great Nancy* from Lifeboat 2.

His rescue was against all odds. He had been adrift for at least five hours when he was picked up, somehow surviving the cold and avoiding a shark attack. A few informal reports, including from the helicopter pilot, recorded that he was stark naked but for his life jacket, which was stuffed with US$15 000 in cash when he was rescued. He had no idea how or when he had lost his clothes, but assured his rescuers that the money was his salary and life savings, rather than proceeds from the casino.

Hoisting continued for much of the morning. The overhead weather conditions improved as the day progressed, although the swell remained huge and unforgiving.

The *Oceanos* was still sinking lower and lower by the bow, increasing the already crippling list to starboard and making it almost impossible for passengers to hang onto the railings without sliding across the deck into the maelstrom. It was also clear that a moment would come when the ship would lose what little stability and flotation were left in the hull, capsize and sink.

By now, all passengers in lifeboats and rubber ducks had been rescued by ships, so the remaining urgency was to evacuate passengers on the deck. There was no other way off the ship than by air and time was becoming critical as more and more water forced its way into and through the stricken ship.

At the stern of the vessel, Paul Whiley steadily continued to load passengers. Each helicopter would take up its station, Paul would grab the wildly swinging strop and place it over the shoulders of two passengers and then signal for the pair to be hoisted up.

Although passengers were hauled up to the helicopters in pairs, it was not always possible to keep travelling companions together. Lou Tolken was eventually evacuated by helicopter, but was separated from her husband Ernie. She waited in fear and unknowing at The Haven for an eternal hour before Ernie's ashen face appeared in a landing helicopter's doorway.

At one stage, Paul summoned George Walton and his wife, Gerda, as the next two to be lifted. Awkwardly, they made their way towards him, with Flight Commander Tony Hunter's aircraft hovering above, ready to whisk the Waltons to safety.

'Lift your arms so that I can fit the harness over you,' commanded Paul. George was carrying a large video camera and bag, which Paul instructed him to abandon. George was having none of it.

'The camera has all my memories. It must go with me.'

The camera and bag seemed to be as important as the desire to be rescued. Paul shrugged and started loading them.

Obediently the couple raised their arms and Paul slipped the harness over them. The ship suddenly lurched and all three of them slipped down the deck. As George tried to grab again for the harness, it snagged on his arm which held the video camera and bag. George shook his arm wildly to let the harness drop over him. The helicopter crew mistook this as a signal to lift. As they heaved, the harness slipped off George's shoulders and the hoist started to lift Gerda only.

She screamed as George flung his arms around her and she tried to grip his heavy body with her legs. Clinging first to her waist, then legs and then sliding down, grabbing her clothing as he went, George slid down her legs and off her feet. The helicopter crew had by then moved over the sea to get away from the ship and tried to lower the chopper to reduce the impact of the fall, but he still plummeted 30 to 40 metres into the black sea.

Paul watched horrified as George dropped like a stone into the water. George kept upright for most of the fall, but finally lost control of his posture and hit the water with a mighty, breath-robbing splash, the sound of the impact lost in the cacophony of wind and waves.

As the helicopter hauled Gerda into its cabin, Paul ran to the higher port side of the ship, jumped down one deck level, waited for the vessel to roll to port so as to reduce the distance to the water and then dived more than 20 metres into the sea. Close to the propeller and at risk of being sucked under the ship, Paul swam as he had never swum before.

He started to scan the water around him, but among the waves and spray he could not see George, who had in the meantime drifted northwards from the ship, driven by the wind, and was lost among the towering waves. Passengers who could see George from their vantage points on the *Oceanos* screamed franticly, blowing their life-jacket whistles and pointing towards him.

Paul looked up at his assistant on the vessel, Piet Niemand, who first gave a confusing signal and then pointed assuredly some way off the stern, in the direction of the wind. A strong swimmer, Paul started swimming as hard as he could, blind to the whereabouts of George, but trusting that somehow he would find him.

He would rise to the top of half-broken waves and sink into the murky troughs as he swam. Some 200 metres downwind from the vessel, Paul eventually bobbed over a wave, surfed down the other side and literally bumped into George, who was now lying face down, winded and only semiconscious. Paul turned him onto his back and revived him as best he could.

George started flailing and kicking his legs. 'Don't do that,' Paul warned him. 'You'll attract sharks.' George quickly settled and allowed his life jacket to keep him afloat.

The moment he had revived, George asked: 'Where is my camera and bag?'

Paul could see the bag floating some distance away and knew it was virtually irretrievable. 'It's gone,' he replied 'Sunk.'

The discussion was closed. It was not worth either of their lives to debate it, let alone try to retrieve the bag. Astoundingly, to this day Whiley still carries a modicum of guilt for not having made some attempt to retrieve the camera case.

Paul then dragged George to the stern of a *Nedlloyd Mauritius* lifeboat, which had managed to manoeuvre over to them in the 20-odd minutes that they had been in the water. The crew on the lifeboat dragged the half-drowned passenger on board while Paul shoved from behind. When he was sure that Walton was safe, Paul swam back upwind a couple of hundred metres to the stricken *Oceanos*, which was now lying with her starboard side almost completely submerged.

Paul had swum towards the stern of the ship, so was now at the point that was highest to scale. With the propellers crashing into the sea dangerously close to him every time the vessel pitched, Paul found himself grabbing for anything that he could find to try heave himself back on board to relative safely.

As the bow lifted and the stern correspondingly dropped with a passing wave, Paul managed to secure a rope that was dangling and had washed down the port side. He was immediately whipped into the air as the ship pitched and yawed back in the opposite direction. Dangling in the air, he tried time and again to climb the rope and pull himself on board, but with the waves and wind beating him harshly against the side of the ship, he eventually surrendered the effort, let go and fell back onto the sea.

The current, running against the wind, carried him along the length of the ship towards the bow. As he was about to pass out of range of the ship, he struck out with what little strength he had left, grabbed a dangling ladder and forced his arms and legs between the rungs so that he would not fall off. Paul hung like that for a while, receiving more of a battering, but too weak to climb the ladder.

As his strength started to return, he climbed up slowly, one tortuous rung at a time, until he finally collapsed onto the deck of the *Oceanos*.

Out of breath with the effort, he clambered up the deck and returned to the head of the queue to help load passengers.

'I'm sorry,' he said apologetically to the awe-struck passengers. 'I just need to take a quick breather before we carry on.' Within minutes he was again loading helicopter harnesses.

Reports flowing back to the command posts were showing increasing numbers of surviving passengers. There was no report yet of any fatality. American media houses were phoning continually for updates.

Brigadier Lord reported to them on the numbers saved, numbers estimated to be remaining on board and the prospects for evacuating the remaining passengers. Journalists were demanding numbers of fatalities. Eventually, Lord apologised for being unable to offer any information about fatalities, but said that he was able to report one sprained ankle.

Once a second evacuation point had been identified near the helideck, TFC staff asked Michael O'Mahoney and Neal Shaw to assist with moving passengers to the forward section of the ship. The ship was by then listing sharply, with ongoing battering by massive waves and gusting gales.

Mike approached one elderly couple in particular, perhaps each around 70 years old. The husband was a small and skinny man, but relatively mobile. His wife was a large lady who walked with great difficulty.

'Grab the ship's railing,' Mike advised as he stood behind her and wrapped his arms around her like a bear, simultaneously grabbing onto the ship's railing. They edged crab style along the deck. It was painfully slow going. They had to stop frequently so she could catch her breath. Her husband followed in a similar fashion, fussing around his wife like a sparrow.

Mike and Neal made numerous such trips to and fro, shuttling and shuffling passengers along the deck until only about 50 passengers were left to be airlifted.

As the numbers dwindled to a handful, Lorraine Betts made her way to them.

'This ship is sinking fast,' she said. 'It could capsize at any moment. We are all going to have to jump overboard. You've done your bit. Go now! Someone will pick you up. Remove your shoes before you jump. Neal, leave your wife's handbag on the deck. Good luck and take care!'

She moved off to warn other passengers to be ready to do the same. Mike and Neal went to the edge of the ship and prepared for their leaps of faith into the boiling waters. They had to trust blindly that somehow someone would pull them from the water.

Both of them were wearing life jackets and the clothes they had been wearing since the drama had begun. Mike also had on his leather flying jacket, which he had collected from his cabin in what later proved to be an inspired defence against the elements.

Waves were smashing into the ship. Timing would be everything in this jump. They watched a few waves crash into and then suck back from the ship. As one hammered onto the hull they leapt. The retreating water sucked them back away from the ship to the relative safety of the blue water.

'Swim, Neal, swim like crazy!' Mike yelled to his friend over the din of the sea and wind.

They had to put distance between themselves and the ship, but as hard as they tried to swim away, they remained largely stationary and entirely at the mercy of the huge waves towering above them. They eventually gave up the uneven struggle, drifting dangerously close to the *Oceanos*, staying just far enough not to be smashed back onto the hull.

Like an angel of mercy, a Navy diver in a rubber duck was by their side within five minutes. The diver hauled them onto the dinghy and then moved on to assist a couple of others who had also jumped. The rubber duck then motored across and gave a tank of petrol to another diver who had run out of fuel in his own dinghy and was bobbing around perilously.

After 20 minutes of hunting for and rescuing survivors, the rubber dinghy ferried the two frozen friends to a nearby lifeboat that had been launched from the *Nedlloyd Mauritius*. By the time they boarded they were both shivering uncontrollably, with their teeth chattering incessantly like pneumatic drills.

When the lifeboat approached the *Nedlloyd Mauritius*, the crew realised that the passengers would be unable to climb up the ship's side, as the sea and wind were too strong. The lifeboat drifted, waiting for the *Nedlloyd Mauritius* to manoeuvre ponderously around to a different angle, creating a lee into which the lifeboat could take some shelter and from which they could disembark.

The adventure was not yet over. The lifeboat's cabin extended from the front of the boat about three-quarters of the way towards the rear. The last portion of the cabin was open. The crew instructed each survivor to climb onto the roof of the cabin.

To disembark, timing was again of the essence. The target was a rope ladder suspended down the side of the ship. The wind was blowing the ladder in random directions back and forth along and away from the side of the ship. Another leap of faith was needed.

Survivors had to wait for the moment the ladder swung closest to them and then jump across the gap from the cabin roof to the ship. Freezing as they were, the wait for each passenger was painfully slow. After a seeming eternity, Mike and Neal each leapt across and scrambled up to the safety of the ship's deck.

Lorraine Betts and JD Massyn leapt into the sea not long after Mike and Neal. They too were picked up by Scoular and Julian Russell in the rubber duck. Their wrist watches both stopped at 10.10 am on Sunday morning.

Robin had stayed on the bridge to continue feeding information to Mobile Rescue 7. As he was speaking, a new voice came onto the radio. Robin recognised it as Captain Avranas, speaking to him from The Haven.

'What degree we are listing at now, Robin?'

Boltman was incredulous. 'What do you mean, *we*?' he asked. The irony was lost on Avranas.

He repeated the question. 'What angle? Look at instrument on the wall,' he instructed.

Robin checked the inclinometer hanging on the wall, which had already reached its limit of 30 degrees to starboard. An inclinometer is a simple instrument that measures the tilt or list on a ship. The faces of the older ones looked a little like an inverted protractor, with degrees marked on the face and a hand that hung loose, like a pendulum, over the face of the instrument. The hand was moved by gravity and pivoted with the tilting or listing of a ship. The angle of list could then be measured against the instrument.

Using a pen, Robin tried to fill in small spaces beyond the 30-degrees marking, following the arc of the pendulum.

'It's about 38 degrees!' he reported.

There was silence from the rescue station. Avranas knew that the ship's stability was virtually gone. Capsize was inevitable and imminent. His silence told Robin everything he needed to know.

A ship's stability is a function of the interaction between the centre of gravity, centre of buoyancy and metacentre of a ship. When a ship is stable, it remains upright and cannot capsize. The job of naval architects is to design ships that will remain stable in all sailing conditions. Avranas did not need to do any calculations to know that a list of 38 degrees and continued flooding would very soon bring about a condition of instability, in which case the ship would capsize and then sink.

Avranas's response, or rather lack thereof, prompted Robin to walk across and let the captain's canaries out of their cage. It was one small act of humanity in anticipation of the inevitable. From the bridge wing, Robin showed one of the birds, sitting on his finger, to Moss, who was still down on the helideck helping to load passengers. Moss looked back, smiling through his fatigue, and gave the thumbs up.

Robin had earlier also rescued the captain's abandoned dog, a spaniel, at some cost to himself. While attempting to pick up the dog and carry him to a lifeboat, it had bitten him on the finger.

Mobile Rescue 7 crackled back onto the radio: 'The helicopters have nearly completed their refuelling,' the calm voice on the other side said. 'How many people are left on board?'

Robin quickly counted: 'Fourteen.'

'Does that include you?' asked Mobile Rescue 7.

'No, make that fifteen!' replied Robin. 'When the choppers come back, don't go to the front, it's nearly under water. I'll move everyone to the pool deck at the stern.'

'Copy,' said Mobile Rescue 7. 'Carry out a last check around the ship, including all the passenger lounges and report back to us.'

Robin quickly set off with one of the jazz musicians employed by TFC. As they passed the bar, Robin took a bottle of Scotch off the shelf. Offering it to him, Robin said: 'I've never been able to buy you a drink, so "Cheers!"'

When they were satisfied that no one was left in the ship, Robin returned to the bridge. On his way he stopped to watch a few passengers and the last of the TFC staff being airlifted. As the dancing girls were being airlifted, Alvon Collison said to Robin: 'I have to go now too … I think my water has broken!'

Back on the bridge Robin announced to Mobile Rescue 7 that he had not found anyone other than those waiting to be airlifted.

The *Nedlloyd Mauritius* called up on the radio. 'Permission to leave the area, please,' asked Captain Dettmar. 'There are no further survivors in the water as far as we can make out.' The other ships started calling in with similar requests.

'Am I the one that must decide this?' asked Robin, unsure of himself.

'You're on the bridge,' replied the *Nedlloyd Mauritius*. 'You must decide.'

'Yes, you have permission to leave. Thank you all for everything you've done for us.'

He then called the NSRI post at The Haven. 'Mobile 7, I'm dressed in a suit and tie. Please don't leave me behind. I need to make my way now to the pool deck at the back of the ship. Thank you and goodbye.'

When Robin reached the pool deck Paul Whiley was there, still glistening wet after his rescue of George Walton. He went off to carry out a last check of the ship and Robin ascended alone in the harness,

This passenger or crew member might have lost everything he took
on board, but not his tuxedo. The photo was taken at the Haven Hotel.

looking down at the ship, her propellers thrusting their lifeless forms up
and out of the water, her bow completely submerged.

It was time to say the last rites for her.

By the time the helicopters started off-loading passengers at The
Haven, five vehicles carrying a team of East London Metro Emergency
Response personnel – mostly medics capable of tending to and stabilis-
ing injured passengers – had arrived by road to join the NSRI and the
Defence Force.

As they were off-loaded, survivors were greeted by military and Metro
personnel and quickly scanned for injuries, exhaustion and hypothermia.

Many couples were separated from each other during
the rescue operation.

Blankets were thrown around them by volunteers. Those who were too
exhausted to walk were stretchered to the hotel. Those who were still
mobile were escorted over the 100 metres or so of grass to the warmth,
comfort and hospitality of this little gem of the Wild Coast.

Passengers were herded through the kitchen, each receiving a cup
of steaming soup, some bread and a rusk. With the volumes of people
requiring sustenance, it was the best the hotel could do. Some passengers
tried to retire to the pub, but everyone had to be herded out again onto
the grass so that they could be counted.

Helicopters arrived periodically, discharging more and more survivors.
Wives were reunited with their husbands, deliriously happy and relieved
to see them again, laughing, crying and hugging. Friends rushed to
helicopters to greet others who had been left behind, unbridled joy

The photo in the middle right shows an exhausted
Moss Hills arriving at the Haven Hotel.

replacing the distress and exhaustion of their earlier experience.

Slowly but surely the numbers on the lawns of The Haven swelled.

And finally a helicopter arrived carrying Moss and Tracy Hills and Robin Boltman. Moss and Tracy had been airlifted together in the same harness. Moss staggered out of the helicopter door, collapsing with exhaustion into the open arms of military and civilian helpers. A cheer went up among the waiting survivors as they saw the three and the crowd spontaneously burst into song: 'For they are jolly good fe-e-llowwws … and so say all of us!'

Moss and Robin were mobbed as the heroes of the hour, recognised for the incredible work they had undertaken on board. Too weak to stand on his own, Moss was wrapped in a space blanket, stretchered to the makeshift field hospital and placed on a drip to treat him for dehydration and exhaustion.

Military doctors pushed through the crowd to the new arrivals.

'Who's Robin?' an officer asked, looking for the mystery voice from the bridge of the *Oceanos*.

'I am,' he replied, 'but I didn't do it!' he added. Despite his all-nighter on the bridge, he could still muster some of his old military-style humour, which was not completely wasted on the gathered military men.

'Let's get you warm and fed and then Major Louter van Wyk needs to have a word with you,' said one of the medics at the scene.

After downing his mandatory cup of soup, Robin was escorted to see Major Van Wyk for a debriefing session. He wanted to know why the captain had not been on the bridge, how Robin had found himself there, whether he believed there could be any passengers left, and a plethora of other things.

Walking into Van Wyk's temporary 'office', still clad in his suit and bow tie for the show that never happened, Robin was greeted by an incredulous officer in command:

'Well, fuck me,' said Van Wyk. 'He's still wearing a suit.'

It did not take the helicopter crews long to gather in the pub, the tension of the past 12 hours slowly slipping off their shoulders. The heroics of the helicopter crews had been extraordinary: that no aircraft crashed and all passengers were rescued in the circumstances of that day were sheer testament to the skill and bravery of the SAAF men.

After the crews had rested, the helicopters and some of the fixed-wing aircraft started making their way to East London or Umtata to refuel for the trips back to their various home. On arrival in East London, they were greeted by a throng of journalists from all over the world, hungry for on-scene information.

It was only then that the Air Force crews realised just how big a story this really was. It was a story with global appeal, and they had been pivotal to the success of the rescue.

Major General Holomisa, who had taken the time and trouble to meet a number of the aircrews who landed to refuel at Umtata, had also been a vital cog in the wheel of success. Much credit must go to him for his willingness to cooperate with his only (and least favourite) neighbours in an act of statesmanship and humanity.

Once Captain Slade Thomas had again refuelled in Umtata, he set out on the two-hour flight back to Durban, exhausted. It was around 5 pm. As he flew out over the coastline, he spotted a lone naval strike craft still ploughing valiantly through the huge swell towards the casualty site, of course now too late even to see the casualty, let alone be of much use to the passengers. Nonetheless, the four naval craft that eventually arrived at the disaster site were set to hunting for survivors or bodies over the next 12 hours or so, as several people remained unaccounted for.

Thomas later heard how irritated the naval crews were with the SAAF.

'You guys never even waited to greet us after our gruelling trip,' was the complaint conveyed to 15 Squadron. It was reported that the seas en route to the casualty were so huge that at least one of the strike craft had had a crane ripped off its superstructure.

Everyone who embarked on the rescue that day was a hero.

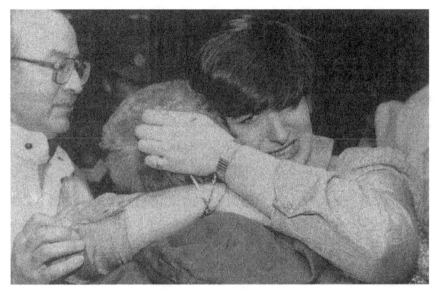

Relieved to be alive ... 22-year-old survivor, Susan Zanoncelli, embraces her
relieved mother while her father looks on.

A survivor gets off the bus at
the East London Holiday Inn.

Another survivor is stretchered off a
helicopter at the Haven Hotel.

CHAPTER 12

GOING DOWN

Paul Whiley and Piet Niemand had stayed on board to search through the vessel for a last time, having got the last passengers, including Piet's son, off the ship earlier. The ship was deserted, but for these two. She was making the sounds of a giant piece of machinery in its death throes. Creaking, twisting, gurgling and lapping sounds reached them as they hurriedly searched the accessible areas of the Jupiter, Apollo and Venus decks one last time.

'Piet,' said Paul matter-of-factly, 'we may have to swim for it.'

They made their way back through the bar area, downing a couple of Cokes on their way to lubricate their dry throats. As they emerged from below onto the weather deck, Paul said: 'Piet, let's get the hell out of here!' He signalled to a helicopter hovering close by. A harness was quickly lowered and they were plucked to safety. The helicopter did a lap around the vessel, now tilted with her bow completely submerged and the stern slowly starting to rise skywards, and then set off for the beckoning coast.

When Whiley stepped off the aircraft at The Haven, throngs of passengers descended on him, cheering and back-slapping him while showering their gratitude on their instant hero. He was bemused by the adulation. In his mind, he had only been doing his job.

By 11.30 am everyone had been evacuated from the *Oceanos* and brought to safety at The Haven. The operations team, with the assistance of the medical personnel, had compiled a list of people rescued.

In the meantime, a ship's manifest had been telefaxed to The Haven for comparison with the on-scene list.

This exercise was not without its challenges, given that 350 people had already been taken on board merchant ships and were bound for various destinations. By comparing numbers, which either were known or had been guessed, the operations team believed that between 10 and 14 people were still missing.

A decision was made to take divers back to the ship and search inside for possible missing persons.

Four volunteers from the Navy vessel SAS *Simonsberg*, who had been airlifted to The Haven, raised their hands, donned wetsuits and were loaded into the choppers.[5] When they reached the *Oceanos*, they scoured the Jupiter weather deck as quickly as they could, knowing that the ship could capsize or sink at any moment. Hampered by the now-critical angle of list, they had to crawl along the deck, hanging onto railings as they went.

Courageously they entered the perilous Apollo deck, just below the weather deck, clambering along the tortuous and half-flooded passages, calling out in the darkness for remaining passengers. Clothing, bottles and passengers' personal effects were everywhere, most afloat in the rising waters.

Deeper access into the ship was now beyond dangerous and further exploration would have been foolhardy. Satisfied that there was no one left in any of the areas they had explored, they quickly returned to the Jupiter deck and were lifted off the wreck at around midday on Sunday.

While the helicopter had been waiting for the divers to complete their search, they noticed diver Gary Scoular and magician Julian Russell still close to the ship in their rubber duck. They were hoisted off their tiny vessel as the final survivors.

A short while later the ship started to slide into the water, tipping herself towards a vertical position. The bow of the ship dug itself firmly into the ocean floor, some 90 metres below sea level. She briefly and

---

5   These men were Lieutenant Commander André Geldenhuys, Chief Petty Officer Frans Mostert, Leading Seaman Luke Dicks and Able Seaman Darren Brown.

The *Oceanos* balances briefly on the ocean bed before toppling
and disappearing into the sea.

almost poetically balanced vertically for a few moments, with about 60
metres of stern and propellers protruding above the water, before she
toppled over and slid quietly into the swell.

As she toppled and slid beneath the waves, clouds of dust poured out
of her exposed decks at the stern of the ship, suggesting that a good
spring clean before she had sailed from East London might have done
her no harm.

At about 1.30 pm the *Oceanos* disappeared completely, leaving just
a mass of deck chairs and other flotsam on the sea as evidence of her
dramatic passing.

A well-drilled crew were waiting for Mike and Neal on the deck of the
Nedlloyd Mauritius as they scrambled to safety. They quickly wrapped
blankets around the survivors and escorted them to their canteen where
they were plied with bowls of steaming soup.

As with the *Kaszuby II*, the crew of the *Nedlloyd Mauritius* could
not have been more helpful or hospitable, doing everything they could

to make the survivors comfortable. After his soup Mike suddenly felt nauseous and made a futile run for the toilets, spewing his soup all over the corridor en route.

Feeling embarrassed, he looked around, found a bucket and a mop and started to clean up the mess. Some of the crew saw what had happened and immediately took over the job. Despite Mike's objections, they would not hear of him doing any more cleaning. He made his way back to the dining area.

When he started to feel a bit better, in fact well enough to want to smoke a cigarette, he discovered that his cigarettes had been reduced to a soggy blend of paper and tobacco. He asked a crew member for a cigarette. In no time, cartons of duty-free Gold Coast cigarettes were being dished out to anyone who wanted them. Crates of beer followed and the survivors sat in the canteen, drinking, smoking and watching TV in real time as the bow of the *Oceanos* dipped into the water and sunk into the depths of the Indian Ocean.

Enjoying the hospitality, Mike pulled over a young Filipino and asked: 'Where can we shower, please?'

'You follow me, sir,' he replied and led them to the ship's sickbay and showed them a bath and shower they could use. Mike and Neal ran a full, steaming-hot bath and both jumped in, to sit and soak in hot water up to their necks like two little boys. As the cold and stickiness of their salty swim left them, they basked in the cleanliness and warmth, grateful for what they usually took for granted.

As they dried themselves off, the young seaman reappeared with a couple of pairs of clean overalls for them and then took them to their sleeping quarters. Mike had been allocated the pilot's cabin. When he entered there was already someone sleeping on his bunk, presumably another survivor, so he dumped his wet clothing on the floor in one corner and headed back to the canteen.

Lorraine Betts, who had jumped into the water with JD Massyn shortly after Mike and Neal and had been rescued in similar fashion, told them that they were bound for East London.

'There will be masses of members of the press there when we arrive,' she said. 'They will want to interview everyone on the ship about the sinking. You are not to say anything to them.'

Someone asked her: 'But what about the captain, Lorraine? He deserted us and the press will want to know about that. I'm not going to keep quiet about that.'

'That's nonsense!' she replied. 'It's ludicrous to suggest that the captain and crew deserted the ship and passengers. We were all there at the time and now we're safe.'

She obviously had her own view of how the rescue had played out. Mike and Neal did not debate it further with her.

Mike made his way back to his sleeping quarters in the pilot's cabin. There was still someone asleep on his bunk, so he found a spare mattress, pulled it onto the floor and fell asleep. On Monday morning he awoke from an almost comatose sleep. He had no sense of time or place, but when he finally regained his full senses he headed back to the canteen, which had become the central meeting point. They were again fed and advised that they would soon be berthing at the East London harbour.

Once all the docking procedures had been completed, they walked down the gangplank to where buses were waiting. A huge contingent of press reporters and camera crews was there. Cameras flashed and journalists clamoured to interview survivors as they stepped onto the quayside.

'Sir, may I have a word with you?' One of the reporters pushed a microphone towards Mike.

'No,' he responded curtly. He was in no mood to be interviewed. The reporter looked disappointed and wandered off looking for another mark, while Mike made his way to the bus.

Under a police escort, which had its lights flashing and sirens blaring, the bus full of survivors set off. It did not stop at traffic lights or stop signs anywhere along the route and soon arrived at the Holiday Inn. The entire hotel had been closed off to host the survivors. On arrival, they were guided to the dining area, and fed again.

Large numbers of South African Defence Force personnel, together with a number of SAA staff were there to assist. At the first opportunity, Mike gave one of the SAA staff his details and asked them to contact his colleagues at Durban's Louis Botha Airport to advise them of his whereabouts.

Each survivor was then interviewed, one at a time, by Defence Force psychologists. They were surprised at how calm everyone was, but warned survivors to be careful of delayed reactions to their traumatic experience and to look out for symptoms in their families as well. The survivors were finally allowed to make their way to the hotel reception and were given the keys to their rooms.

Still barefoot since jumping into the sea, Mike walked into his room, immediately picked up the phone and called his father at work: 'Dad, it's me and I'm fine.'

His father broke down and sobbed with relief into the telephone. No relatives knew at that time whether Mike and Neal were dead or alive as communications about the survivors had been vague and difficult to source.

'Yvette and the children are fine, Mike. They are due any minute in Durban Harbour. Yvette's parents are waiting there to collect them.' This was the first time he had had any direct news about his family and he felt the latent tension leave him.

Mike and Neal then rendezvoused with hotel staff who provided toothbrushes, toothpaste and sandals.

'Mr O'Mahoney, you have time for a shower and short rest. You will then be collected, taken to the airport and flown home.' The end of this extraordinary journey was in sight.

When the buses dropped them at the airport they walked to the check-in counter. Mike saw an SAA colleague.

'Johan,' he said to his colleague, 'I need you to take care of something for me.' He pulled a ship's flare from his jacket pocket and handed it to Johan for safekeeping. Johan looked bemused, but Mike knew it would not be allowed on board the aircraft. He and Neal then boarded the flight with no worldly possessions whatsoever, save for the clothes they were wearing.

Yvette O'Mahoney with 3-month-old baby Meghann after they were rescued.

Mike's SAA colleagues seated them in Business Class and they took off for Durban. Soon after take-off, the captain announced that wreckage from the *Oceanos* could be seen below the plane. Plastic deck chairs and other flotsam were clearly visible, bobbing on the sea. A lifeboat had washed ashore. A shiver ran through Mike. He might otherwise have been among the flotsam.

Less than an hour later they landed at Durban, greeted by a huge welcoming committee. They were mobbed by family, friends and colleagues. Thirty-six hours of pent-up, exhaustion-fuelled emotion spilt out as Mike was greeted by Yvette, his children, parents and brothers. He could not wait to get home.

The *Oceanos* had been expected in the port of Durban at 6 am on the Sunday morning. Duncan Starke, the executive branch manager for Polaris Shipping, the ship's agent, knew that many relatives of passengers would not be aware of the drama at sea and might come to collect passengers when the vessel docked. He thought it best to go down to the port and explain to relatives what had happened.

He also decided that he would need to meet each rescue ship as it arrived so that he could personally thank the captains for what they had done. He set off for the harbour at 5 am, having briefed his Port Elizabeth office to follow the same protocols and instructed a subagent in East London to do likewise.

After meeting the master of the *Great Nancy* shortly after his ship berthed, Duncan went to advise friends and relatives waiting at the passenger terminal about what had happened. While some had an inkling of the drama at sea, most greeted the news with disbelief. Once he had briefed the waiting friends and families, he went and checked that Telkom had set up the telephones he had requested, that rooms were available for doctors and that the transport to hospitals was ready and waiting.

One of the biggest risks run by ships agents is that they incur huge costs on behalf of their principals, which are paid to them either long after the expenses have been incurred or, if the principal is in financial trouble, never. Agents therefore usually ask for money on account before they will do anything. However, faced with this emergency, Polaris started running up costs in good faith.

Early on Sunday morning, Polaris Shipping were notified by Epirotiki that the latter had sent them US$75 000 on account of expenses to be incurred. Despite this payment, it was clear to Phillip Simpson, the managing director, that the costs were mounting and would continue to climb rapidly. Port marine services for rescue ships, doctors, post office services, transport, agents along the coastline and the like were rapidly draining the Polaris coffers.

Phillip voiced his concern to his colleagues.

'You know, we're spending an awful lot of money. We could be in trouble here.'

'That's no problem, Phillip,' said Mike Brown. 'I'll phone Silvermine and tell them to call off the rescue.'

Mike's response prompted a half-panicky response from Phillip, who could never be sure whether Mike was joking.

'No, of course you can't do that. I was just saying.'

However, Epirotiki kept Polaris in funds for the duration of the rescue, repatriation and investigation effort. They were a model principal in that sense.

One of the greatest challenges for the Polaris team was establishing whether all the passengers had been rescued. Lists of rescued passengers were being sent to their office from rescue ships by telefax. The TFC staff who had been rescued were still on duty, drawing up lists and seeing to the passengers. As there were no immigration records, they were completely dependent on the lists coming from the rescue ships, records of bookings for the voyage from East London to Durban and the Cape Town ship's manifest.

Once the ship had started sinking, a new problem arose. Apart from a dearth of knowledge about which passengers had not boarded the ship in East London, there was of course also no accurate record of which passengers had left the ship on which lifeboats and who had ended up on which rescue ship. A number of passengers had by then also been evacuated from the *Oceanos* by helicopter, and those records were being compiled as passengers came ashore.

The challenge of reconciling the numbers of passengers who had sailed from East London with the numbers of rescued passengers was enormous. Duncan had to liaise with every rescue ship and the SAAF to try and gather people's names and reconcile those with whatever other information he had.

Eventually, when the rescue was complete, there were 11 people missing according to the combined records. Duncan tried calling the homes of some of the missing passengers to see whether they were missing at sea or simply missing in the records. Slowly he was able to start accounting for them. Some of the missing people were back home, having left the ship in East London or never having joined it in the first place. Duncan put out a message that a few passengers remained unaccounted for.

While he was hunting for missing passengers, Duncan received a call from a passenger who had boarded in Cape Town.

'Mr Starke, this is Allan Forster. I'm supposed to be on the *Oceanos* with my wife. However, the weather was so poor in East London that we didn't reboard the ship and instead flew back to Durban. If you happen to be looking for me among rescued passengers, you won't find me.'

That was two accounted for and it gave him hope that there were others who were in a similar situation, rather than missing at sea.

As many of the passengers who had been on the ship were SAA staff, the national carrier had opened up their Disaster Control Centre in Johannesburg. The latter is a permanent establishment, which is on stand-by in respect of every flight into and out of South Africa. They had set up a contact centre and were compiling and maintaining the lists of passengers and crew who were supposed to have been on the vessel and who had been rescued. They were dealing with queries, contacting relatives and generally keeping track of who was where. They were also liaising with Polaris.

The employees at the contact centre experienced two moments of discomfort while calling around. The first was when they called Marlize Venter*, car dealership MD Johan Venter's wife, and the second when they called the wife of his colleague, Piet Mynhardt. In each case, the conversation went something like this:

'Mrs Venter, this is the South African Airways Disaster Control Centre. We are calling on behalf of the charterers of the *Oceanos*, TFC Tours. We had you booked on the ship with your husband for a voyage from East London to Durban. We thought you were missing. Are you able to clarify and confirm that you and your husband are both home and safe?'

'I don't know what you're talking about. We were never booked to be on any ship,' came the response. 'My husband is on a business trip in the

Eastern Transvaal with Piet Mynhardt as far as I know.'

After a moment of silence, the caller from SAA said: 'But we have a record of you and your husband boarding the ship in East London. However, we can't work out what happened after you boarded and once the ship had sunk.'

Mrs Venter was taking some time to digest this information. 'So, if you say he was on the *Oceanos*, he's not in the Eastern Transvaal?'

The SAA caller could almost hear Mrs Venter's synapses trying to connect.

'Yes, as I say, we have a record of you and him boarding the ship.'

'I don't know what to say ...' replied Mrs Venter, slowly cottoning on. 'But I hope he's drowned. And Mynhardt as well.' With that the phone went dead.

After the call, Marlize Venter, in a fit of rage, pulled a pair of scissors from a drawer and made her way to her husband's wardrobe. There she cut off the sleeves and trouser legs of all his business suits.

Not yet done, she then reversed his Mercedes out of the garage, put the automatic gear shift into drive and floored the accelerator, ramming the back garage wall. Just to ensure the job was complete, and as part of her cathartic cleansing process, she repeated the exercise twice more before phoning some friends to get advice on the best divorce lawyer in Port Elizabeth.

Her anger was compounded when she watched the TV news later that day and saw Johan, Janet, Piet and Mary-Anne disembarking from the *Kaszuby II*.

In the end, with SAA's help and some of his own sleuth work, Duncan had reduced the list of missing passengers to three, which included two children. Duncan was at a loss and feared the worst. He continued the hunt, trying to think through and follow up on every possibility.

In the aftermath of the rescue, with ships arriving in East London and Durban on the Monday, Polaris had to arrange to house passengers in hotels, organise flights home, separate the crew from passengers and arrange accommodation for the latter. They then had to start repatriating some of the junior crew members, transport crew to venues where they were to be questioned by lawyers, investigators and the marine division of the Department of Transport, all the while keeping the owners and TFC appraised of developments.

Later on the Monday afternoon, when the *Kaszuby II* had called at Durban to discharge her survivors, Duncan was in the passenger terminal. The parents of the two missing children came to see him.

They had been separated from their children during the rescue and were in a state, stricken with the anxiety of what might have happened. The parents were so traumatised by the prospect that they had lost their children that Doctor Robertson had to administer some medication to calm them down and they were then both hospitalised. Duncan was distraught.

After the parents had been taken to hospital, the children's grandparents came to the terminal. Duncan and TFC staff started hunting among the passengers in the terminal, checking every child to see if he or she was accompanied or not. Eventually, the two children were found. They had been on the *Great Nancy*, but had not known they had to give their names in for recording when they boarded. That reduced the tally to one.

The grandparents were joyfully reunited with the children and the parents discharged from hospital. A moment of deep gloom among the Polaris directors had turned to sheer joy.

In dealing with the press, Phillip Simpson had more than a few challenges. Media houses were calling in every few minutes, demanding updates on the drama. Around midday on the Sunday, Phillip received a call from an American reporter. After identifying himself, the journalist said, 'Mr Simpson, have they rewritten the maritime protocols in South Africa?'

'What do you mean?' he asked.

'Well, on the *Birkenhead* it was established that women and children should always be first off the ship, but we have heard that Captain Avranas left early on one of the first helicopters. Can you comment on this?'

'No comment,' replied Phillip. Whether this was true or not, what else was there to be said?

Duncan had arranged with the owners of the Beach Hotel in Durban to make the entire hotel available. The hotel owners made arrangements to relocate guests and take the entire crew of the *Oceanos* into the hotel. Filipinos were separated from Greeks. Who took that decision, and why, remain a mystery.

The last piece of passenger rescue business for Polaris was to deal with Captain Avranas's spaniel, which had been pulled from a lifeboat by one of the rescue ships. Duncan felt a certain measure of antipathy towards the dog, given that it had tried to bite him when he went on board the *Oceanos* at the time the ship was last in Durban. As it had also bitten Robin Boltman on the finger when he was trying to round the dog up for the evacuation earlier, it was clear its behaviour was neither entirely predictable nor sociable.

The ship's doctor looked after the dog in the harbour until plans had been made to repatriate it. Eventually, Mike Brown drove out of the harbour on Monday afternoon with the spaniel in his boot to avoid the awkward and most likely unhelpful attentions of the Customs authorities. Arrangements were then made to repatriate the animal to Greece.

After returning to the office that evening, Mike stayed there until 5 pm on the Tuesday afternoon, trying to solve the mystery of the missing passenger. He finally did: the passenger had made his way home from East London to Port Elizabeth, but had been uncontactable until then. Mike had been in the office since 11 pm on Saturday night. Although his role had largely been as liaison between all the maritime authorities, owners and operations people, he also made himself indispensable in some of the investigative aspects of trying to account for all passengers.

After locking up on the Tuesday evening and bidding the other two farewell after their marathon, he set out for home. In his exhaustion, he rolled his car on the highway, but somehow survived the accident almost unscathed.

CHAPTER 13

SURVIVORS AHOY!

It was a typical Sunday evening at the Pike household on 4 August. With bath time done, it was all hands on deck to get our children fed. It would still be a little while before my wife, Kazalette, and I could manage to wolf down some food ourselves, move towards story time and get the kids to sleep, before finally spending some quality time with each other.

Stefan, our 5-month-old boy, was perched in a baby seat on the kitchen countertop. Kazalette was trying to shovel down some form of gruel and whatever else very small boys can be persuaded to eat.

I was supervising our daughter, Jeśka, who was just over two years old. Obstreperous and far too talkative, she was devising new and creative ways of getting egg and soldiers down the hatch.

The phone rang and I grabbed the receiver with a free hand. It was my partner Shane Dwyer, head of our shipping department and undisputed South African doyen of maritime casualties, sounding very businesslike. He was not in the habit of calling on Sunday evenings.

Shane had been instrumental in developing the maritime jurisdiction laws that set South Africa apart from the rest of the world in terms of what is legally possible when it comes to arresting ships to obtain security for litigation or arbitration in other shipping jurisdictions. He was known to many shipping people around the globe and regarded as one of the best maritime lawyers in the world.

Shane had also been involved with most of the major maritime casualties in southern Africa over the preceding 20 years and was acclaimed as the shipping go-to lawyer in the country. My firm, Shepstone & Wylie, represented most of the P&I Clubs in the world together with many of their members, the shipowners themselves.

'Andy, I am going to need your help. There is a passenger liner that has sunk near Coffee Bay and it's a big mess.' There is never any beating about the bush with Shane.

'The ship is called the *Oceanos* and we are acting for the owners, Epirotiki Lines of Greece. They are entered with the UK Club and our instructions are coming from Norton Rose [law firm] in London. I'm in East London because some of the survivors are being landed here.'

'I need you to meet rescue ships, which should start arriving in Durban at around 3 am tomorrow. You are going to need a team to start interviewing passengers and crew. Start lining up lawyers in the firm – we'll need to use everyone we have. I will be in touch later.'

With that, he was gone. There were no cellphones in South Africa at the time, so I had no idea when I would hear from him again.

Shane had travelled to East London with Captain Chris Green of P&I Associates. They were accompanied by Captain Roy Martin, a local ship surveyor and ex-master mariner. Shane had been told that passing cargo ships, which had picked up some of the survivors of the disaster, would be calling at East London, Port Elizabeth and Durban to disembark survivors.

I told Kaz what was happening and, for the umpteenth time, handed over to her the child management and containment programme and dropped everything to deal with a new shipping crisis. I pulled out the firm's contact list and started dialling.

We had a small and adequate team in the shipping department, but it was clear that we were going to need a lot of additional help to cope with the almost 400 passengers and 200-odd crew who had been rescued. I started calling associates, first those in the shipping department, thereafter those in the litigation department, then I moved on to associates in the commercial and other departments. I also asked all the trainees to be on standby, telling them that they might expect a call to go down to the harbour at 3 am.

In particular, I called Carol Searle, a young trainee who had been at the firm for only seven or eight months.

'Carol, I might need your help very early tomorrow morning with statement taking and I don't know what else. It's unlikely, but just to give you the heads-up that you should be on stand-by.'

No sooner had I put the phone down, than it rang back. It was Carol.

'I am coming with you,' she said. 'You don't have to charge me out to the client, but I want to be involved for the experience.'

I doubtfully thanked her for her offer, put the phone down and carried on calling people. Eventually I had about 15 lawyers lined up on stand-by. Carol called me again an hour or two later to ask what time we were leaving. Despite my lukewarmness, she was so persistent that I finally surrendered and agreed to take her along.

The rest of my evening was taken up calling ships agents, port authorities and anyone I could think of who might have some information about the rescue mission and when the first ships carrying survivors might arrive. Eventually I learned that the *Great Nancy* would arrive at around 4.30 am the following morning and berth at the passenger terminal in Durban. I let Carol know and told her to meet me at the terminal. It was midnight by then and telephones around the country continued to buzz off their hooks.

I lay down to try and nap for a couple of hours, but I was too wired and restless to sleep. I got up to figure out what I would need to find out from whom and start planning for what would turn out to be the biggest shipping investigation and response effort in my career.

I stood on the quayside with Carol under the watery lights of the passenger terminal, watching the *Great Nancy* being nudged onto her berth by the tugs. It was 5 am and I was buzzing with excitement.

The bulk carrier *Great Nancy* was sailing in ballast (meaning she had no cargo on board) and sat with a huge freeboard high out of the water and her main deck probably some 10 to 15 metres above the waterline. It was hard to gauge exactly from the shore side, but the ship loomed enormous above us. As I stood there watching the shore gangs tying up the head and stern lines onto the tired-looking shore bollards, I wondered what I was actually going to achieve by meeting this ship.

Although Shane had wanted me to meet the vessel and try to take some statements, I suspected that passengers who had already survived a 30-something-hour ordeal would be less than enthusiastic to have to spend another hour talking to a lawyer before they disembarked, and they certainly would not be willing to stand in line and wait their turn. Giving statements would be the last thing on their minds. Nonetheless, I thought that perhaps I would get an opportunity to have some informal chats and get a feel for their experience. I also knew that the master of the ship would probably be willing to give me a statement and make his crew available if necessary.

One of the things that we do as maritime lawyers is to investigate casualties and incidents on board ships. It is standard procedure that the master and senior officers such as the chief officer and chief engineer will make themselves available to give statements to lawyers, provided that they do not believe they are compromising themselves or their employers in any way.

Carol and I watched the Chinese crew on the deck busying themselves to release and lower the aluminium gangplank tethered to the side of the ship. The crew were battling to free it, when suddenly it dropped a few metres before they regained control of it. Slowly they lowered it to the ground and started installing the regulation safety nets beneath. I noticed that the gangplank was slightly skew and not flush on the ground, but assumed that was just the way it was installed. In any event, it looked climbable.

As soon as it was down and the nets were in place, I said to Carol: 'Okay, let's do this thing!'

We set off towards the ship. Observing gentlemanly protocol, I allowed Carol to walk ahead of me onto the gangplank and we slowly made our precarious way up the side of the ship.

As we neared the top, and when Carol was about three or four steps from the deck, the crew started pulling the gangplank up again for some reason, despite our being on it. The entire staircase tilted over and away from the side of the ship and, in my shock, it seemed certain that we were going to be shaken off and plummet onto the tarred quayside metres below.

In that moment of realisation I saw Carol literally leap over the last few steps onto the deck like a mountain goat. I sprinted the last few steps to avoid being tipped onto the beckoning – and very solid – quayside below, or worse, into the gap between ship and quay wall. Somehow we both made it onto the ship, with hearts in our mouths and heaping abuse onto the crew. Not quite the gracious embarkation I had planned, but one of the occupational hazards of being a maritime lawyer.

As I tried to recompose myself and make sure I had not dropped anything off the gangplank, I saw a queue of survivors, many with life jackets still around their necks, waiting to disembark. It seemed certain that they were not planning to hang around and be interviewed by lawyers.

'Oh well,' I thought, 'I'm sure we'll have another chance to interview them later.' Which, of course, we did not.

In any event, I introduced myself to the passenger waiting at the front of the queue to disembark.

'Good morning, I'm Andrew Pike. I am a lawyer representing the owners of the *Oceanos*. I am really sorry about the ordeal you have gone through.'

He replied incredulously: 'You're a lawyer? What are you doing here?'

'Would you be willing to tell me about your experience?' I asked.

'It was awful and I'm going home.' With that he pushed past me and his fellow survivors followed him onto the gangplank.

I briefly exchanged a few words with the odd passenger who seemed willing to chat. Everyone had a story. As people were walking past me, I saw a woman carrying a tiny baby. I later learnt that her name was Gail Adamson, who had been on Lifeboat 2 with Debra le Riche.

'How old is the baby?' I asked.

'Just over two weeks,' she replied. I felt shocked.

'How did you get onto the ship from the lifeboat with such a small baby?' I asked.

'The crew of the ship lowered a bucket on a rope to the lifeboat. I put the baby in the bucket, stuffed some warm clothes on top and they pulled him aboard. I then had to climb up a rope ladder.'

Suddenly the enormity and reality of this rescue started dawning on me. This was not just a question of people clambering out of lifeboats onto a big ship. This had been a near-death experience for most. Seeing a 2-week-old baby who had survived with everyone else brought home to me that there had been nothing short of a miracle at sea. I carried on along the queue of disembarking survivors, entered the accommodation section and climbed the four or five flights of narrow and awkward stairs to the master's office.

The Le Riche family disembarked and were taken to a local hotel by TFC-organised shuttles, where they managed to shower and get some rest until they were flown back to Port Elizabeth via Bloemfontein.

As soon as she reached the hotel, Debra called her father. 'Dad, it's me and we're safe,' she said, her bravado finally overcome with emotion.

'I've been waiting for your call,' he said. 'I never doubted that you would be just fine.'

Debra packed up her family and belongings, such as they were, to head for the airport. Her only keepsakes from her trip on the *Oceanos* were the key to her still-locked cabin and the whistle she had removed from her life jacket.

At the top of the stairs in the accommodation section of the *Great Nancy*, I saw the captain's title inscribed on a plaque fastened to the open door of his cabin, which was on the same level as and close to the ship's bridge. I knocked and then entered.

'Good morning, Captain,' I said, respectfully handing over my business card, as I had done so many times before on other ships. 'I'm the lawyer representing the owners of the *Oceanos* and their P&I Club. May I talk to you?'

'Ah, lawyer!' replied the Asian-looking captain, fully and smartly dressed in his uniform, even at that hour of the morning. It never fails to amaze me how alert and ready for business the captains of most ships are, no matter what time of day or night I need to deal with them. He gave me his card: Captain Foo Chio Hong.

Ships' captains are a special breed. They carry a huge responsibility, perhaps not quite on the same level as aircraft pilots, but the conditions under which they operate are hazardous, often unpredictable and, quite frankly, would terrify me at some level, which is perhaps why I never went to sea (leaving aside a lifetime's plague of seasickness).

I don't know how many ships' captains I have met over the years, but they all seem to share a commonality of authority, responsibility and a complete integration with the huge pieces of machinery with which they have been charged, understanding that, on their turf, they have the last word, and usually also the first. Most are also impeccable in their record keeping and have a finger on the pulse of every activity on the ship.

There is a reporting hierarchy on every ship, from the ratings through the officers to the master. Everything that happens on board is recorded either on an instrument or in a log book, whether the occurrence is in the engine room, on the bridge, main deck or in a cargo hold. On modern ships there are digitised data recorders and other equipment that also keep track of much of the important activity on a ship. There is therefore usually a strong document and data trail that provides objective evidence during an investigation.

It therefore never fails to surprise me how often ships' captains will try to mislead lawyers and investigators when something has happened on board that is not going to reflect well on the master. Perhaps it is human nature to behave in an exculpatory way and perhaps ships' captains think that they can run circles around maritime lawyers because of their home-ground advantage.

However, what they sometimes forget is that we often have years of investigative experience and access to expert resources such as retired master mariners, naval architects, engineers and surveyors, who know exactly how ships work, exactly what equipment is on board, what each instrument records, what its readings mean and what documents should be available. In every investigation, the truth eventually comes out.

Based on our meeting, my impression was that Captain Foo was probably not one of those who tried to mislead the lawyer interviewing him. He had no reason to do so. To the contrary, he had an extraordinary and good story to tell, so we got started.

'Captain, I need to take a statement from you. Would it be in order to do that now?' I asked.

My approach with every ship's captain – indeed with everyone in my life, but particularly ships' captains – is to be courteous and respectful. They are busy and often do not particularly enjoy being interviewed and sometimes informally cross-examined.

They are also professionals who know a whole lot more than I about what they do and are worthy of respect, not only for what they do and know, but as human beings who live in a rough environment. I have seen enough bullying and cajoling in my profession to know that, for the most part, the technique rarely delivers the results you want.

'Please could you write down your full names, address and contact details, Captain? I will also need a copy of your Seaman's Book.'

A Seaman Record Book is a continuous record of a seaman's service. This document certifies that the person holding it is a seaman as defined in the International Convention on Standards of Training, Certification and Watchkeeping for Seafarers. Every seafarer must carry this document while on board, which is also an official and legal record of his sea experience. It is one of the most important documents while a seaman is travelling on board.

So I started with the dreary early formalities of statement taking: biographical details, where the ship had originated, where she was headed, whether she was carrying any cargo on board, how many crew she carried, requesting documents such as a crew list and log book extracts. Finally, I got onto the meat of what happened and what they had seen and heard.

The captain explained: 'We were 6 mile southeast of *Oceanos*, steam north for Richards Bay, when chief officer receive Mayday signal and request for assistance from South Africa. Approximately 22:50 local time. They say *Oceanos* take water and abandon ship order given.'

'What was the sea state and weather like when you received the call?' I asked.

'Beaufort 11 to 12, 60-knot wind gust to 80. In 33 years at sea, I never see such waves. Average 20 metre, extreme spray, waves breaking. It was worst storm ever,' he said calmly, but clearly reliving the experience as he told me.

The Beaufort scale was devised in 1805 by a Royal Navy officer, Francis Beaufort (later to become Rear Admiral Sir Francis Beaufort), and was standardised for use on Royal Navy ships in the 1830s. Sailors use the scale to describe the sea state at any given time. The scale ranges from 1 to 12, with 1 meaning that the sea is calm and mirror-like and 12 meaning there are hurricane-force winds in excess of 64 knots (118 kilometres per hour) and the sea is generating waves in excess of 14 metres and is completely white with foam and spray.

It is not often that ships' masters show much excitement about the factual state of the sea, because any captain who has been at sea long enough will have seen pretty much the best and worst of what the ocean has to offer, and then more than once. So, for Captain Foo to say that this was the worst that he had ever seen was a clear statement that any ship would have been challenged in those circumstances.

Captain Foo told me how they had responded to the Mayday call and, on instructions from the coordination centre at Silvermine, had sailed towards the *Oceanos*. As they approached the stricken vessel, they used spotlights to start searching for survivors.

He spoke of the lifeboats that they had spotted being tossed around in the huge seas and how it had been impossible for him to manoeuvre the ship to get close to the lifeboats or vice versa. It had also been dangerous to approach the *Oceanos* for fear of a collision. Eventually, he had manoeuvred his vessel in a way that created shelter from the wind for some of the lifeboats. The lifeboats then made their way into the lee of the ship.

Captain Foo told me about the lifeboats crashing against the hull of his ship and starting to break up while passengers were still on board, despite the boats being on the sheltered side of the *Great Nancy*. One boat slid along the shipside towards the stern, where its great propeller was turning over, emerging from the water as the empty vessel surged on each passing swell. 'I thought the lifeboat was going to be chopped up,' he said.

With his ship being in ballast and high out of the water, and the surrounding wave action causing the stern to rise out of the water every time a wave passed under the vessel, the spinning propeller became a hazard for all lifeboats in the vicinity. He explained how his crew had had to lower buckets on ropes to haul children out of the lifeboats while adult passengers scrambled up rope ladders that had been suspended overboard.

I finished interviewing Captain Foo at around 7 am. He then told me that he believed there was still an elderly passenger in one of the crew cabins. Given his age and state of exhaustion, he had been put to bed in the cabin to sleep and recover some strength.

I went down to the cabin, where I found Mr Joseph Bonner*.

'How are you feeling?' I asked, introducing myself as I had already done so many times that morning.

Joseph Bonner appeared to be in his early eighties. Still dressed in the same clothes as when he had boarded the lifeboat, he was dishevelled and simply worn out, even taking his age into account.

'I'm feeling better after some rest,' he said. 'The crew very kindly put me in this cabin to sleep.'

'A strange thing happened just now,' he continued. I was all ears.

'I heard voices in the cabin, which woke me. I opened my eyes, without moving, and there I saw six stark-naked Greek sailors. They were crew from the *Oceanos*, just sitting naked on the other bunk beds, sharing out money between them. I thought it prudent just to close my eyes again and pretend I was still asleep.'

It seems there is still some honour among thieves.

As we spoke a bit more about his experience and how he had managed to board the ship from one of the lifeboats, he said something odd to me.

'You know, there was a bad smell on this ship when she was sinking.'

'What did it smell like?' I asked.

'I'm not really sure,' he said. 'Maybe rotting cabbage or sewage.'

I was not sure what to do with that information, but jotted it down anyway. As it happened, several passengers and entertainers said something similar over the next few days during our investigation. It had to have been significant, but we had no idea how a sinking ship and a bad smell would fit together. It was one of those pieces of evidence that made sense only when we eventually understood what had actually happened on the ship.

On my way off the ship I noticed *Oceanos* life jackets lying around on the deck of the *Great Nancy* and the quayside, abandoned by survivors. I grabbed four or five of different makes and sizes and threw them into the boot of my car. I had already heard so much complaining about the quality of the life jackets and inadequacy of the rescue equipment that I suspected these might become important evidence in an enquiry. At worst, they would make pretty neat souvenirs.

CHAPTER 14

THE INVESTIGATION

By 5 am on Sunday morning, the Durban office of P&I Associates was fully staffed. Open lines had been established with the coordination centre at Silvermine and the UK Club. P&I Associates staff started setting up what would be known as the 'War Room' for the next few weeks, extending their existing office into a large unlet space. The War Room was to become a major logistics hub in the investigation.

Given the enormity of the casualty, Captain Chris Green, managing director of P&I Associates, realised that they were going to be facilitators rather than investigators, as it was almost certain that Phil Nichols, the lawyers of the international law firm Norton Rose and a team of foreign investigators – the so-called 6 000 milers[6] – would descend on the office. In that context he ordered his staff to ensure that additional telephone lines, photocopiers and telefax machines were set up, desks and chairs were hired and workstations created for the anticipated influx of English and Greek investigators.

I was then a relatively newly admitted partner of Shepstone & Wylie, having recently returned to South Africa after a four-year stint abroad, working first at a leading London maritime law firm and later at a Luxembourg-based foreign law firm.

Chris had explained the situation and circumstances to my partner, Shane, by phone and suggested that they should probably go to East

---

6   The distance most of them would have had to travel to South Africa.

London and see what they could find out as he had learnt that some survivors were on their way there, either by bus from The Haven or being carried by rescue ships.

By lunchtime, news had reached Chris that the ship had sunk and all passengers were believed to have been evacuated. By then he had chartered a light aircraft and he, Shane, Captain Roy Martin, and two officers from the Department of Transport flew directly to East London. Roy was an independent maritime consultant and ship surveyor, predominantly providing his services to Shepstone & Wylie.

He had come ashore after a number of years at sea with the then South African national carrier, Safmarine, where he had ended his career as a master mariner. After leaving Safmarine, Roy had exchanged his captain's uniform for overalls, boots, temperature monitors, a camera, hammer and whatever else was needed to become an independent ship surveyor and ship auctioneer. When he was not helping lawyers to investigate accidents on ships, Roy was selling distressed and abandoned ships that had been arrested in South Africa for unpaid debts and other legally frowned-upon practices.

As what he termed 'a charitable gesture', Chris also offered David Fiddler of the Department of Transport and his colleague, Captain Robert Zanders, a seat on the six-seater Cessna. At that stage, the only news on the airwaves was whatever Moss Hills had been feeding to the media, which was largely centred around the passenger evacuation. Information on the cause of the sinking was scanty at best and generally unreliable.

The trip to East London was intended as an information-gathering expedition so that Chris could provide something more substantive to the UK Club. Chris gave the pilot of the Cessna the last known coordinates of the stricken *Oceanos* and they headed south into the wind to see what was still afloat and what they could establish in East London.

As they approached and then circled the site of the casualty they could see flotsam on the sea – tables, chairs, the odd empty life jacket bobbing around ominously, ropes, unrecognisable pieces of smashed timber, a couple of lifeboats. Although they already knew that the ship had sunk earlier, they were somehow still disappointed to find so little trace of a ship of such substance.

As soon as they arrived in East London, the three investigators for the UK Club hurried off in a taxi to the local Holiday Inn, where they knew survivors would be dropped off. In the meantime, Shane had lined up a legal team from a local law firm to assist with whatever logistics would be required. The Department of Transport representatives hung back, intent on making their own plans for the meantime.

...

On waking that fateful Sunday morning, David Fiddler, the principal officer of the Durban office of the Department of Transport's marine division, switched on Radio 5. His blood ran cold as he listened to the news.

'Radio 5 has received reports of a Greek passenger liner named the *Oceanos* which is sinking off the Transkei coast. Information is scanty at this stage, but passengers are said to have abandoned ship and South African Air Force helicopters are in attendance. It is not known how many passengers were on board, but it could be as many as 600.'

This was a disaster on a scale never before seen or handled by the Department, or indeed by any agency in the country. Six hundred passengers adrift in lifeboats tossing in tumultuous Transkei seas could only spell disaster.

The Marine Division of the Department of Transport was responsible for all maritime transport, but in particular safety issues relating to ships. The division had officers in every port along the South African coastline and Fiddler was responsible for Durban. He was also Acting Chief Ship Surveyor for the eastern zone of South Africa, which encompassed the entire coastline from Durban to Port Elizabeth, some 1 000 kilometres. The Transkei lay between these two cities and so this particular ship casualty fell squarely into his area of responsibility.

One of the roles of the division was to randomly inspect ships to check for safety issues, as happens typically with port state control inspections in most ports around the world. Although he was well aware of the vessel's operations in South African waters, Fiddler did not know offhand if any of his surveyors had actually inspected the *Oceanos* since she had arrived and started operating in the region, although it seemed likely.

A concern flitted across his racing mind: if his division had indeed inspected this ship, it could prove more than embarrassing for the Department if something had been missed. He put the thought out of his mind: he had a bigger crisis on his hands and the buck stopped with him.

Fiddler immediately made a few calls to verify what he had heard on the radio and then called the Director General (Shipping) of the Department of Transport, Willem Kempen. The latter was the highest-ranking civil servant in the Department at the time, reporting directly to the minister.

'Mr Kempen,' said Fiddler, 'I am sorry to disturb you on a Sunday morning, but I have just heard a report that a passenger ship called the *Oceanos* is sinking off the Transkei coast.'

'Ja?' replied Kempen after considering for a moment what he had just heard. 'How many passengers are on board?'

'As many as 600,' replied Fiddler. He could hear a sharp sucking of breath at the other end of the line.

'What is the plan?' asked Kempen. Fiddler had been waiting for this question, knowing that whatever answer he gave would not be very convincing. In keeping with his approach to life, Fiddler decided that transparency would be the safest approach. He could not mislead Kempen: it would not take long before he was found out and that could be even more career limiting than saying that there was no complete plan.

'Mr Kempen,' he replied, 'the Marine Division has never planned fully for the sinking of a passenger ship in our waters. We have so few passenger liners calling here that this has always seemed remote and not as much of a priority as dealing with cargo ships.' He waited for the blast from the other end. It did not come.

'And …?' asked Kempen.

'As you know, we have dealt with cargo ship casualties frequently,' replied Fiddler. 'We currently have little idea of the extent of the casualty. Without further information it is difficult to make a proper assessment of the situation. The safety of passengers and crew is, as always, paramount.

'My immediate plan is to liaise with all stakeholders and urgently gather whatever further information is available to enable us to make the right decisions. Our biggest challenge will be resources. One or two salvage tugs might save the ship, but if there are hundreds of people in the water or in lifeboats, tugs will be insufficient, the numbers will be beyond the NSRI and in any case the casualty is probably beyond their range. Quite frankly, Mr Kempen, we will need the help of the Defence Force.'

He knew it was unnecessary to remind Kempen of the constraints under which he worked. The Department placed major restrictions on the division's expenditure, offices were audited monthly, no one – not even principal officers – had credit cards and hopelessly insufficient budget was allocated to the Marine Division to acquire and maintain the resources needed to deal with a major casualty.

'I see,' said Kempen, without offering more. After a long pause he asked: 'What do you need me to do?'

Fiddler, knowing the levels of bureaucratic resistance through which he usually had to burrow to procure resources from the Department, took the gap.

'I will need a car from the Government garage – a large one, please. I also need the Minister to send a jet to Durban to get me to the scene of the casualty,' said Fiddler, more in hope than believing the latter request would actually be granted.

'You don't ask for much,' growled Kempen. 'I'll see what I can do. The jet is unlikely. Keep me posted.'

He was gone, so Fiddler started busying himself on his fact-finding mission, calling around to anyone who might have information for him.

By mid-morning he had mustered some staff into the office to help out and also had a far clearer picture and the outline of a plan. He knew he had to get to the scene of the casualty as well as to East London, where he understood survivors on rescue ships would be disembarked. He also knew by now that there was not much more to be done in the rescue effort. The Air Force was on the scene, airlifting passengers from the stricken vessel, ships in the area had picked up many of the survivors from lifeboats and the Marine Division would not have any further real role in the rescue.

What Fiddler now had to do was find out why the ship had foundered. Apart from ensuring safety at sea, a large part of the Department's mandate was to conduct postmortems, so to speak, on ship casualties, find out why they had happened and make recommendations to avoid future occurrences.

Fiddler needed to talk to passengers and, more particularly, the officers and crew.

He had by now secured a car – a large one – from the Government garage, but that was not going to get him to East London anytime soon. The port city was a good ten or so hours away by car, requiring him to traverse an often treacherous route through the unkempt and potholed roads of the Transkei. He needed wings, but Kempen had not come through with the jet. Well, not yet, anyway.

As so often happens when you declare your need to the universe, life delivered right on cue.

His phone rang. 'Fiddler,' he said, answering in his habitual style.

'Dave, it's Chris.' It was Captain Chris Green from P&I Associates. 'We've chartered a plane to East London. Would you like a ride?' This was manna. David's plea for help had been answered.

'Thank you, Chris. Is there room for Rob? I need a navigation expert with me.' David Fiddler was asking for a ride for Captain Robert Zanders. He was a no-nonsense, straight-talking Dutch ex-master mariner and at that time Fiddler's second-in-command in the Durban office.

'Yes, I think we can do that,' said Chris with gracious largesse.

The Department of Transport was often a thorn in the side of a shipowner because of its formalistic insistence on standards being upheld, giving no leeway on minor technical infringements. The Department irritated P&I Associates particularly because they, P&I Associates, were always the ones to clean up the mess after non-compliant shipowners had been caught out by the Marine Division.

However, Chris knew only too well that the shipping community in Durban, indeed South Africa, was a small one, that the Department would be stretched for resources and that it could never do any harm to put himself in credit with them. Eventually he would want to call in a favour in return and this act of generosity would stand him in good stead in the future.

'We'll see you at Virginia [airport] in half an hour.'

Neither David Fiddler nor Robert Zanders had an overnight bag, but they knew it was now or never. If they spurned Green's offer they might never get to East London. 'Thanks, Chris. We'll see you there.'

Quickly, they threw together whatever they thought they might need to record statements and set out in Fiddler's big Government car for the short 20-minute drive out to Virginia.

In the late afternoon on Sunday the first buses from The Haven started arriving at the hotel, laden with survivors. Other survivors had been disembarked from the *Nedlloyd Mauritius* at East London harbour and had been taken to the Holiday Inn by shuttle. Chris, Shane and Roy tried to speak to a few of the passengers as they arrived at the hotel, but for the most part the survivors were exhausted, distressed and the information they were giving was largely confusing and garbled.

Chris was constantly in contact with Phil Nichols in London, relaying whatever he had found out and eventually was given the instruction by Nichols to return to Durban and manage the crisis from there. He called the air charter company who had carried them to East London.

'Can you send a plane to collect us?' asked Chris.

The voice at the other end replied apologetically: 'I'm sorry, Captain

Green, but the Cessna is currently in use and the only aircraft we have available is the Learjet.'

'Send the jet in that case,' said Chris with conviction. It was clear that money would have to be thrown at this particular problem.

Chris in the meantime had been contacted by Epirotiki and a dedicated telephone line had been established for them. Everyone was trying to contact and locate Captain Avranas. He was said to be on a bus headed for East London, but had clearly gone to ground.

Back in the P&I Associates offices in Durban, the War Room had been fully established. Phil Nichols and three lawyers from the London office Norton Rose were on an aeroplane headed for South Africa, representatives of the hull-and-machinery (H&M) underwriters were en route, an Epirotiki superintendent was headed in from Greece and the Department of Transport had been given limited access to whatever information was available.

By Monday mid-morning, the full investigation team from London had arrived. Richard 'Dickon' Daggitt, a naval architect, had also arrived from Cape Town, having been summoned by Shane the previous afternoon. In addition, the Greek superintendent, Spiros Evthakio, most memorable because of a laryngectomy that required him to speak through a microphone pressed against his throat, had arrived a couple of hours after the English team bearing the ship's plans and the stability book.

Dickon Daggitt had been appointed by Shane as an independent naval architect to assist in the investigation of the sinking. He had studied Mechanical Engineering at the University of Cape Town and had then gone on to study a Master's degree in Ship Technology in London. This qualified him as a naval architect, which enabled him to design ships and understand the paradox that water could make a ship both float and sink.

On his return to South Africa, he worked for a company called Sandock, a ship builder based in Durban, and was later transferred to Germany to assist in ship building work, designed to circumvent the apartheid sanctions in place at the time.

The shipowners, Epirotiki Lines, had to prove to their insurers that the ship had sunk on account of a so-called peril of the sea and not because of wear and tear. The latter was conceivable given that the ship was almost 40 years old. If Epirotiki failed to prove their point to the insurers, they would not be paid for the loss of their ship. They were looking at a potential loss of somewhere around US$15 million, a significant sum even today, let alone in 1991.

There were also potential passenger claims – almost 400 of them – with which the owners and their P&I Club would have to deal. The cause of the ship's sinking would determine whether Epirotiki or TFC Tours was liable. TFC Tours and Epirotiki would have to battle out liabilities under the charter party agreement between them and TFC would have to consider refunding passengers for their tickets and so on.

Other interest groups also wanted to know what had happened. The Department of Transport was investigating the accident and the war risks underwriters, mindful of the bomb threat made at the time of the Sahd wedding, needed to understand whether any war risk had occurred – a bomb explosion for example – to determine if they were liable.

The stakes were high and we needed Dickon Daggitt to help us determine the cause of the loss. It was already becoming apparent to us that the officers and crew were not going to be very helpful. As a naval architect, Daggitt was the person on the owners' South African team to bring understanding of ship design and behaviour to the investigation table and answer the questions everyone was asking. With the physical evidence truly submerged at sea, Daggitt would have his work cut out, having to rely on whatever documents still existed and a host of witnesses of varying credibility.

Shane and I were available as local lawyers. We had also rounded up another 20 or so lawyers in the firm, who were all on stand-by to assist. There was also Carol Searle, our candidate attorney, who had by then made herself indispensable and could provide us with whatever support we needed at the War Room while working with the Norton Rose lawyers and Daggitt.

Together we were the owners' and Club's team and probably made up around 30 people. In addition, a local representative from the Salvage Association, Ian Lloyd, had been appointed to conduct the investigation on behalf of the H&M underwriters. The Salvage Association was formed to protect the commercial interests of underwriters and so remains the first choice investigator on behalf of marine insurers around the world.

The H&M underwriters must be distinguished from the UK P&I Club. Whereas the Club essentially covers third-party risks, the H&M underwriters keep the owners of the ship insured against loss of or damage to the ship or her machinery (engines, generators, equipment such as cargo cranes, and so on). There is often a tension between shipowners and their H&M underwriters in the sense that the owners must prove that the loss of or damage to the vessel arose within the parameters of the risks covered by the insurance policy and is not what is termed an 'excluded risk'.

Older policies – such as the one that covered the *Oceanos* – required losses to be caused by perils of the seas (as defined in the policy). The most important perils of the seas did not include every loss that occurred on the sea, but only accidental, unanticipated losses occurring through extraordinary action of the elements at sea (such as storms and rogue waves), as well as errors in navigation such as a collision with another vessel or running aground. Ordinary action of the wind and waves and usual wear and tear were not perils of the sea.

So, in the case of the *Oceanos*, Epirotiki had to demonstrate to their H&M insurers that the sinking of the ship came about as a result of a peril of the seas, while, in turn, the H&M insurers would have far preferred to avoid the claim by showing that the sinking was as a result of an excluded cause, such as wear and tear.

The owners' team would need to investigate the matter to prove the perils of the seas loss, while the Salvage Association were in attendance either to satisfy the H&M underwriters that a peril of the sea was indeed the cause or to show that the loss was an excluded risk.

Once everyone was present in the P&I Associates offices, the owners' team immediately had a round-table meeting, and thereafter once or twice daily, to delegate tasks, determine who required what support and assistance, ascertain who had learnt what information and generally ensure that the investigation followed particular protocols and formats.

What became immediately clear was that Norton Rose wanted to interview every single crew member from the ship, about 180 in total. All crew by this time had been moved from The Haven or transported by ship to East London or Durban and had been sequestered at the Beach Hotel in Durban, from where they needed to be ferried around Durban to face various interviews.

Different interest groups wanted to speak to different crew members for different reasons. For example, the P&I Club was keen to speak to the chief engineer because they knew exactly what should have been in his cabin, having just finished paying him out for all of his personal effects lost in the previous Epirotiki ship casualty. Part of the function of the Club was to validate claims of crew members when there had been a casualty.

One of the responsibilities of P&I Associates was to check on the liability exposure to the P&I Club in respect of passengers. The P&I Club realised that they would be on the hook for passenger claims and were desperate to ensure that there was some control over these. P&I Associates had in fact taken the liberty of video recording passengers as they came off the rescue ships, with a view to report what they were carrying so that there would be no risk of claims for appliances such as cameras that had in fact not been lost.

This footage was eventually used together with the claim forms that some passengers had completed for the ship's agents, Polaris. In addition, we (Shepstone & Wylie) also invited passengers to complete claim forms after the dust had started to settle, so we were able to check for inconsistencies in claims.

As soon as Spiros Evthakio, the Epirotiki Superintendent, had made the ship's stability book and general arrangement plan available to him for reference, Dickon Daggitt set to redrawing the ship on his computer. The stability book is a vital document, approved by the Administration of the flag under which a ship is registered, and shows all the calculations required to determine whether a ship is stable or not in particular conditions.

For example, it will enable the master of a ship to determine a ship's stability in calm seas, rough seas, with or without a load, and so on. A ship can make adjustments to its stability by, for example, filling or emptying ballast tanks with sea water, depending on the amount of cargo and fuel on board, prevailing sea conditions and so on.

Whether a ship is stable or not determines whether the ship will remain upright and floating or capsize and sink. Daggitt required the stability book to determine, working from what would have been a completely stable ship, how much water in which parts of the ship would have caused her to list to the angles she did and eventually heel over and sink, as well as over what period.

In a twist of irony, the *Oceanos* was very lively when at sea, reported by many passengers to pitch and roll a lot, especially in heavy weather. So when her hull filled with water it provided an element of stability to the vessel, which helped the rescue effort as the ship's movement in the big seas would have been reduced.

The general arrangement plan describes, graphically, how a ship has been built and is laid out. It shows every part of every deck, together with all the dimensions of the ship. With the ship's documents at hand, Daggitt was able to reverse engineer the vessel's sinking by reference to the evidence we were able to gather from those who were on the ship.

Once he had created a computer model of the ship, which he would be able to flood and sink on screen, he and I started to interview one crew member after the next, starting with the most senior deck and engineering officers and then working our way down to the lower ranks. Daggitt would ask all the technical questions and I would get clarity on some of the navigational and other information as far as necessary.

As Shane and the Norton Rose people had already interviewed each crew member, I did not want to revisit too much of what they had already covered. However, we discovered that we were faced with an unusual situation: we had at least five interest groups who wanted to interview crew members. Other than ourselves, representing the UK Club and Epirotiki, the other groups were as follows:

- As charterers of the vessel, TFC Tours of course wanted to know where they stood relative to the owners of the vessel. They had a charter party with Epirotiki and, if it materialised that the ship was unseaworthy prior to her voyage, it could bring about a significant claim by the charterers against the owners.

- The H&M underwriters wanted to gather information because Epirotiki would be bringing a claim against them for the loss of the ship.

- The war risks underwriters were interested in the casualty because of the bomb threat that had been made when the ship was in East London. If a bomb had caused the sinking of the ship, this would have been an exclusion under the H&M policy, but would then have been covered by the war risks underwriters. Their lawyer, of course, wanted access to anyone who might have had knowledge of a bomb on board the ship.

- The Department of Transport believed they had jurisdiction to conduct a preliminary enquiry into the sinking of the vessel and, in due course, a Court of Marine Enquiry, which had already been ordered by the Minister of Transport. They therefore wanted access to the crew, in particular the senior deck and engineering officers. However, David Fiddler had the grace to stand to one side and not push his department's angle too hard while everyone else was trying to access the crew. Little did we know at the time that he had already informally garnered vital evidence about the sinking, which may have partly explained why he was so gracious at the start.

In the context of so many stakeholders, each crew member was therefore being subjected to four or five interviews, one after another in assembly-line fashion.

What we quickly discovered, however, was that the senior crew members were very coy with their information, being deliberately obtuse in some of their responses or else simply vague and contradictory. Given that we were trying to assist the owners to prove an insurance claim, we expected the crew to assist and cooperate with us. However, it seemed they were hiding from us something which would not have reflected well on them or their owners.

No sooner had Shane and the Norton Rose people completed an interview, than the crew member would be surrounded by his colleagues, clearly doing a full debriefing and telling colleagues what questions had been asked and what answers had been given. Although most of the caucusing was in Greek, and so at first we could not understand what was being said, we had a good idea of what was going on.

The result was that the next crew member would come for an interview and where the first had given a vague and implausible response to a particular question, the next crew member would answer the same question with much the same answer, but be far more confident, have greater conviction in his response and sound more plausible. Other than obvious inconsistencies and impossibilities, it was hard to tell when we were being lied to and when we were hearing the truth.

We had to devise a plan to address this and came up with two mitigation strategies. One of our solutions was to double up the interviews. Once Shane and the UK lawyers had completed an interview, the crew member was immediately sent to Daggitt and me for a second, independent interview, without knowing what had been said before. The crew member would also not have had a chance to caucus with his colleagues before the second interview. I would record the statement we took and we would then be able to compare notes later and identify inconsistencies.

Our second solution to the problem was to employ a translator, Captain Davut Leylek, whom we borrowed from a local survey company to help with the interviews. Leylek spoke both Greek and Arabic, which made him very useful to us. Although he performed some functions as an interpreter, he was also instructed where possible to mingle, act as a 'spy' and tell us what was going on, especially among the Greek crew members.

The crew spent a lot of time discussing among themselves the issues about which they were most worried and did not want to divulge to the lawyers. Leylek was instructed that the crew members must not know that he understood Greek. He would then hang around and report back to us what he was overhearing.

This ploy worked well, with the crew members generally speaking openly among themselves when he was around. Leylek dutifully reported back to us what he had heard, which then allowed us to plan the next round of questions and to put the same questions to different crew members more or less simultaneously. This meant that crew members were asked about the thing they most did not want to tell us and were not able to concoct a story by caucusing with each other. This way we were able to extract more of the truth than we would otherwise have been able to do.

The only thing we were absolutely sure of was that there was a big secret among the officers, which was purposefully being kept from us. What it could be, we could not say, but we suspected that the crew – the engineers in particular – had done something blameworthy.

In the meantime, I had lined up a number of other associates from our firm. They were also based at the P&I Associates offices and they were responsible for sitting in on the interviews by the H&M underwriters, TFC Tours and the war risks underwriters.

This was a condition we placed on other parties who wanted to interview the Epirotiki crew members: the owners had to be privy to whatever the crew said to the other stakeholders. It was a take-it-or-leave-it offer and everyone agreed to the arrangement. Once again, this was important for determining inconsistencies in statements and also ensure that other stakeholders did not stumble upon information that had not been given to us.

By the time a crew member had completed a round of interviews, he was quite punch-drunk. But at least we had points of reference and comparison to help us get to the truth.

The Department of Transport asked if they could start interviewing crew. We objected. For a start, the crew did not want to be part of an investigation by the Department. It was clear that something had happened on board the ship to which we had not been made privy. The crew obviously thought that whatever they had done was wrong and they were terrified that if they revealed any fault on their part to the Department they might be arrested and detained in South Africa. We were instructed by Epirotiki to resist a Department enquiry under the Merchant Shipping Act.

At the time, the Department had sweeping powers, in terms of the Merchant Shipping Act, to interview whomever they wished in whatever circumstances they wished and also to conduct a preliminary enquiry. The preliminary enquiry is a precursor to a full-blown Court of Marine Enquiry. It is usually conducted as a relatively informal enquiry, with the Department investigators sitting around a table with witnesses and trying to form a preliminary view on what in fact happened.

Soon after the Department started this process, we told them that they were not allowed to continue because they had no jurisdiction over the casualty given that the ship had sunk in foreign, that is, Transkeian waters. Realising that we probably had a good point, the Department then contacted the Transkei Government and asked the latter to instruct them (the Department) to conduct an investigation in Durban.

The Transkei Government had no marine investigation capability and as they clearly wanted to have some involvement in whatever reflected glory there might be, they were only too happy to give such an instruction to the Department of Transport. In the meantime, we (Shepstone & Wylie) were preparing court papers to interdict the Department against continuing with the investigation.

The debate raged for a few days until eventually the crew left Durban quietly and surreptitiously. The Department were in practical

Two crew members of the *Oceanos* at the Beach Hotel in Durban.

terms then prevented from carrying on with the investigation as all the witnesses, or at least those who were most intimately involved with the ship, were gone.

Sitting with Daggitt, I learnt so much about how and why ships float or sink. He would question, for example, the chief engineer about how much fuel had been taken on at which port and placed in which tank, how much had been used, how much was left in particular tanks, what other liquids had been distributed around the ship and so on. With that information, together with numbers of passengers, estimates of baggage weights and so on, he was able to calculate the ship's stability at any given time.

It was important for him to understand the ship's stability before the vessel got into trouble so that he could then understand what subsequently made the ship unstable and caused her to list and later to sink.

Some of the key evidence that emerged at this time was from Moss Hills's video camera. It revealed the listing of the ship at different times, but more importantly the amount of water that had entered the ship, the level of the water as it rose from deck to deck and the exact whereabouts of the water.

This, coupled with evidence given by passengers, TFC staff and some of the more junior crew, enabled Daggitt to sink the model he had generated on his computer. From the general arrangement plan he had determined what pipes ran where and how water would make its way through the ship once it had entered from the auxiliary engine room.

He knew where the water had come in, how it would have had to flow to make the ship list the way it did and subsequently make it sink. What Daggitt did not know was why it came into the ship in the first place or how it got past watertight bulkheads.

One part of the mystery seemed to unfold from an unexpected quarter. Two days after the *Oceanos* sunk, Shane told me that David Gordon, SC of the Durban Bar had called the office and asked to speak to him. We would later find out he had been on an *Oceanos* cruise to Mauritius and Réunion a few months before. 'He says he's got important information for us. Some video he took on the ship a while ago. I think we need to meet with him later.'

Despite being awash with ongoing interviews and other *Oceanos* work, Shane and I left the '6 000 milers' that afternoon and returned to our offices to meet with David.

He then told us about his experience in Réunion. 'When I heard that the ship had sunk I knew that the grounding must have had something to do with it,' he said in his resonant, booming voice.

A video recorder and screen had been set up and David then gave us a private screening of his footage. As we watched it was clear to see mud swirling around in the water on the port-side mid-section of the ship, more or less where the hull of the ship housed the auxiliary engine room. There was no way of telling how hard the ship had touched the bottom, but there was no doubt that either there had been some contact or that the ship had passed through such shallow water that mud had been stirred by her motion.

Either way, this might prove to be a decisive factor in the investigation. It at least offered some sort of explanation of why water came in through the side of the ship. If a shell plate had kinked when the ship touched the bottom, there would have been an inherent weakness in that part of the hull. Given what we knew by then, this information had a smoking-gun feel to it.

'David,' said Shane, 'we might have to call you as a witness if there is litigation.'

David immediately complained ruefully, 'In that case I suppose I can't accept any professional brief on this matter: I now have a conflict of interest as a potential witness.'

After two intensive weeks of interviewing the crew and one or two entertainers, no one was much closer to learning the truth of why the ship had sunk. Our days were both intense and long. Typically, we would arrive each day at the P&I Associates office at 7 am. Over a cup of coffee we would have a general discussion on the strategy for the day ahead and who would be speaking to whom and how we would divide up our tasks.

Chris Green's team from P&I Associates helpfully kept topping up our coffee and provided lunchtime sandwiches. At 6 pm, the mandatory pizzas and Coke – a dietician's dream – were delivered for the team. At around 8 pm, we would gather together for a debrief and comparison to see what we had all learnt, checking on consistencies, and inconsistencies, and considering the significance of any new information that had been shared by any of our witnesses.

We would then knock off at 9 pm, Shane and I typically heading back to our own offices at Shepstone & Wylie to put in a couple of hours of work and try to deal with the regular day-to-day business of our practices. I generally arrived home around midnight, put in a few hours' sleep, took a shower and started all over again at 7 am. By the end of the first week we were exhausted, but still with no end in sight.

The English lawyers were slave drivers, even giving Dickon Daggitt some light counselling when he had the temerity to take off an hour or two on Sunday to watch a Grand Prix on TV.

After nearly two weeks of toil, all we really knew was that water had come pouring in through the side of the ship, probably through the sea chest, which was part of the generator cooling system. We speculated that the cause of the breach in the shell plating had been the impact of a particularly large and unpleasant wave, but other than the circumstances of the weather at the time and David Gordon's video shot in Réunion, even that was impossible to prove.

Nonetheless, it was the most likely explanation and would probably carry the day if the hull underwriters were ever to reject the claim by the owners. The only other suggestion might have been that, because the ship was nearly 40 years old, a shell plate had simply fallen off due to wear and tear. This was less plausible and we were reasonably sure that if a court were ever asked to make a finding, it would conclude that the likely cause of the loss of the shell plate was a large wave, which would qualify as a peril of the sea.

We also knew that the engineers had been doing some work in the auxiliary engine room at the time when the water came through, but they were more than a little vague about what exactly they had been doing and what the state of repairs was at the time of the flood. The one thing they were adamant about, however, was that when the water came flooding in, they closed the watertight doors behind them when they left the area.

What they were unwilling to tell us was how the water got out of a watertight space and spread to the rest of the ship or how they knew that the ship was going to sink. As Captain Roy Martin said to me wryly after the first day's investigation: 'When you see an engineer standing on the weather deck of a ship wearing a life jacket, you can be pretty sure that there's nothing more that he can do to stop the ship from sinking and that the ship is going down. They know something that they aren't telling us.'

One of the junior Filipino crew members who had been working in the auxiliary engine room from time to time, suggested that there might have been a small hole through the forward watertight bulkhead, but we were never able to verify this and could not even be sure that we had properly understood what he had said because of language challenges. The mystery persisted and the crew flew home.

We had made a first cut of the evidence in Durban, but now the local investigation was over.

On the second Sunday after the *Oceanos* had sunk, Daggitt was back home in Cape Town when he received a call from Shane, informing him that the investigation was moving to Piraeus. 'Can you book yourself a flight and be in Piraeus by tomorrow morning?'

Daggitt scurried around to get himself organised and managed to get a flight to Greece that evening. The crew had been evacuated towards the end of the previous week, with the Greeks being repatriated to Greece and the Filipinos back to the Philippines. On arrival in Piraeus, Daggitt met up with Shane, the Norton Rose lawyers, investigators from the well-known London casualty investigation firm, Brookes Bell, and senior Epirotiki staff of course, including the owner, Captain Andreas Potomianos.

And so the investigation began all over again, this time with Brookes Bell leading the evidence and robustly testing every assertion made by the crew. The investigation raged on for another two weeks, with the only respite being the first weekend.

That Friday, Captain Potomianos asked the team: 'Do you want to go back to London or would you rather just laze around on my island?' No one for a moment doubted that, being the owner of Epirotiki, he did in fact also own an island.

As one, the team chose the island over a long-haul weekend trip back to London. The ubiquitous blue Peugeots, the signature mode of transport for Epirotiki, loaded everyone up and took them to the Piraeus port to catch a ferry to Captain Potomianos' island.

There the team was loaded onto his yacht. As it motored around the blue Aegean Sea, Daggitt and one of the Brookes Bell consultants insisted that the motor be stopped and the yacht continue under sail. And so the *Oceanos* team briefly lived the dream, before flying back to Athens on the Monday. That week saw the team back on its brutal schedule, starting work at 7.30 am, continuing until 8 pm and then being fetched by Potomianos at 9 pm to start dinner, which saw them back in bed at around 2 am each morning.

A week was about as much as they could manage.

Once they were done in Piraeus, the team flew back to London to debrief, evaluate the new information that Brookes Bell had managed to squeeze out of the crew, consolidate all the evidence and present the Epirotiki Line's total loss claim to the hull underwriters.

CHAPTER 15

'ABANDON IS FOR EVERYBODY'

The Cessna carrying Chris Green, Shane Dwyer and Roy Martin, along with David Fiddler and Robert Zanders, landed at East London early on Sunday afternoon. Upon disembarking, Green, Dwyer and Martin walked quickly towards the airport building, intent on getting themselves to the local Holiday Inn where survivors were gathering. Fiddler and Zanders found themselves alone on the airport apron.

Chris Green had flown them to East London, but he certainly was not going to invite them to join in and attend interviews of crew members. Those were legally privileged and Fiddler was not particularly surprised that further cooperation had been suspended for the meantime.

As they stood and discussed their next move, a man dressed in an Air Force pilot's uniform approached them. 'Are you Mr Fiddler?' he asked. David nodded.

'I have instructions to fly you to wherever you need to go.'

Fiddler looked at Zanders, who looked as bemused as Fiddler felt by this approach. 'Kempen must have organised this,' surmised Fiddler.

'Follow me,' said the pilot, Captain Jacques Hugo. They walked towards a military Puma helicopter.

As they boarded the pilot apologised. 'Sorry, Sir. There's not much space at the back. We have to carry a lot of equipment.' Fiddler and Zanders were met with an enormous tank of aviation fuel in the back of the helicopter, on which they had to sit for the ride to the casualty site.

They again flew over the casualty site, just in case there was anything more to be seen, but by then much of the debris they had seen earlier had dispersed and there was little evidence of the drama that had unfolded over the past 20-odd hours. The pilot then flew them to The Haven.

Fiddler and Zanders started hunting for the captain of the ship. They had heard some stories about his behaviour on board, so needed to verify those for a start, but in any event the captain would (or at least should) have been the person having the most knowledge of the casualty and evacuation, so he was the obvious departure point for their investigation.

Captain Avranas was nowhere to be found. The managers of the Haven Hotel, Boet and Lynette Jacobs, suggested that he must have holed up in a room somewhere. However, given the chaos they had had to contend with since early morning, they were unable to say where exactly he might be.

Fiddler and Zanders temporarily abandoned the search, principally to fend off a loyal Filipino crew member who was harassing – almost manhandling – them in his defence of the captain and attempts to persuade them that the captain was actually a good bloke. Fiddler had no patience for this. His mission was to find out what had happened, not to start attributing or apportioning blame. All he wanted was a quiet word with the master of the ship.

They spent the night in the lounge at The Haven, chatting to the few survivors who were still around and gleaning what they could from the managers of the hotel before catching a disturbed and uncomfortable few hours of sleep.

The following morning they established the room in which the captain had billeted himself. Fiddler knocked on his door: 'Captain Avranas, this is David Fiddler of the Department of Transport. We need to speak to you.'

Avranas refused to open the door. They could hear him moving around inside. Following one more attempt and warning him that they would have to take steps to force him to speak to them, they broke down the door and entered. After introducing themselves, informing Avranas about their wide powers under section 9 of the Merchant Shipping Act and warning the master that he could be imprisoned if he did not cooperate, Fiddler told him: 'Captain, we are conducting a preliminary enquiry. We need you to answer some questions.'

'What you want to know?' he asked sullenly.

'We want to know why the ship sank.'

Avranas gave a characteristic shrug of his shoulders.

'I do not know,' he said. 'I do nothing wrong.'

Fiddler quickly realised that whatever cooperation he was likely to get in his investigation was not going to be forthcoming from Captain Avranas.

After a few more futile attempts, Fiddler gave up. 'Let's go, Rob,' he said in disgust, walking out to the helicopter that had brought them to The Haven. Most of the helicopters had by then demobilised and flown back to their respective bases. A few minutes later they were airborne.

When they arrived in East London, Fiddler met Green at the airport. 'So much for fucking cooperation,' growled Green, obviously annoyed that Fiddler and Zanders had been to The Haven without them. They were not offered a ride back to Durban.

Fiddler and Zanders waited for a commercial flight to take them back home. They went straight into the office and convened their regular Monday morning meeting, a little late, with the other senior surveyors to discuss further strategy. A robust approach was agreed upon.

Fiddler ordered that the captain and chief engineer be brought to the Marine Division offices in town. The two officers were then collected by Department officials and marched into the office. Fiddler opened the conversation in his usual straightforward manner:

'Captain, Chief Engineer, I must warn you both that it is an offence under the Merchant Shipping Act not to cooperate with us. You can be fined or go to jail if you do not cooperate or if you withhold information. The Department of Transport has convened a preliminary enquiry under the Act and this entitles us to request information and documents from you.'

Fiddler, using his *ex officio* role as commissioner of oaths, then required both officers to swear an oath to tell the truth and started with his questions.

Chief Engineer Panayiotis Fines had brought with him a set of ship's plans that he had salvaged off the vessel before leaving in one of the lifeboats. These he immediately surrendered to Fiddler. It was clear that he was going to be more helpful than the captain.

Fines told a harrowing tale. He explained how the sea chest had broken off the side of the ship and water had suddenly and unexpectedly come pouring through the gratings with massive pressure and in a huge volume, quickly filling the generator room space. Fiddler surmised that it must have been corroded: sea chests do not simply pop off well-maintained ships.

'I hear terrible noise and run to generator room from engine room,' said Fines. The main engine was adjacent to and forward of the generator room.

'I try to stop water. I push sea chest back onto the hull, but pressure too high and sea chest keep coming off. Look, my arms!'

Fines showed Fiddler deep cuts all over his forearms, which he said had been caused by trying to push the sea chest back onto its fitting. When he realised that the bilge pumps were unable to cope with the flood, he frantically called the bridge, advised the captain what was happening and fled with the other engineers, closing the watertight doors behind them.

'If you closed the watertight doors, why did the ship sink?' asked Fiddler. Again, the Mediterranean shrug, this time from the chief engineer.

Captain Avranas remained as unhelpful as ever, responding to questions mostly in monosyllables and answering with the minimum of information, volunteering nothing more than he was asked.

'There are reports that you were one of the first off the ship by helicopter, Captain. Is that correct?' asked Robert Zanders.

'No, I leave with everyone else,' replied Avranas.

'We understand that you left a lot of passengers behind on board, Captain. Why was that?'

'I leave ship to coordinate rescue from the shore,' replied Avranas. 'I come back in helicopter later.'

After the two *Oceanos* officers left, Fiddler set about studying the plans the chief engineer had left behind. He could see that, forward of the generator room bulkhead, was a sewage collating tank in the engine room. On the plan, a 10-centimetre venting pipe ran up the bulkhead of the generator room and through the bulkhead into the engine room. This he knew would have been to allow noxious gases to escape.

It was apparent to him that sewage and grey water from the forward and aft cabins drained into inlet pipes and then into the sewage tank.

Fiddler pondered over the plans, noting that the vessel used to be a cargo ship and ferry that carried cars. He knew that, as a car carrier, the bottom deck would have been just above the sewage tank. He had also been told by some of the passengers at The Haven that those on the lower deck of the ship complained of a smell of sewage.

Suddenly, as he was looking at the plans, he had an epiphany. Running down to his government garage car, he sped off to the Beach Hotel, to which the chief engineer had been returned after his interview. He found out from the receptionist where Fines' room was and ran up the stairs, bursting in on him.

'Chief,' he demanded, a little breathlessly, 'tell me truthfully: was the venting pipe in place when the sea chest came off?'

Chief Engineer Fines hung his head a bit, unable to look Fiddler in the eye.

'No,' he replied wearily, 'it was not. We remove a part of it.'

'Why not?' asked Fiddler.

'That pipe, it was often blocked. The passengers, they complain of shit smell. I always have to remove pipe and clean it. When the water come, there was no time to replace.'

'So you knew that the water in the generator room would pass through to the engine room when it reached the level of the venting pipe hole?' asked Fiddler rhetorically. 'And you knew that the water would flood forwards through the ship and it would sink after you closed the water-tight doors?' Fiddler pressed him.

'Yes. There was nothing we could do.'

'Why did you not close off the valves on the inlet pipes of the sewage tank?' asked Fiddler. That would have stopped the water from flowing back.

'Controls are in mess room. There was no time.'

Just then the door was pushed open behind him. Fiddler looked over his shoulder to see Ian Lloyd, the Salvage Association representative who was investigating the loss of the ship for the H&M underwriters, standing in the doorway. Lloyd looked surprised and uncomprehending.

'You're not supposed to be here,' he said menacingly. 'You can't talk to the chief.'

'I can talk to whomever I like and do whatever I like,' countered Fiddler aggressively. 'Have you not read section 9? And I can have you arrested for obstructing an investigation by the Department,' he added as a parting shot.

Lloyd was furious: 'Don't you threaten me,' he shouted. 'Now get out of here.'

Fiddler knew his powers under the Merchant Shipping Act, but he also knew he would never use them on Ian Lloyd, one of the respected elders in the maritime fraternity. He had the answer he needed from Chief Engineer Fines. He also knew he had not played strictly by the unspoken rules of the game and decided that a strategic retreat might serve the Department's cause best at this stage. Bidding Lloyd a curt good day, Fiddler left for his office to start writing a report.

The information Chief Engineer Fines gave David Fiddler was never provided to the legal investigation team in South Africa: this was the big secret being withheld from us.

The information about the sewage venting pipe was first revealed to me when I was researching this book and I interviewed David Fiddler. Unsurprisingly, it was never shared with the legal teams working in South Africa on the investigation at the time. This is because any initial investigation of the Department of Transport into a casualty is preliminary in nature. The Department will make initial findings from the investigation, but they rarely make that information available at the time because the release of the findings might pre-empt findings of the next stage in an investigation, the Court of Marine Enquiry.

A preliminary enquiry report is usually submitted to the Minister of Transport, who then considers, in light of the preliminary findings, whether to convene a Court of Marine Enquiry. This next stage in an investigation is usually ordered when the casualty is sufficiently serious.

It would therefore be embarrassing for both the Minister and the Department if third parties (lawyers, media and so on) became aware of the preliminary findings before the Minister did. The withholding of information by the Department is therefore not so much a reluctance to cooperate with other investigating teams as it is protocol. (The initial findings may even prove to be wrong when tested in a Court of Marine Enquiry.)

However, it is difficult to understand the crew's reluctance to share the information with the owners' lawyers. It might be that they thought withholding the information would protect their owners' from adverse publicity or that they did not understand the potential adverse effect on the insurance claim. A more plausible reason, however, might have been that they did not trust us (as foreign lawyers) to keep their information confidential. They may have feared that if we leaked it to the authorities it could place them at risk of being arrested in South Africa for negligence.

Crews are frequently arrested by local authorities in the jurisdiction where there has been a shipping casualty, especially if pollution is involved. (Thankfully, pollution was not a significant factor in the *Oceanos* casualty.) Arrests of crew in Africa are not infrequent as it usually gives the local authorities some leverage over the shipowners. The *Oceanos* crew would have been alive to this.

Avranas never did cooperate with the Department of Transport or Fiddler. The tragedy is that he genuinely seems to have thought that his actions were perfectly normal. He stuck to his story of leaving the ship to coordinate the rescue from the shore. One version by Avranas was that he in fact rejoined a helicopter after he had been landed at The Haven and flew around with it to ensure that the airlift was effectively carried out. Boet and Lorraine Jacobs were adamant that he never left his room at the Haven Hotel after his arrival.

In an interview with the South African Broadcasting Corporation soon after the incident he defiantly declared: 'When I order abandon ship, it doesn't matter what time I leave. Abandon is for everybody. If some people like to stay, they can stay.'

This was later quoted in the *New York Times*. The interview remains on social media to this day and epitomises not just a fundamental arrogance by Avranas, but also a complete lack of respect for the passengers and crew under his care. Furthermore, Avranas's statement ignores the fact that neither he nor any other member of crew ever gave the order to abandon ship.

This also opens the question whether the modern day ship's captain is still required to be the last to leave a sinking ship. In January 2012, Captain Francesco Schettino was one of the first off the infamous *Costa Concordia*, which sunk off Isola del Giglio in Tuscany after striking an underwater rock. Judging by the universal outrage and condemnation of Schettino's actions, it remains bad form for the captain of a ship to abandon his passengers.

The *Oceanos* owners, Epirotiki Lines, supported the captain's narrative. The following quote (in the public domain) is attributed to the then head of Epirotiki Lines: 'As regards the captain abandoning the vessel, this is untrue and he has maintained his position throughout in assisting the rescue in the most effective way ...'

He also said the following when asked about senior crew members who were first onto the lifeboats: 'Of course the crew members assigned to the boats have to enter first in order to assist the embarkation of the passengers.' That might have been plausible had the passengers ever been ordered onto the lifeboats.

CHAPTER 16

LESSONS FROM BLACK SWANS

Back in South Africa, we reviewed the ticket conditions and concluded that the conditions on all the passenger tickets were sufficient to enable Epirotiki Lines to avoid paying much, if any, compensation to passengers.

After a heated debate over whether compensation should be paid, reason prevailed, with the view that both decency and the risk of further tarnishing Epirotiki's reputation required that some compensation be paid to passengers. A decision was made to pay 50% of reasonably proven losses, despite the legal view being that Epirotiki was not liable to pay anyone.

There was no particular magic in the figure of 50%: it was just a number that sounded about right. The payment was to be *ex gratia*: that is, as a gesture despite the absence of legal liability for the owners. At Shepstone & Wylie we started the overwhelming task of gathering and assessing passenger, entertainer and crew claims.

Some passengers had already completed claim forms when they stepped off the rescue vessels in Durban and East London. These had been provided by the ship's agents and were generally regarded as most likely to be reliable rather than exaggerated, but nonetheless were all devoid of proof.

We then put out a general invitation to all passengers, using TFC Tours as our intermediary, asking them to submit claim forms and any proof they had of what it was they had lost. We invited them to submit invoices, if those were still in their possession, photographs of passengers holding the items which they claimed had been lost or anything else that would reasonably verify what they were claiming.

We accepted that they had all lost clothing and suitcases – that seemed like a reasonable assumption – and tried to imagine what would have been a reasonable amount of clothing for the duration of the trip for each passenger. For example, someone who had travelled from Durban to Cape Town and intended returning to Durban would have required sufficient clothing for about a week, whereas someone sailing from East London to Durban would have needed only an overnight bag and perhaps something smart for the Saturday evening.

With about 400 claims pouring into our offices, we had a dedicated team processing each one as it arose. Spreadsheets were created detailing passengers' names, ports of embarkation and disembarkation, lists of what they had claimed, references to the proof they had submitted and so on. The paper management was enormous.

As we started generically grouping lost items together, it became apparent that we were going to have to try get our own valuations. Cameras and video cameras were difficult to value. Some were older than others and we had to apply our minds as to how values should be discounted for the age of a lost item. Eventually we appointed a local camera shop as our consultant and presented them with lists of cameras and ages as best we knew and asked them to value the equipment.

Watches were a bit more difficult: there was no one shop that carried the makes and models of all watches which were said to have been lost. Inevitably, we were also faced with what seemed like a disproportionately high number of claims for Rolexes and other high-value items. Apart from common sense, logic and some discretion, we also had to apply a healthy dose of cynicism to some of the claims.

Claims for cash were rejected: there was simply no way to verify cash and, on any basis, the ticket conditions were clear that cash could not be reimbursed if it was lost. One claim seemed so implausible that it was probably true: a passenger averred that he had placed six gold Kruger rand coins in the ship's safe as he was moving house from East London to Durban. Thankfully, we were not required to tell the passenger that we simply did not believe him. Kruger rands, we decided, were equivalent to cash and therefore were part of the excluded claims.

Over a number of months we steadily worked our way through the claims. The UK Club had placed funds into our client trust account and we were authorised to assess and settle claims as we saw fit.

Not everyone was happy with what they received. Some, like Michael O'Mahoney, were able to replace what really mattered with their payouts for the loss of personal effects. Michael was particularly upset about the lost camera equipment – a wide-angle lens, a zoom lens, a flash unit and aluminium case – because he had borrowed the equipment from a friend. Shopping around in South Africa he quickly realised that the compensation paid was not going to cover the missing equipment. Thinking creatively, he was instead able to use the money to purchase an air ticket at a 90% staff discount, fly to Hong Kong and buy the replacement equipment at a discounted price there.

The biggest obstacle to settlement with some of the passengers came from a Johannesburg lawyer who represented a large group of Johannesburg-based passengers. No matter how we tried to settle those passengers' claims, he rejected every offer, threatening to sue if the offer was not increased.

In the end, we made final offers to all of his clients. These were rejected, yet we never heard from him again. Sadly, therefore, one group of passengers were never compensated at all owing to the sterling efforts of the group's lawyer. And we wonder why our profession gets such a bad rap from time to time!

With the exception of the Johannesburg group, we finally tied up all of the passengers' and entertainers' claims about 15 months after the incident.

The *Oceanos* rescue was a triumph. It was, and remains, one of the greatest maritime rescues in history, by any measure. It is hard to imagine a similar event happening again in similar circumstances anywhere in the world and having the same outcome, even in today's world of better communications, safer ships and more effective rescue patterns and preparation.

In as much as the *Oceanos* foundered and sank in a perfect storm, with all of the worst weather elements of the Wild Coast rolled into one, the success of the rescue may also be attributed to that perfect storm: one that arose from the coming together of preparedness, willingness, human spirit, selflessness, courage, resilience, doggedness and determination of many of the good citizens of South Africa.

There are some lessons in this for us and future generations, all of whom are struggling to deal with the challenges and crises dished up by a changing and unpredictable world.

The 'Black Swan' theory was conceived by Nassim Taleb, the risk analyst, as a metaphor to describe an event which is unexpected, has a significant impact and can somehow be explained only after it has occurred and all the facts are to hand. The expression is based on the ancient thought that black swans were presumed not to exist, until the first one was seen.

The theory refers to events of large magnitude, which have major consequences and play a dominant role in history. Although originally the theory was confined to financial events, Taleb extended the idea to all major historical events in 2007. There are three significant aspects to a black swan event. First, it has to be an 'outlier' – something that is way beyond the realm of the ordinary and predictable. Nothing in the past can convincingly point to its occurrence as a possibility. Secondly, it is associated with an extreme effect. Finally, human nature prompts us to concoct explanations for its occurrence after the fact, despite its status as an outlier, so that it then appears both predictable and capable of being explained.

Whether the *Oceanos* would have been a classic black swan event is hard to say, but it does tick a number of the boxes. The casualty was something completely out of the ordinary, something that could almost never have been expected and which completely changed the way people thought about things relating to maritime rescue and passenger ships.

When we think back on cataclysmic disasters at sea, the one that comes most easily to mind is the *Titanic*. The ship sank in deep, freezing and remote waters; there were limited rescue facilities and inevitably there was significant loss of life. Upon her launch, the *Titanic* was heralded as unsinkable, yet she sank. If ever there was a maritime black swan, that was it.

Three years after the *Oceanos*, the *Achille Lauro* caught fire and sank off Somalia with no loss of life, principally because it happened on relatively calm waters and all lifeboats were able to be launched. More recently, the *Costa Concordia* grounded and then sank, but in shallow waters. Even with all her modern equipment, sinking in shallow and calm waters and with rescue forces not far away, there was still loss of life. Other than those three, there are very few major peacetime passenger liner losses.

Only a few passenger ships sank in the 18th and 19th centuries. The *Waratah* and *Titanic* sank at sea within three years of each other, 1909 and 1912. However, ships later became safer with regard to construction, safety management and operations. Very few passenger liners sank thereafter, and none on the South African coastline, so the idea of a passenger liner sinking in South African blue water in 1991 was anathema.

When the *Oceanos* sunk, she was an outlier. It had been over 80 years since the last major passenger catastrophe in southern African seas (the *Waratah*) and no one expected one in modern-day 1991. Inevitably, therefore, no one had planned for such an event. That is the way it is with black swans: because we do not expect them, we do not plan for them. It is only afterwards that people can see that it was inevitable.

The consequences of a black swan event can be, and usually are, considerable, disastrous. How then, in the face of a maritime black swan, did South Africa manage to avoid the loss of even one life?

Inevitably, there was an element of good fortune. Call it the grace of God or whatever you want. Recall the story of the casino dealer who was picked up miles from the *Oceanos*, for example, or the child who was swept out of one of the lifeboats and plucked out of the sea by another passenger. Recall the stories of children being lifted in buckets, lifeboats being chipped away by spinning propellers of rescue ships or crashing against the sides of rescue ships, and a myriad of other incidents.

An element of fate and fortune pervaded all the extraordinary stories of the rescue, but ignoring that and focusing holistically on the event itself, the rescue remains one of the most successful in history. One therefore has to look at the rescue as a whole to figure out what went right for the miracle to have happened.

Perhaps the starting point is to say that, in the context of any industry – be it financial, aviation, maritime or anything else – one has to imagine the very worst thing that could possibly happen and then ask whether the processes, institutions, support structures and response units are adequate to deal with whatever comes, even if we cannot imagine what it is that might come.

At the time, *Lloyd's List*, the world-renowned and influential shipping newspaper, described the rescue effort thus: 'If the [*Oceanos*] had to get into distress, it was only on the South African coast, virtually on the whole continent, that such succor for her passengers and complement would have been available'.

Lloyd's List paid particular tribute to South Africa's search-and-rescue infrastructure and, more particularly, the skill, professionalism and extensive training of the aircrews. Although they were pivotal to the success of the rescue, we need to look at the wider picture to understand what was in place to create the resilience shown in the face of this outlier incident. In risk management terms, the word 'resilience' is defined as an organisation's readiness to respond to risk.

Let us start with South Africa's coastal radio stations. These were all operational at the time, were able to communicate with one another and with the Maritime Rescue Coordination Centre at Silvermine and were the first line of defence for ships in trouble on that stretch of coastline. It is also instructive that a worldwide radio network exists, so that a ship in trouble at the tip of Africa was able to broadcast a Mayday signal to a Norwegian radio station more than 10 000 kilometres away.

The centre at Silvermine itself was well drilled in shipping disaster management, although they had never contemplated having to rescue 600 passengers off a sinking passenger liner in hostile waters. They had lines of communication to all possible rescue services in the region and so became the hub in the middle of the rescue wheel.

One then starts to look at all the other institutions involved. One such was the NSRI. With its primary mission being to save lives at sea, it already offers the skeleton of a rescue infrastructure that can offer support.

The East London Metro Rescue Services was an emergency service provider which is replicated in every town around the country. Once again, when you create a significantly resilient rescue and emergency infrastructure, it lends itself to responding to any disaster, no matter how unusual.

And then there was the South African Defence Force. Exceptionally well trained and willing to place themselves above safety, the heroes of the various helicopter squadrons involved in the rescue were fundamental to the success of the rescue. Most interesting, however, was that, on their own version, the inland helicopters were ill-equipped to perform the roles they did. Not only were they ill-equipped, but they were technically acting illegally in the task they undertook.

The helicopters of 15 Squadron were just about adequate for the job, but ultimately it was the pilots and crew of all the helicopters who made the rescue possible. Their skill was attributable to their intense, extensive and competent training, but beneath that was a spirit of rescue, adventure, selflessness and discipline.

The calibre of leadership in the Defence Force at that time was exceptional. The responsiveness of Brigadier Dick Lord, the precision and methodology of Brigadier Theo de Munnink and the leadership of the flight commanders gave rise to a system which, when tested in the extreme, was able to stand up to the disaster it faced.

In our world, every industry, organisation and sector has to show resilience in the face of adversity. Over the last few decades, it has been a trend to integrate business continuity systems into organisations to create the resilience necessary for unplanned and unwanted disasters. Business continuity is about ensuring that business continues, if not as usual, then at least in a functional and operational manner as soon as possible after the occurrence of a disaster.

The *Oceanos* rescue, while not categorised as such an operation, illustrates beautifully how business continuity can happen. In the *Oceanos* rescue, every system in the South African search-and-rescue armoury was tested thoroughly. The only one found wanting was the ship herself.

Despite the behaviour of the captain and many of the senior crew and the sinking of an ostensibly seaworthy ship, it was largely business as usual for the passengers within a day of the event, although there were of course many who were severely traumatised. This can be attributed to the resilience of the systems in place at the time.

So, what were some of the biggest lessons to be learned?

- **Imagine the individual consequences, not the events.** By their nature, black swans generally cannot be imagined, but if you want to plan for one, it is usually possible to imagine for the worst possible consequences, and then put in place resources to mitigate those.

- **The first line of defence must be both responsive and secure.** The first line must be an early-warning system, one that is able to start the wider process of business continuity, rescue or disaster response at the earliest possible moment. Port Elizabeth Radio, East London Radio, Cape Town Radio and Durban Radio were the primary elements of that early-warning system.

- **Ensure that the second line of defence is so well versed in the possibility of disaster that, even when there is no specific plan for the actual event, it has sufficient experience elsewhere to respond in an appropriate manner.** The Silvermine coordination centre was staffed with incredibly well-trained people: people who had experience in all possible areas to which they would need to respond in a maritime emergency, people who had a passion for their jobs and who, provided they followed particular procedures, would be able to respond to the black swan when it swam by.

- **The last line of defence must be impenetrable, well drilled and properly resourced.** That was the idea of course with the famous Maginot Line built after the First World War. Massive reinforcements were built along the eastern border of France to keep the Germans out, but failed because the plan did not contemplate every circumstance of attack. The French were so focused on a ground-based attack from the Germans in a particular direction that their plan overlooked air-based attacks and being out-flanked in other directions.

  In the case of the *Oceanos*, the only possible resource that was sufficiently large to deal with a crisis of this magnitude was the South African Defence Force and, more specifically, the SAAF. On its own, the Air Force might have been a Maginot Line of sorts. However, when Navy divers were added in, people were placed on the shore and all stakeholders interfaced. The last line of defence held.

- **Be flexible.** The participation of the Defence Force in the *Oceanos* rescue raises an interesting question. Why should they have been involved in a civilian casualty? The answer is that sometimes one has to draw on resources that are operating outside their usual sphere of duty because the scale of the disaster is such that the regular resources are simply not able to respond.

  The regular resources in this case were the NSRI and the Metro Emergency Services. Although their supporting roles were invaluable, they were simply insufficient to deal with anything on this scale. The wider institution, South Africa Inc., therefore has to be willing to be sufficiently flexible to deploy resources that would normally never be used for civilian operations, if it is to respond appropriately to a large-scale disaster.

  In the World Trade Center disaster, one of the lines of defence was the New York Fire Department. A fire department is largely about fighting fires, not dealing with buildings falling down. Yet they were the heroes in that event because they were flexible, ready, able and properly trained to respond to what was New York's black swan.

- **Ensure that there are ancillary response services to support the overall efforts.** This is about creating an holistic approach to dealing with black swans. No single institution can deal with a black swan on its own, so the correct preparation for such an event is to ensure that various supporting institutions can be called on. Those included not only the NSRI and East London Metro in this case, but also several others.

- **Leadership is paramount.** The leadership of Brigadier Dick Lord was exemplary; read about his leadership in his book *Standby*. But lest you be sceptical about him describing his own role in the rescue, speak also to the people who knew him. Without fail, they sing his praises as an extraordinary leader with vision, method and experience.

   Ultimately, dealing with black swans is about dealing with people, ensuring that existing systems are properly utilised and deployed. Whereas Dick Lord and Theo de Munnink were appointed in leadership positions and were expected to lead by virtue of their roles, Robin Boltman and Moss Hills were thrust into these roles; a lead guitarist and magician would not usually be thought of as leaders on a ship. Nonetheless, they stepped into a vacuum of leadership, displayed initiative, courage and decisiveness and delivered the better part of 600 people to safety through their actions.

   Paul Whiley, a 22-year-old able seaman, foisted into the biggest modern maritime drama in South African history, took his leadership cue and created order and calm where a recipe for disorder and panic awaited.

- **Provide unquestioning support to your leadership.** Beneath each of the leaders was a group of other leaders and implementers, such as the flight commanders like captains Goatley and Thomas, operational coordinators like Major Louter van Wyk, and so on.

The question then is: what sort of leaders are needed in the face of a disaster? The answer seems to be: skilled, decisive, courageous, visionary, creative, able to think outside the normal parameters, acting within their authority (both personal and delegated). But ultimately, every leader needs to be fully empowered to do whatever is necessary to deliver the organisation.

- **Ensure that every stakeholder in every organisation completely owns his or her role.** The staff of TFC Tours – Lorraine Betts, entertainers such as Moss Hills, Robin Boltman and others – were completely engaged in their roles. They understood that their primary role was to direct cruises or run the entertainment. Nonetheless, they were willing to take a wider ownership of the well-being of the passengers whom they served.

It would have been easy for the TFC staff and entertainers simply to have left the ship at the earliest possible opportunity. No one would have criticised them for that. However, they took ownership of their roles as stewards when faced with a crisis created by a deserting captain and senior crew. They stepped up to a situation which they could never have envisaged.

One has to attribute a massive part of the success of the operation to the calm presence of mind, integrity and commitment of the TFC staff. Courage followed. If any of them were asked beforehand whether they would have the courage to manage all the passengers on a sinking ship, they would probably have given a blank stare. However, 'cometh the hour, cometh the man'.

- **Engage all possible stakeholders in the response to a black swan event.** The rescue ships were stakeholders engaged in maritime rescue by maritime codes that apply to mariners. Every mariner is required both by convention and tradition to support people in distress at sea. An entire industry had geared itself for this very moment, not knowing when it would happen, how it would happen or in what circumstances. Yet the international maritime industry knew that black swans were possible and that they have to look after their own.

There were so many other stakeholders, supporters and interested people in this operation: the ship's agents, the managers of The Haven, Major General Bantu Holomisa of the Transkei, ordinary citizens who happened to be in the vicinity, SAA. The list goes on and on. Every one of them had an important role and many of them did so voluntarily, simply out of a sense of duty to their fellow man. That sort of engagement cannot be taught; it can only be lived.

- **Never underestimate the human spirit.** Credit must go to everyone who participated in the rescue, unbidden, for purely humanitarian reasons. Translating this into, say, a business context, ultimately it is about the culture of the organisation faced with a crisis. This was about the culture of South Africans when faced with a crisis. People simply mucked in because it was the right thing to do. The lesson is to get the culture right in an organisation, an industry, a country.

How many times in the past have we seen South Africans of all descriptions, colours and creeds pulling together to create a result that could never have happened without the collective spirit of giving and humanity? Even though there were those who turned their back on the incident – such as Captain Avranas and some of his senior officers, who saw the incident only in terms of self-preservation – the greater spirit of the collective prevailed. It was that culture of giving and caring which ultimately led to the greatest maritime rescue.

- **Know who you can trust.** It is people who are willing to get their hands dirty, people who are willing to engage with a problem and deal with whatever is presented to them, who you can count on. Those who flee the scene, those who distance themselves from the action cannot be counted upon and it is important to distinguish between the two when deciding who will step up.

Paul Whiley told me that Piet Niemand had insisted on staying behind on the vessel until the very end to completely fulfill his role as Paul's assistant. Paul described him as someone you could totally count on, no matter what. When you read about people like Michael O'Mahoney, Neal Shaw, the Le Riche family, Robin Boltman, Moss

Hills, Lynne Greig, JD Massyn, Lorraine Betts and the many, many others in this epic account, you realise that the human spirit is incredible. But often times, people have some weakness, lack the courage or are too occupied with their self to acknowledge others, and ultimately it will show up under duress. Plan then sufficient resources to manage, even if some fail.

Examine the behaviour of people, the resilience of institutions and the part played by the wider stakeholder group in any major disaster and you will be able to understand why the disaster ended in triumph rather than tragedy.

The *Oceanos* rescue was a modern-day miracle. It reflects the best of what South Africa had to offer at the time. In a way, with its history going back a couple of centuries, South Africans have frequently had to deal with unexpected events and challenges. At times they have dealt with them appallingly – think about the white response to Sharpeville in 1960 and Soweto in 1976. But at other times, South Africans have been extraordinary in their resilience. Think about Nelson Mandela and the millions of oppressed blacks during the apartheid era. Think about civil society and the South African press who, under intense pressure from many quarters, finally managed to topple a despot president in 2018.

Ultimately, we represent a country and community which is about rising above the unexpected. Whether the country in its current state, weakened by poor leadership, rampant corruption and neglect of resources, would be able to respond to another black swan remains to be seen, but I nonetheless believe that we have the will, the people, the courage, the commitment and the spirit ultimately to triumph over whatever disasters may befall us.

POSTSCRIPT

On reconciliation, 571 passengers sailed from East London. Of these, 221 were airlifted by helicopter, the rest evacuated by lifeboat. There were no deaths. The few recorded injuries were minor in nature. The time from the first water ingress to the eventual sinking of the ship was about 17 hours, making the rescue that much more remarkable given the remote location of the casualty.

The fate of the captain and his officers

Information on the fate of the captain and his crew is sparse. The Greek Transport Ministry held a maritime enquiry when the crew returned to Greece, but the formal report has never been made public. I have plumbed a number of potential sources in Greece for the report, but have met with a dead end each time. The Greek authorities have told me, categorically, that the report is not a matter of public record and I may not see it if I have no current legal interest in the matter.

Nonetheless, it is understood that Captain Yiannis Avranas, Staff Captain Christos Nikolaou, Safety Officer Costas Skourlis, Chief Engineer Panayiotis Fines and Second Engineer Antonis Varvarigos were tried in Greece by a tribunal of some sort. The Wikipedia entry for the *Oceanos* records that '[T]he captain and some of the crew were convicted of negligence for fleeing the ship without helping the passengers' and cites the *New York Times* as its source.[7]

Captain Avranas is understood to have been shunted sideways for a period after the *Oceanos* sinking and placed in command of a small

---

7   See https://en.wikipedia.org/wiki/MTS_Oceanos.

ferry boat called the *Panagia*. Later he was given the command of another Epirotiki passenger liner. All was apparently forgiven. In fact, if the public face of Epirotiki Lines was to be believed, they actually thought that Captain Avranas did a sterling job on the *Oceanos*.

Publicly they claimed that, but for the control and diligence which he exercised over the rescue, many passengers might have lost their lives. The fact that no lives were lost was apparently testimony to Avranas's leadership.

To the contrary, the absence of any senior deck officers from the ship during the evacuation made the boarding and launching of the lifeboats perilously dangerous, far more so than if they had been present and assisting in the stabilisation of the lifeboats. Only good fortune prevented serious injury or death. It is possible that they were not given access to the reaction of the South African and other world media, but it seems more likely that a brave face was required in an attempt to salvage the reputation of Epirotiki Lines.

Loud bangs and conspiracy theories

There has long been speculation that the sinking of the *Oceanos* may have been as a result of more than just bad weather and bad luck. Many people on board reported a loud bang shortly before the lights went out. No one has been able to say categorically what caused that noise.

One crew member has insisted, emphatically and categorically, to me that the noise was caused by a bomb in the engine room. He claims that 'all the crew knew and were sworn to secrecy'. He maintains that the sinking was in fact a scuttling to enable the owners to make an insurance claim.

Save for what appears to have been a hoax bomb threat during the wedding ceremony at sea, and despite asking a number of people to try and determine whether there was a deliberate explosion, I have encountered no other evidence of a bomb.

A South African television channel sent divers down onto the wreck not long after the sinking to see if they could find evidence of a bomb. The ship was lying on her port side (the side through which the water

MAYDAY OFF THE WILD COAST

came into the ship), so there was nothing visible of the breach in the hull. The divers were also unable to access the engine room area, so their dive shed no further light on the sinking. Ironically, the only loss of life associated with the sinking of the vessel arose when one of these divers sadly lost his life during the dive.

The ship's war risks insurers conducted investigations in parallel with those in which I was involved. They likewise found no evidence of a bomb on board the ship. I doubt very much that the ship was deliberately scuttled. While it does happen from time to time, quite frankly no seaman in his right mind would have scuttled his ship in circumstances where his survival was doubtful at best.

The three other possible explanations for the loud bang are as follows:

- A huge wave crashed into the side of the ship, which could have made a banging sound on impact. (This is Moss Hills's theory. Interestingly, one passenger reported that the ship lurched and more or less came to a stop when she heard the bang. This might have been consistent with a massive wave smashing so hard into the ship that it almost stopped her forward momentum.)
- A loud noise occurred when the sea chest was breached and water came pouring into the auxiliary engine room.
- There was an explosion of sorts when water in the auxiliary engine room rose to the level of the generators and caused a massive electrical short.

The jury is still out.

Passenger after-effects

Different people react differently to the same situation. Some passengers, like Michael O'Mahoney, emerged from the disaster with no mental scarring. Lou Tolken, in contrast, was so shattered by her experience that, in the grip of post-traumatic stress, she was hospitalised and sedated for four days after her return to Durban.

Other passengers reported recurring nightmares and sleepless nights. Incredibly, from what I can glean, most passengers were able to get on with their lives, largely unscathed. Some were grateful for what they had previously taken for granted while others were angry with TFC, the crew and anyone else they could blame.

The one common theme among those I have spoken to is that the event was unforgettable by any standard and the rescue effort and result nothing short of miraculous.

Military honours

Captain Slade Thomas watched Able Seaman Paul Whiley's landing and working on board. He wrote in the citation for his bravery award of Whiley's heroic deeds and how he went way beyond any call of duty:

> [Whiley] was the first diver to be lowered aboard the MV *Oceanos*, and although he was severely beaten against the ship's superstructure, he reached the deck.
>
> Under extremely trying conditions he then succeeded in creating order and stability among the passengers. He then started hoisting passengers, on the first lift he accompanied a survivor up to the helicopter, after which it took a further 10 minutes of nerve-racking hovering to get him back on the deck.
>
> During this manoeuvre, after being severely battered against the railing of the ship he was flung out of the hoisting strap and fell to a deck lower than intended. Thereupon a male survivor also fell out of a hoisting strap and fell 40 metres into the mountainous swells. AB Whiley, disregarding his own life, dived into the treacherous seas and on reaching the semi-conscious passenger, revived him and assisted him into a rescue craft.
>
> Not quite finished Paul Whiley then swam back to the sinking ship and was confronted with the further difficulty of climbing back on board. Whilst scaling a ladder draped over the ship's side, he was repeatedly beaten against the ship's hull. However, his perseverance paid off and he managed to return to the deck to continue his vital task.
>
> After six hours aboard the *Oceanos* Able Seaman Whiley was one of the last persons to be hoisted from the stricken vessel.

For this Whiley earned the *Honoris Crux (Gold)*, the highest military honour then to be awarded. Only six of these were ever awarded by the South African Defence Force.

Other military honours included:
- *Honoris Crux (Silver)*: AB Gary Ian Scoular
- *Honoris Crux*: Lt Cmdr André Geldenhuys; PO Frans Hugo Mostert; LS Darren Malcolm Brown; LS Luke James Dicks (all from the South African Navy, Divers School)

In addition to *Honoris Crux*, the following decorations for bravery and actions above the call of duty were awarded to South African Air Force personnel for their contributions on that day:
- *Air Force Cross decoration*: Cmdt Eric Brennan Elphick; Cmdt Anthony Charles Hunter; Maj Phillip Fenwick; Maj Anthony Wright Johnson; Maj Martin Johannes Hugo Louw; Maj Hermanus Frederik Steyn; Maj André Stroebel; Capt Anton Botha, Capt René Martin Coulon; Capt Peter Evans Haynes; Capt Charles Glen Goatley; Capt Hendrik Meintjies; Capt Jacques Hugo; Capt Tarri Jooste; Capt Johannes Meintjies; Capt Slade Christopher Thomas; Capt Francois Johann Weyers; Lt Mark Graig Fairley; WO2 William James Riley; F/Sgt Norman Herbert Askew-Hull; Capt Len Pienaar; F/Sgt Frans Campher; F/Sgt Daniël Francois Bezuidenhout; F/Sgt Daniël Roedolf Jacobs; F/Sgt Christoffel Jacobus Pedlar; F/Sgt Philip Davey Joseph Scott; F/Sgt Frans Schutte; F/Sgt Willem Hendrik Steyn
- Mentioned in *Dispatches*:
- South African Air Force: Brig TJM de Munnink, SD; Brig RS Lord, SD; Col GA Hallowes; Col BJ Kriegler; Col LE Weyer; Cmdt DB Janse van Rensburg; Maj WHW van Wyk
- South African Navy: Capt (N) PC Potgieter; Capt (N) RD Stephen; Cdr AG Absolom; WO1 P Hutchinson
- All *Oceanos* helicopter crews were jointly awarded the prestigious Igor

I Sikorsky award for humanitarian service. The award is sponsored by the Helicopter Association International, a not-for-profit professional trade organisation with some 2 500 member organisations, which provides programmes to enhance safety and professionalism in the helicopter industry and is intended to foster professionalism. The Association also promotes through publication the unique contributions by helicopters for the benefit of society.

- The award was made in 1992, for only the third time in its 20-year history. It was received at a ceremony in Las Vegas by the then SAAF attaché, Col 'Monster' Wilkens and the then South African Ambassador to the United States, Mr Harry Schwartz. The citation on the award reads: 'Presented to the person(s) who best demonstrates the value of civil rotorcraft to society and their operators through the saving of life, protection of property and amelioration of distress.'

Civilian awards and accolades

Moss Hills, Robin Boltman and several TFC Tours staff were nominated for the Woltemade Decoration for Bravery, the highest civilian award for bravery at the time. However, for whatever reason they never heard anything more after the nomination. (It is speculated that there may have been political considerations at the time, but no clarity was ever given.)

Robin Boltman received the following awards and acknowledgements:
- An award for bravery by the Magic Council of South Africa, for providing the ultimate service to magic. He was made an honorary member of the Council.
- After 9/11, the Society of American Magicians brought out a medal called the Heroism and Patriotism Award to honour magicians who contributed to rescue services. Boltman was nominated for the medal and was only the fourth recipient, and the first and only non-American ever to receive such an award. The magician Bill Gleeson received the medal on his behalf.

In July 2020, 29 years after the event and as a direct consequence of the publication of this book in South Africa, the National Sea Rescue Institute of South Africa (NSRI), finally gave the TFC staff and other civilians the recognition that they so richly deserved. After reading the book and researching their own operations documents and a number of other sources, NSRI made the following awards:

Award	Awardee
Bravery Bronze	Geraldine Massyn
Bravery Bronze	Liezel Louw
Bravery Bronze	Lynne Greig
Bravery Bronze	Michael O'Mahoney
Bravery Bronze	Neal Shaw
Bravery Bronze	Piet Niemand
Bravery Bronze	Terry Lester (posthumous)
Bravery Gold	Julian Russell
Bravery Gold	Lorraine Betts
Bravery Gold	Moss Hills
Bravery Gold	Robin Boltman
Director's Thanks	Hilton Schilder
Director's Thanks	Peter Niemand
Director's Thanks	Tracy Hills
Director's Thanks	Tom Hine (posthumous)
Director's Thanks	MFV Kaszuby II
Director's Thanks	MV Nedloyd Mauritius
Director's Thanks	MV Reefer Duchess
Director's Thanks	MV Great Nancy
Director's Thanks	MFV Anik
Meritorious Service	NSRI Station 7

This represents the most Bravery Awards ever issued at one time by NSRI.

Organisations and people involved in the *Oceanos* rescue

While it is tempting to credit the success of the rescue to one or two organisations and individuals, such as the South African Air Force, the South African Navy, Moss Hills and Robin Boltman, ultimately it was the collective effort of many who turned a potential tragedy into a triumph. These included:

Civil aviation airfields, including:
- Jan Smuts Airport (now OR Tambo International Airport)
- Louis Botha Airport (then Durban's International Airport)
- East London
- Port Elizabeth
- DF Malan Airport (now Cape Town International Airport)
- Bloemfontein
- Umtata

Civil Protection
Coastal radio stations (Durban, East London, Port Elizabeth, Cape Town) and Rogeland Radio (Norway)
Department of Foreign Affairs
Department of the Environment
Department of Transport
Major General Bantu Holomisa and the Transkei Government
The Haven Hotel
Hospitals
- Entabeni
- St Augustine

Metro rescue services (Border, East, West)
National Sea Rescue Institute
P&I Associates (Pty) Ltd
Polaris Shipping (ships agents)
Port captains in Durban, Port Elizabeth and East London

RCC Piraeus (Greece)
South African Airways
South African Air Force, including:
- Maritime Rescue Coordination Centre, Cape Town
- Air Force Command Post
- Mobile Air Operations Team
- various Air Force bases
- various Air Force squadrons

South African Army, including:
- Eastern Province Command
- Group 8, Eastern Province

South African Medical Services, including:
- Head Office: Operations
- Medical Command, Eastern Province
- Medical Command, Natal
- 1 Military Hospital, Pretoria

South African Navy, including:
- Naval Command Post
- 4 strike craft
- 14 divers
- Silvermine Communications Centre
- various naval bases

South African Police
TFC Tours
An unknown Mother Superior at a Catholic mission in the Transkei and numerous other anonymous volunteers who opened their doors and hearts to the survivors of the *Oceanos*

BIBLIOGRAPHY

Printed sources

Boltman, R. 2007. *Do these stairs go up or down?* Noordhoek: Captains and Kings Publishing.

Lord, D. 2010. *Standby! South African Air Force Search and Rescue.* Johannesburg: 30 Degrees South Publishers.

Uys, I. 2010. *Oceanos – Survivors' Stories.* Knysna: Fortress Network.

Electronic sources

Wikipedia. 2019. https://en.wikipedia.org/wiki/MTS_Oceanos

Oceanos Survivors & Friends. 2012. www.facebook.com (accessed: 25 January 2019)

Hills, M. 2018. Oceanos *Sinking.* https://www.oceanossinking.com/stories-a

Rose-Marie Rowe. 2010 May 28. The sinking of the *Oceanos* – 4th of August 1991. http://oceanossinking.blogspot.com/2010/05/what-happened-to-captain-yiannis.html

Michael O'Mahoney. 2011 August 4. The *Oceanos* sinking – My Experience. http://oceanossinking-myexperience.blogspot.com/2011/08/20-year-anniversary.html

ACKNOWLEDGEMENTS

My acknowledgements and thanks to all the people who allowed me to interview them, who corresponded with me from around the world or otherwise gave me assistance, leads and background information, including:

Alec McAlery (lawyer)

Angela Trollip (wedding guest)

Chantelle Oosthuizen (journalist)

Capt Chris Green (Managing Director, P&I Associates)

Daphne Osborne (Director, TFC Tours)

David Fiddler (Principal Officer, Department of Transport, Maritime Division, Durban)

Capt Davut Leylek (translator and surveyor)

† David Gordon, SC (advocate)

Debra le Riche (passenger)

Duncan Starke (ships agent)

Eduardo Abellar (*Oceanos* crew)

Geoff MacGregor (National Sea Rescue Institute)

Geraldine 'JD' Massyn (hostess, TFC Tours)

Capt Jacques Hugo (South African Air Force)

Jesse Gillitt (*Oceanos* enthusiast)

Juliet Blanch (English arbitrator, one of the Norton Rose solicitors investigating the *Oceanos* in South Africa and Greece)

Lou Tolken (Manager, TFC Tours, Durban)

Lynette Jacobs (hotel manager)

Mercia Schultz (travel agent and passenger)

Michael O'Mahoney (passenger)

Moss Hills (entertainer, TFC Tours)

Capt Nick Sloane (Director, Resolve Marine Group and Salvage
   Master, *Costa Concordia*)
Paul Whiley (diver, South African Navy)
Paul Williams (English solicitor, lead Norton Rose partner
   investigating the *Oceanos* in South Africa and Greece)
Peter Leonard (operator, Durban Radio)
Philip Scott (flight engineer, South African Air Force)
Phillip Simpson (ships agent)
Richard 'Dickon' Daggitt (naval architect)
Robin Boltman (entertainer, TFC and acting cruise director)
Rose-Marie Rowe (passenger)
Capt Roy Martin (ship surveyor and investigator)
Capt Saroor Ali (Acting Deputy Chief Operations Officer, South
   African Maritime Safety Authtority)
Shane Dwyer (lead South African lawyer with Shepstone & Wylie)
Sobantu Tilayi (acting Chief Executive, South African Maritime
   Safety Authority)
Capt Slade Thomas (helicopter pilot, South African Air Force)
Capt Tarri Jooste (helicopter pilot, South African Air Force)
Tarryn Ford (helicopter operator)
Brig Theo de Munnink (Maritime Rescue Coordination Centre
   command, South African Air Force)
Capt Tony Crabbe (port authority tug pilot, East London harbour)

In particular, a huge and sincere thanks to Carol Campbell, for the prod she gave me to get this book written, and to my dear friends: Steve Woodward, for his ever-incisive, insightful comments and editorial contribution, and Prof. John Hare, for his thoughtful commentary and encouragement.

A massive thank you as well to my publisher, Annie Olivier of Jonathan Ball Publishers, for her professional yet gentle directing of the publication, and to my editor, Linda Pretorius, for her impeccable and invaluable contribution to the book.